Setting the Agenda

Third Edition

For Betsy
Maxwell McCombs

For Tere, Simón, Camilo, and Santiago
Sebastián Valenzuela

Setting the Agenda

The News Media and Public Opinion

Third Edition

Maxwell McCombs
Sebastián Valenzuela

polity

First published in 2004 by Polity Press
This edition published in 2021 by Polity Press

Polity Press
65 Bridge Street
Cambridge CB2 1UR, UK

Polity Press
101 Station Landing
Suite 300
Medford, MA 02155, USA

ISBN-13: 978-1-5095-3579-8 (hardback)
ISBN-13: 978-1-5095-3580-4 (paperback)

A catalogue record for this book is available from the British Library.

Library of Congress Cataloging-in-Publication Data

Names: McCombs, Maxwell E., author. | Valenzuela, Sebastián, author.
Title: Setting the agenda : the news media and public opinion / Maxwell
    McCombs and Sebastián Valenzuela.
Description: Third edition. | Cambridge, UK ; Medford, MA : Polity Press,
    2020. | Includes bibliographical references and index. | Summary: "An
    anticipated third edition of the go-to text on agenda-setting"--
    Provided by publisher.
Identifiers: LCCN 2020017655 (print) | LCCN 2020017656 (ebook) | ISBN
    9781509535798 (hardback) | ISBN 9781509535804 (paperback) | ISBN
    9781509535811 (epub)
Subjects: LCSH: Mass media and public opinion. | Mass media--Social
    aspects. | Mass media--Political aspects. | Mass media--Influence. |
    Public opinion.
Classification: LCC P96.P83 M38 2020 (print) | LCC P96.P83 (ebook) | DDC
    302.23--dc23
LC record available at https://lccn.loc.gov/2020017655
LC ebook record available at https://lccn.loc.gov/2020017656

Typeset in 10.5 on 12pt Plantin
by Fakenham Prepress Solutions, Fakenham, Norfolk NR21 8NL
Printed and bound in Great Britain by TJ Books Limited

For further information on Polity, visit our website: politybooks.com

Contents

Boxes

Foreword: 'Messages and Residues'

Even as children we know instinctively that a message, such as a cry, generates a response. This comprehensive book makes clear that many messages, especially those from news media, are not random but are ordered by journalists and others in prioritized ways, from most to least important, and that audiences have to read, watch, listen, and learn. Agendas provide priorities, not just information.

In our personal lives we live in real worlds with family and friends and street addresses, jobs, schools, and hospitals, and deserts and mountains. In our civic lives we live in imagined worlds that we learn about from others, including media. These worlds overlap, of course. There is a continuum from touching to visualizing. Information from others, including traditional and social media, providing prioritized agendas. In media the priorities are evident. Newspapers give the biggest headline to the most important topic, a presidential election result, or a tearing tornado. Television leads off with the topic, or even breaks into regular programming with 'breaking news'. Social media lead off with the topic and stay on that topic, gathering others into the informational web like an expanding spiderweb in the attic.

Agenda setting is often described as the press telling us what to think about rather than what to think. We have long known that media coverage can magnify topics, or even people, as P. T. Barnum in the nineteenth century made an apparently good singer, Jenny Lind, into a world-famous star, the Swedish Nightingale. The power of a message, or an amplified voice one way or the other, has been known for centuries, but agenda-setting scholars have provided specific evidence of the many ways this phenomenon occurs – across time, nationalities, and political systems. Communication scholars Maxwell McCombs and Sebastián Valenzuela have surveyed a vast literature in a single volume in a way that teachers and scholars can use. This is a text and a major book of scholarship.

Agenda-setting scholarship was a long time in coming. Wilbur Schramm of Stanford more or less invented the field of mass communication scholarship seventy years ago with his own writing and collections of key insights about media and mass communication. These collections served as early texts and research guides. Scholars of journalism conducted legal and historical scholarship in the first years (as they still do) and borrowed the methods of sociology and social psychology. They also employed content analysis, the one method that naturally belongs to journalism scholarship. Decades ago, Wayne Danielson of Stanford, North Carolina, and Texas, and Guido Stempel of Ohio University, among others, began to link content with computers and find ways to generalize research samples to large populations. Schramm early on sketched a model of a communicator-to-message-to-audience message direction, with a weaker feedback loop. It was, and remains, a universe to discover.

With content analysis, one could read messages backwards to discern details of audiences and even cultures, but also could look forward more precisely at effects on audiences. Of course, there was the message itself. The agenda-setting work of McCombs and his colleagues connected content analysis with audience effects more exactly than ever before. One could make predictions, the first step in theory building. If we had time and resources, we could trace historically how the voice of a Swedish singer grew from filling auditoriums in towns and cities to filling the imagined air of listeners everywhere, with echoes even today, more than a century later. Agendas leave residues. Agenda setting provides tools as well as concepts. Agenda setting goes forwards and backwards, even as we stand, so to speak, on messages themselves.

Citation analysis of the original article of McCombs and Donald Shaw demonstrates the growth in the concept of agenda setting, along with the resistance to the simple idea it represented – if a cognitive stimulus, then a cognitive response – in a period, the 1950s and 1960s, when attitude change was the dominant paradigm. We remember reading one literature review which detailed this resistance like the lines left by the receding tides on an Atlantic beach, from: (1) there is no message residue, to (2) there is a slight, but artifactual, residue, to (3) there is a residue, but we have long known about it, to (4) there is a message effect but it's mostly trivial and can be accounted for by other causes. That is, the review hinted, agenda-setting research is not significant, at least to those most interested in attitude change and behaviour. The first paper on agenda setting, based on the 1968 presidential election study in Chapel Hill, was rejected by the Association for Education in Journalism (now AEJMC). It was not published until 1972, slightly revised, in *Public Opinion Quarterly.*

But agenda-setting research continued, perhaps because of its conceptual simplicity, and by now there are more than 500 articles around the world, numerous books, and thousands of papers. The 1972 McCombs and Shaw article has drawn more than a million hits on Google. There are now different branches of agenda setting, such as attribute agenda setting, intermedia agenda setting, and agenda-melding, among others. With study of agenda-setting levels 2 and 3, one can see how the attributes of media messages are reproduced in the minds of audiences and perhaps wonder what the implications are, as China, among other nations, pulls the strings of traditional and social media content producers. The United States has its first Twitter president, but probably not its last. There is also evidence that audiences mix information from traditional and social media to find a blend that is personally comfortable, not necessarily one that is factually accurate. John Milton's plea assumes that truth will defeat falsehood, even as we may be slipping into a post-factual society. If so, media still have the power to set agendas with messages based on facts or opinions.

Agenda setting on occasion can be a complex social topic that reaches far beyond news media and audiences. Rita Colistra of West Virginia University has explored the importance of agenda-cutting. Consider that Southern white newspapers did not carry news about African American activities in certain periods of our history, unless African Americans were associated with crime or accidents. Japan has seemingly ignored its aggressor role in the Second World War, while Germany has acknowledged its part in their history books, and history is a major agenda setter. If you are not on the news agenda in contemporary life, you do not exist in civic culture, at least to people who don't know you personally.

There is an activist side to agenda setting. What if news media created a regular local beat about climate change, or about ending poverty and generating opportunity? Journalists would produce stories regularly. In time, audiences would think more about these topics, although this alone would not guarantee civic action. Agenda setting is the necessary first step in social change. Telling people what to think about is a considerable power. Is that not the job of teachers, parents, religious and political leaders, bosses, and even friends?

Agenda-setting scholarship has sometimes employed sophisticated methods, but the concept of communicator-to-message-to-receivers remains its simple core. This book organizes the literature and field into clear segments in a way that makes the power – and evolution – of this research discipline clear. This version of the book, the third, is different because the book, like the field, has evolved. No one knows research on agenda setting as well as Max McCombs, and now Sebastián Valenzuela. Their portrayal of agenda-setting research is emerging piece by piece, like tracing the numbers on a 'What Am I?' page. The third edition of this book is the most complete story yet, a rich contribution to our understanding of the processes involved in agenda setting.

We are pleased to have been contributors to this ongoing stream of communication research for the past half century, along with our students and our students' students and many others. David Weaver remembers creating the need for orientation construct with Max McCombs in 1973, from studies of social psychology that suggested the importance of relevance and uncertainty in information seeking. It was exciting to see the data from the 1972 Charlotte study fitting the predictions of the NFO model so well, both in terms of media exposure and strength of agenda-setting correlations.

Donald Shaw remembers the afternoon in Chapel Hill, North Carolina, when Max came down the hall with the news that their AEJ paper on agenda setting had been rejected. What to do? One option was to drop the paper into the trash can and move on. After all, common sense had long made clear that news did have an impact. Who needed the precision of agenda setting? Max had a different idea. So, he tells students today that when you get a rejection of a scholarly paper or article, take a closer look at your idea: You may really be on to something.

Donald L. Shaw, University of North Carolina,
David H. Weaver, Indiana University

Preface

Setting the agenda is now a common phrase in discussions of politics and public opinion. This phrase summarizes the continuing dialogue and debate in every community, from local neighbourhoods to the international arena, over what should be at the centre of public attention and action. In most of these dialogues the news media have a significant and sometimes controversial role. Should there be any doubt about this long-standing and widespread role of the news media, note the *New York Times'* description of twentieth-century British press baron Lord Beaverbrook as a man 'who dined with prime ministers and set the nation's agenda'.[1] Or former *New York Times* executive Max Frankel's description of his own newspaper:

> It is the 'house organ' of the smartest, most talented, and most influential Americans at the height of American power. And while its editorial opinions or the views of individual columnists and critics can be despised or dismissed, the paper's daily package of news cannot. It frames the intellectual and emotional agenda of serious Americans.[2]

The enormous growth and expansion of these media institutions that are now such a compelling feature of contemporary society was a central aspect of the last one hundred years. To the host of newspapers and magazines spawned in the nineteenth century, the twentieth century added ubiquitous layers of film, radio, television, and cable television. In its closing years came the internet and, in the twenty-first century, a kaleidoscopic mix of new communication technologies – most notably social and mobile media – have continued to blur the traditional boundaries between mediated and interpersonal communication, and between the various media and their content. These new channels redefine 'mass' communication and enlarge its agenda-setting role in society. Mass communication once meant the large-scale distribution of identical messages, particularly through newspapers, television, and radio. The new communication channels, such as Facebook, YouTube, Instagram, and Twitter, are massive, too, in that large proportions of society use them, but the messages flowing through these channels are personalized.

Although everyone talks about the impact of these emerging technologies in the current media landscape, the enormous social influence of communication was already apparent decades before Mark Zuckerberg invented Facebook. In *The Making of the President, 1972*, American journalist Theodore White described the power of the news media to set the agenda of public attention as 'an authority that in other nations is reserved for tyrants, priests, parties, and mandarins'.[3] In the years since White's cogent observation, social scientists across the world have elaborated the ability of the news media and an expanding panoply of communication channels to influence many aspects of our political, social, and cultural agendas.

One of the most prominent and best-documented intellectual maps of this influence is the theory of the agenda-setting role of the communication media, which is the subject of this book. Theories seldom emerge full-blown. They typically begin with a succinct insight and are subsequently elaborated and explicated over many years by various explorers and surveyors of their intellectual terrain. This has been the case for agenda-setting theory. From a parsimonious hypothesis about the effects of the news media on the public's attention to social and political issues during election campaigns, agenda setting has expanded to include propositions about the psychological process for these effects, the influences that shape communication agendas, the impact of specific elements in their messages, and a variety of consequences of this agenda-setting process. Expanding beyond the traditional news media, agenda-setting theory has become a detailed map of the effects of the flow of information about public affairs through a growing plethora of communication channels.

The immediate origins of this idea began with a casual observation about the play of news stories on the front page of the *Los Angeles Times* one day in early 1967. There were three big stories that day: internationally, the unexpected shift from Labour to Conservative in the British county council elections; nationally, a budding scandal in Washington; and locally, the firing of the Los Angeles metropolitan area director of a large federally funded programme that was a keystone in President Johnson's national 'War on Poverty'. Not surprisingly, the *Los Angeles Times* put the local story in the lead position on page 1 and relegated the other two stories to less prominent positions on the front page. Any one of these stories – in the absence of the other two – easily would have been the page 1 lead, a situation that led to a speculative conversation over drinks among several young UCLA faculty members at their Friday afternoon 'junior faculty meeting' in the lobby of the Century Plaza Hotel. Is the impact of an event diminished when a news story receives less prominent play, we wondered? Those speculations grounded in a scattered variety of ideas and empirical findings about the influence of the media on the public were the seeds for the theory of agenda setting.

The formal explication of the idea of agenda setting began with my move that autumn to the University of North Carolina at Chapel Hill, where I met Donald Shaw and began what is now a fifty-year plus friendship and professional partnership. Our initial attempt at formal research on this idea built literally on those speculations in Los Angeles about the play of news stories. We attempted to construct an experiment based on actual newspapers that played the same story in radically different ways. The *Charlotte Observer* was a widely respected newspaper in North Carolina, which produced a series of editions during the day, early ones for points distant from Charlotte, the final edition for the city itself. One result of these multiple editions was that some stories would begin the day prominently played on the front page and then move down in prominence in subsequent editions, sometimes moving entirely off the front page. Our original plan was to use these differences from edition to edition as the basis of an experiment. However, the shifts in news play from day to day proved too erratic – in terms both of the subjects of the stories and in the way that their play in the newspaper changed – for any systematic comparison of their impact upon the public's perceptions.

Despite this setback, the theoretical idea was intriguing, and we decided to try another methodological tack, a small survey of undecided voters during the 1968 US presidential election in tandem with a systematic content analysis of how the news media used by these voters played the major issues of the election. Undecided voters were selected for study on the assumption that, among the public at large, this group, who were interested in the election but undecided about their vote, would be the most open to media influence. This was the Chapel Hill study, now known as the origin of agenda-setting theory.[4]

A fundamental contribution of the Chapel Hill study was the term itself, 'agenda setting', which gave this concept of media influence immediate currency among scholars. The late Steve Chaffee recalled that, when I saw him at the 1968 annual meeting of the Association for Education in Journalism and told him about our study of agenda setting, the term was new and unfamiliar but he immediately understood the focus of our research.

Since Donald Shaw was trained in history, you might expect us to have exact records on the creation of the term 'agenda setting' – the 'One Tuesday afternoon in early August …' kind of sentence – but, ironically, neither Donald nor I recalls exactly when we came up with that name. We did not mention 'agenda setting' in our 1967 application to the National Association of Broadcasters (NAB) for the small grant used in partial support of the research, but our 1969 report to the NAB on the results of the Chapel Hill study uses the term as if it had been around forever. Sometime during 1968 the name 'agenda setting' appeared,[5] and Steve Chaffee undoubtedly was one of the first 'referees' to acknowledge its utility – perhaps the very first outside the immediate Chapel Hill circle involved in the project. Further corroboration is provided by the Google Books Ngram Viewer, which shows that 1968 was the first year in which the phrase 'agenda setting' was used systematically. Chapter 1 presents the details of the Chapel Hill study as well as some of the key intellectual antecedents of this idea.

To paraphrase Sherlock Holmes, with the success of the 1968 Chapel Hill investigation, the game clearly was afoot. There were promising leads in hand for the solution to at least a portion of the mystery about the precise effects of the media upon public opinion. Subsequently, many detectives began to pursue these clues about how public attention and perception are influenced by the media and how various characteristics of the media, their content, and their audiences mediate these effects. Much like the adventures of Sherlock Holmes, whose cases fill nine lengthy volumes, a wide variety of links in this vast intellectual web has been chronicled. However, because the marketplace of ideas in communication research is very much one of laissez-faire, elaboration of the agenda-setting role of the communication media has not always proceeded in an orderly or systematic fashion. There have been many detectives working on many cases in a variety of geographical and cultural settings, adding a bit of evidence here and another bit there over the years. New theoretical concepts explicating the idea of agenda setting emerged in one part of this intellectual web, then in another.

For many years, the primary emphasis was an agenda of public issues. Especially in its popular manifestation of polls in the news media, public opinion is frequently regarded in these terms. Agenda-setting theory evolved from a description and explanation of the influence that the news media have on public opinion about the issues of the day. An open-ended question used by the Gallup Poll since the 1930s, 'What is the most important problem facing this country today?', is frequently used for this research because polls based on this question document the hundreds of issues that have engaged the attention of the public and pollsters over the decades.[6] Perhaps for the first time in modern history, in 2020 this Most Important Problem (or MIP) question yielded the exact same response in all polls across the world: the coronavirus crisis.

Moving beyond an agenda of issues, agenda-setting theory has encompassed public opinion about political candidates and other public figures, specifically the images that the public holds of these individuals and the contributions of the media to those public images. This larger agenda of topics – public figures as well as public issues – marks an important theoretical expansion from the beginning of the communication process, what topics the media and public are paying attention to and regard as important, to subsequent stages, how the media and public perceive and understand the details of these topics. In turn, these stages are the opening gambit for mapping the consequences of the media's agenda-setting role for attitudes, opinions, and behaviour.

And, in recent decades, investigation of agenda-setting effects and their consequences have expanded beyond the domain of public affairs to explore settings as diverse as sports, religion, and business. All of these media effects upon the public are presented in this volume, not just theoretically, but in terms of the empirical evidence on these effects worldwide.

In contrast to the piecemeal historical evolution of our knowledge about agenda setting since the seminal 1968 Chapel Hill study, the chapters of this book strive for an orderly and systematic presentation of what we have learned over those years, an attempt to integrate the vast diversity of this evidence – diverse in its historical and geographical settings, mix of media and topics, and research methods. Presenting this integrated picture – in the words of John Pavlik, a *Gray's Anatomy* of agenda-setting theory[7] – is the central purpose of the book. Much of the evidence forming this picture is from an American setting because the 'founding fathers' of agenda setting, Donald Shaw, David Weaver,[8] and myself, are American academics, and the majority of the empirical research until recently has been conducted in the United States. However, the reader will encounter considerable evidence from Western Europe, East Asia, Latin America, and the Middle East. One of the great strengths of agenda-setting theory is this geographical and cultural diversity in the evidence replicating the major aspects of this influence on society.

Beyond the immense gratitude to my best friends and long-time research partners, Donald Shaw and David Weaver, this book owes a great debt to the host of scholars worldwide who created the accumulated literature that is catalogued here. Prominent among these scholars is a leading Latin American scholar, Sebastián Valenzuela, who joins me as the co-author of this third edition. An associate professor in the School of Communications at Pontificia Universidad Católica de Chile in Santiago, Sebastián brings an important international voice to *Setting the Agenda*. He continues the significant contributions to agenda setting made by University of Texas at Austin scholars over the past three decades.

The theory of agenda setting is a complex intellectual map still in the process of evolving. Although the emphasis in this book is on an empirically grounded media-centric map of what we now know about the role of the media in the formation of public opinion, there also is discussion in the later chapters of the larger context in which this media influence occurs. This agenda-setting role of the media has been a rich lode for scholars to mine for more than fifty years, and yet much of its wealth remains untapped. However, even the existing theoretical map already identifies exciting new areas to explore, and the flux in our contemporary public communication system has created a plethora of new opportunities for elaborating the map presented here.

Even within the original domain of public opinion, there is more to consider than just the descriptions and explanations of how the media influence our views of public affairs. For journalists this phenomenon that we now talk about as the agenda-setting role of the news media is an awesome, overarching ethical question about what agenda the media are advancing. 'What the public needs to know' is a recurring phrase in the rhetorical repertoire of professional journalism. Does the media agenda really represent what the public needs to know?[9] In a moment of doubt, the executive producer of ABC News' *Nightline* once asked: 'Who are we to think we should set an agenda for the nation? What made us any smarter than the next guy?'[10] To a considerable degree, journalism is grounded in the tradition of storytelling. However, good journalism is more than just telling a good story. It is about telling stories that contain significant civic utility.[11] The agenda-setting role of the media links journalism and its tradition of storytelling to the arena of public opinion, a relationship with considerable consequences for society. And the expanding media landscape and evolution of journalism and political communication presents significant questions about the formation of public opinion.

Maxwell McCombs
Austin, Texas, March 2020

1 Influencing Public Opinion

The American humourist Will Rogers was fond of prefacing his sardonic political observations with the comment, 'All I know is just what I read in the newspapers.' This comment is a succinct summary about most of the knowledge and information that each of us possesses about public affairs, because most of the issues and concerns that engage our attention are not amenable to direct personal experience. As Walter Lippmann long ago noted in *Public Opinion*, 'The world that we have to deal with politically is out of reach, out of sight, out of mind.'[1] In Will Rogers' and Walter Lippmann's day, the daily newspaper was the principal source of information about public affairs. Today we have a vastly expanded panoply of communication channels, but the central point is the same. For nearly all of the concerns on the public agenda, citizens deal with a second-hand reality, a reality that is structured by journalists' reports about these events and situations, which in turn are amplified, transformed, and commented upon by users across digital and mobile media.

A similar, parsimonious description of our situation vis-à-vis the news media is captured in sociologist Robert Park's venerable phrase, the 'signal function' of the news.[2] The daily news alerts us to the latest events and changes in the larger environment beyond our immediate experience. But the news media do considerably more than signal the existence of major events and issues. Through their selection and display of the news, journalists focus our attention and influence our perceptions of what are the most important issues of the day. This role of the news media in identifying the key issues and topics of the day and their ability to influence the salience of these issues and topics on the public agenda has come to be called the agenda-setting role of the news media.

News media communicate a host of cues about the relative salience of the topics on their daily agenda. The lead story on page 1 of a newspaper, the placement of a story on a website, the length of a story, even the number of social media interactions garnered by a story – all communicate the salience of topics on the news agenda. The television news agenda has a more limited capacity, so even a mention on the evening television news is a strong signal about the high salience of a topic. Additional cues are provided by its placement in the broadcast and by the amount of time spent on the story. For all the communication media, the repetition of a topic day after day is the most powerful message of all about its importance.

The public uses these salience cues from the media to organize its own agenda and decide which issues are most important. Over time, the issues emphasized in news reports become the issues regarded as most important among the public. The agenda of the news media becomes, to a considerable degree, the agenda of the public. In other words, the news media largely set the public agenda. Establishing this salience among the public, placing an issue, event, public figure, or other major element in the news on the public agenda so that it becomes the focus of public attention and thought – and, possibly, action – is the initial stage in the formation of public opinion.

Discussion of public opinion usually centres on the distribution of opinions: how many are for, how many are against, and how many are undecided. That is why the news media and so many news users are so fascinated with public opinion polls, especially during political campaigns. But, before we consider the distribution of opinions, we need to know which elements are at the centre of public opinion. People have opinions on many things, but only a few really matter to them. The agenda-setting role of the news media is their influence on the salience of an object of attention in the news, such as a controversial topic or a political candidate, an influence on whether a significant number of people regard it as worthwhile to hold an opinion about that object.

While many issues compete for public attention, only a few are successful in doing so, and the news media exert significant influence on our perceptions of what are the most important issues of the day. Within professional news outlets, this is not a deliberate, premeditated influence, as in the expression 'to have an agenda'. Premeditated attempts at influence are the realm of the partisan media, propaganda, advertising, so-called 'fake news' sites, and other forms of communication that seek to persuade.[3] Professional news media seek to inform, not persuade. And their agenda-setting role stems not from efforts at persuasion, but rather is an inadvertent influence resulting from the necessity of the news media to select and highlight a few topics in their reports about the most salient news of the moment.

This distinction between the influence of the professional news media on the salience of objects in the news and on specific opinions about these objects is summed up in Bernard Cohen's observation that the news media may not be successful in telling people what to think, but they are stunningly successful in telling their audiences what to think about.[4] In other words, the news media can set the agenda for public thought and discussion. Sometimes the news media do more than this. Other times, the news media fail at setting the public agenda. Hence, we will find it necessary in later chapters to expand on Cohen's cogent observation. But first, let us consider in some detail the initial step in the formation of public opinion, capturing public attention.

Our pictures of the world

Walter Lippmann is the intellectual father of the idea now called, for short, agenda setting. The opening chapter of his 1922 classic, *Public Opinion*, is titled 'The World Outside and the Pictures in our Heads', and summarizes the agenda-setting idea even though Lippmann did not use that phrase. His thesis is that the news media, our windows to the vast world beyond direct experience, determine our cognitive maps of that world. Public opinion, argued Lippmann, responds not to the environment, but to the pseudo-environment constructed by the news media.

Still in print nearly a century after its original publication, *Public Opinion* presents an intriguing array of anecdotal evidence to support its thesis. Lippmann begins the book with a compelling story of 'an island in the ocean where in 1914 a few Englishmen, Frenchmen, and Germans lived'. Only the arrival of the mail steamer more than six weeks after the outbreak of the First World War alerted these friends to the fact that they were enemies.[5] For Lippmann, who was writing in the 1920s, these are contemporary updates of Plato's Allegory of the Cave, with which he prefaces the book. Paraphrasing Socrates, he noted 'how indirectly we know the environment in which nevertheless we live [...] but that whatever we believe to be a true picture, we treat as if it were the environment itself'.[6]

Contemporary empirical evidence

Empirical evidence about the agenda-setting role of the communication media now confirms and elaborates Lippmann's broad-brush observations. When agenda setting was first proposed, it ran counter to the prevailing paradigm among communication scholars that the mass media had limited effects in changing people's perceptions and attitudes. Agenda setting, on the contrary, showed that the news media can have strong, direct effects in the short term by influencing not what people think, but what they think about.

However, the empirical currency of agenda setting as a theory about the formation of public opinion came much later than Lippmann's essay. When *Public Opinion* was published in 1922, the first scientific investigations of the influence of mass communication on public opinion were still more than a decade in the future. Publication of the first explicit investigation of the agenda-setting role of mass communication was exactly fifty years away.

Systematic analysis of mass communication's effects on public opinion, empirical research grounded in the precepts of scientific investigation, dates from the 1940 US presidential election, when sociologist Paul Lazarsfeld and his colleagues at Columbia University, in collaboration with pollster Elmo Roper, conducted seven rounds of interviews with voters in Erie County, Ohio.[7] Contrary to both popular and scholarly expectations, these surveys and many subsequent investigations in other settings over the next twenty years found little evidence of mass communication effects on attitudes and opinions. Two decades after Erie County, Joseph Klapper's *The Effects of Mass Communication* declared that the so-called Law of Minimal Consequences prevailed: 'Mass communication ordinarily does not serve as a necessary and sufficient cause of audience effects, but rather functions among and through a nexus of mediating functions and influences.'[8]

However, the early social science investigations during the 1940s and 1950s did find considerable evidence that people acquired information from the news media even if they did not change their opinions. Voters did learn from the news. And from a journalistic perspective, questions about learning are more central than questions about persuasion. Most journalists are concerned with informing. Persuasion is relegated to the editorial page and, even there, informing remains central. Furthermore, even after the Law of Minimal Consequences became the accepted conventional wisdom, there was a lingering suspicion among many social scientists that there were major media effects not yet explored or measured. The time was ripe for a paradigm shift in the examination of media effects, a shift from persuasion to an earlier point in the communication process, informing.

After Lippmann, other authors in the social sciences alluded to the idea that the news media influence what people deem to be the relevant issues of the day.[9] However, it was only when two young professors at the University of North Carolina's School of Journalism launched a small investigation in Chapel Hill, North Carolina, during the 1968 US presidential campaign, that the notion was put to proper empirical testing. Their central hypothesis was that the 'mass media' set the agenda of issues for a political campaign by influencing the salience of issues among voters. These two professors, Donald Shaw and Maxwell McCombs, also coined a name for this hypothesized influence of mass communication, 'agenda setting'.[10]

Testing this agenda-setting hypothesis required the comparison of two sets of evidence: a description of the public agenda, the set of issues that were of the greatest concern to Chapel Hill voters; and a description of the issue agenda in the news media used by those voters. Illustrated in Box 1.1, a central assertion of agenda-setting theory is that those aspects emphasized in the news come to be regarded by the public over time as being important. In other words, the media agenda sets the public agenda. Contrary to the Law of Minimal Consequences, this is a statement about a strong causal media effect on the public – the transfer of salience from the media agenda to the public agenda.

To determine the public agenda in Chapel Hill during the 1968 presidential election, a survey was conducted among a sample of randomly selected undecided voters. Only undecided voters were interviewed because this new agenda-setting hypothesis went against

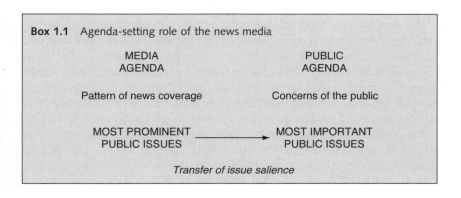

Box 1.1 Agenda-setting role of the news media

MEDIA AGENDA	PUBLIC AGENDA
Pattern of news coverage	Concerns of the public
MOST PROMINENT PUBLIC ISSUES	MOST IMPORTANT PUBLIC ISSUES

Transfer of issue salience

the prevailing view of media effects. If this test in Chapel Hill failed to find agenda-setting effects under rather optimum conditions, voters who had not yet decided how to cast their presidential vote, there would be little reason to pursue the matter among the general public, where long-standing psychological identification with a political party and the process of selective perception often blunted the effects of mass communication during election campaigns.

In the survey, these undecided voters were asked to name the key issues of the day as they saw matters, regardless of what the candidates might be saying. The issues named in the survey were ranked according to the percentage of voters naming each one to yield a description of the public agenda. Note that this rank ordering of the issues is considerably more precise than simply grouping sets of issues into those receiving high, moderate, or low attention among the public.

The nine major news sources used by these voters were also content analysed. This included five local and national newspapers, two television networks and two news magazines. The rank order of issues on the media agenda was determined by the number of news stories devoted to each issue in recent weeks. Although this was not the very first time that survey research had been combined with content analysis to assess the effects of specific media content, their tandem use to measure the effects of mass communication was rare at that time.

Five issues dominated the media and public agendas during the 1968 US presidential campaign – foreign policy, law and order, economics, public welfare, and civil rights. There was a near-perfect correspondence between the rankings of these issues by the Chapel Hill voters, and their rankings based on their play in the news media during the previous twenty-five days. The salience of five key campaign issues among these undecided voters was virtually identical to the salience of these issues in the news coverage of recent weeks.

Moreover, the idea of powerful media effects expressed in the concept of agenda setting was a better explanation for the salience of issues on the public agenda than was the concept of selectivity, which is a keystone in the idea of limited media effects. To be clear, agenda setting is not a return to a 'magic bullet' or 'hypodermic needle' theory of all-powerful media effects. Nor are members of the public regarded as automatons waiting to be programmed by the news media. But agenda setting does assign a central role to the news media in initiating items for the public agenda. Or, to paraphrase Lippmann, the information provided by the news media plays a key role in the construction of our pictures of reality. And, moreover, it is the total set of information provided by the news media that influences these pictures.

In contrast, the concept of selectivity locates the central influence within the individual and stratifies media content according to its compatibility with an individual's pre-existing attitudes and opinions. From this perspective, it is often assumed that the news media do little to alter the issue priorities of individuals because individuals maximize their exposure to supportive information and seek out news about issues that they already deem important. For instance, during an election, voters are expected to pay the most attention to those issues emphasized by their preferred political party.

Which does the public agenda more closely reflect? The total agenda of issues in the news, which is the outcome hypothesized by agenda-setting theory? Or the agenda of issues advanced by a voter's preferred party, which is the outcome hypothesized by the theory of selective perception?

To answer these questions, those undecided Chapel Hill voters who had a preference (albeit not yet a firm commitment to vote for a candidate) were separated into three groups – Democrats, Republicans, and supporters of George Wallace, a third-party candidate in that election. For each of these three groups of voters, a pair of comparisons was made with the news coverage on the CBS television network: the issue agenda of that voter group compared with all the news coverage on CBS, and the issue agenda of the group compared with only the news on CBS originating with the group's preferred party and candidate. These pairs of comparisons for CBS were repeated for NBC, the *New York Times*, and a local daily newspaper. In sum, there were a dozen pairs of correlations to compare: three groups of voters times four news media.

Which was the stronger correlation in each pair? The agenda-setting correlation comparing voters with all the news coverage, or the selective perception correlation comparing voters with only the news of their preferred party and candidate? Eight of the twelve comparisons favoured the agenda-setting hypothesis. There was no difference in one case, and only three comparisons favoured the selective perception hypothesis. A new perspective on powerful media effects had established a foothold.

The accumulated evidence

A year after publication of the Chapel Hill study, Theodore White's last instalment of *The Making of the President* series details the agenda-setting influence of the news media in the excerpt shown in Box 1.2. Since the modest beginnings in Chapel Hill during the 1968 presidential election, more than 500 separate scientific works on agenda setting have accumulated, spanning all six continents, including political and non-political settings, across a variety of media, and dozens of issues.[11] In 2011, the 75th anniversary celebration of *Public Opinion Quarterly* noted that the Chapel Hill study was the most cited article ever published in the journal.[12] By March 2020, this article alone had over 12,000 citations in Google Scholar. Some authors even speak of the 'agenda-setting juggernaut'[13] to highlight the popularity of the agenda-setting concept when studying the influence of journalists and the news they produce. And it may well be the only theory in journalism studies to have a scholarly journal entirely devoted to it, *The Agenda-Setting Journal*.

Despite reams of published research, the basic idea of the theory has remained straightforward: Agenda setting refers to the process by which the elements (e.g. issues, public figures, companies, or government institutions) that are deemed relevant by the news media as well as the attributes used to describe these elements often become

---

Box 1.2   The power of the news

The power of the press in America is a primordial one. It sets the agenda of public discussion; and this sweeping political power is unrestrained by any law. It determines what people will talk and think about – an authority that in other nations is reserved for tyrants, priests, parties and mandarins.

No major act of the American Congress, no foreign adventure, no act of diplomacy, no great social reform can succeed in the United States unless the press prepares the public mind. And when the press seizes a great issue to thrust onto the agenda of talk, it moves action on its own – the cause of the environment, the cause of civil rights, the liquidations of the war in Vietnam, and, as climax, the Watergate affair, were all set on the agenda, in the first instance, by the press.

Theodore White, *The Making of the President*

In the stream of the nation's capital, the *Washington Post* is very much like a whale; its smallest splashes rarely go unnoticed. No other newspaper dominates a city the way the *Post* dominates Washington. . . . There are complaints that the paper has lost energy since Benjamin C. Bradlee retired as editor, in September 1991, but nothing seems to have diminished the influence that the *Post* holds over the nation's political agenda; and nothing has diminished the paper's almost mystical importance to the city's permanent population of malcontents, leaders, and strivers.

The New Yorker (21 and 28 October 1996)

relevant to public opinion, too. Importantly, the basic agenda-setting hypothesis has been widely documented. The latest meta-analysis – a technique that pools in a statistically meaningful way the results of separate studies – found an average correlation of +0.49 between the media and public agendas.[14] To put this number in perspective, consider that the mean effect estimate for human communication phenomena is +0.21.[15] This robust collection of evidence also documents the time-order and causal links between the media and public agendas in finer detail. Here is a sampling of that evidence.

The 1972 US presidential election in Charlotte

To extend the evidence for agenda setting beyond the narrow focus on undecided voters in Chapel Hill and their media sources during the autumn 1968 election, a representative sample of all voters in Charlotte, North Carolina, and their news media were examined three times during the summer and autumn of 1972.[16] Two distinct phases of election-year agenda setting were identified. During the summer and early autumn, the daily newspaper was the prime mover. With its greater capacity – scores of pages compared to half an hour for network television news – the *Charlotte Observer* influenced the public agenda during the early months. Television news did not. But in the final month of the campaign, there was little evidence of agenda setting by either the local newspaper or the television networks.

In addition to documenting the agenda-setting influence of the local newspaper on the public, these observations across the summer and autumn of that election campaign eliminated the rival hypothesis that the public agenda influenced the newspaper agenda. When there are observations of the media agenda and the public agenda at two or more points over time, it is possible to compare simultaneously the cross-lag correlations measuring the strength of these two competing causal hypotheses. For example, the influence of the newspaper agenda at time one on the public agenda at time two can be compared with the influence of the public agenda at time one on the newspaper agenda at time two. In Charlotte, the agenda-setting hypothesis prevailed.

The agenda of issues during the 1972 presidential campaign included three very personal concerns – the economy, drugs, and bussing to achieve racial integration of the public schools – and four issues that were more remote – the Watergate scandal, US relations with Russia and China, the environment, and Vietnam. The salience of all seven issues among the public was influenced by the pattern of news coverage in the local newspaper.

The 1976 US presidential election in three communities

An intensive look at an entire presidential election year followed in 1976 and again highlighted variations in the agenda-setting influence of the news media during different seasons of the year.[17] To capture these variations, panels of voters were interviewed nine times from February through December in three very different settings: Lebanon, New Hampshire, a small town in the state where the first presidential primary to select the Democrat and Republican candidates for president is held each election year; Indianapolis, Indiana, a typical midsized American city; and Evanston, Illinois, a largely upscale suburb of Chicago. Simultaneously, the election coverage of the three national television networks and the local newspapers in these three sites was content analysed.

In all three communities the agenda-setting influence of both television and newspapers was greatest during the spring primaries, when voters were just beginning to attend to the presidential campaign. A declining trend of media influence on the public agenda during the remainder of the year was particularly clear for the salience of seven relatively remote issues – foreign affairs, government credibility, crime, social problems, environment and energy, government spending and size, and race relations. The salience of more personal matters, such as economic issues, remained high for voters throughout the campaign, regardless of their treatment by newspapers and television. Personal experience can be a more powerful teacher than the news media when issues have a direct impact on people's lives.

Although these detailed examinations of the issues on the public agenda help us understand the variations in the agenda-setting influence of the news media, the specific issues change from election to election. So it is useful to have a summary statistic that will allow us to compare the degree of agenda setting taking place in different settings. One of the most common measures used by scholars exploring the agenda-setting role of the news media is the correlation statistic. This statistic summarizes precisely the degree of correspondence between the ranking of issues on the media agenda – which issue received the most news coverage, which issue the second most coverage, etc. – and the ranking of those same issues on the public agenda – which issue most members of the public regard as most important, which issue ranks second among the public, etc.

The possible range of scores for the correlation statistic is from +1.0 (perfect correspondence) through 0 (no relationship at all) to −1.0 (a perfectly inverse relationship). Agenda-setting theory predicts a high positive correlation between the media agenda and the subsequent public agenda.

Using this correlation statistic to summarize a key finding from the intensive year-long look at the 1976 presidential election in three different communities, we see that, during the spring primaries when the agenda-setting influence of both television and newspapers was at its peak, the correlation between the national television agenda and the subsequent voter agenda was +0.63. That is a significant degree of influence. In contrast, the correlation between the agendas of the three local newspapers read by these voters and the voters' agenda of public issues was only +0.34. Nevertheless, this was the peak period for the newspapers. Although it is fashionable to attribute great influence to television in many aspects of life, do not rush to generalize this particular finding about the relative influence of television and newspapers. The final section of this chapter will present a more cautious and comprehensive picture of the agenda-setting role played by various communication media.

These extensive observations of the 1976 presidential campaign across the entire election year provide another opportunity to compare the core hypothesis of agenda-setting theory that the media agenda influences the public agenda with the competing causal hypothesis that the public agenda influences the media agenda. In contrast to the agenda-setting correlation of +0.63 noted above for national television during the spring, over the same time period the correlation between the public agenda and the subsequent national television agenda is only +0.22. The difference between the two is further amplified by comparison with the Rozelle–Campbell baseline, a statistic indicating the value to be expected by chance alone. In this instance the Rozelle–Campbell baseline is +0.37. The agenda-setting correlation is far above this baseline. Its rival is below the baseline. For newspapers, the rather low agenda-setting correlation of +0.34 nevertheless compares quite favourably with the rival correlation of +0.08. The Rozelle–Campbell baseline in this instance also is +0.08. In both of these instances, the evidence corroborates the causal influence of newspaper and television issue agendas on the public agenda.

These initial empirical efforts to map the agenda-setting role of the mass media encompassed three consecutive US presidential campaigns. Election settings were not selected because of any assumption that agenda-setting effects are limited to elections, but rather because national elections create a natural laboratory for the examination of media effects. During a national election there is a continuing massive barrage of messages on public issues and other aspects of politics. If these messages are to have any significant social effects, the effects must occur by election day.

In addition to these advantages for studying media effects, there is also an enduring tradition of scholarship on the role of mass communication in national elections that began with the seminal studies of Lazarsfeld and his colleagues, first in Erie County during the 1940 US presidential election and then in Elmira, New York, during the 1948 US presidential election. For all these reasons, the initial examinations of agenda setting were conducted in election settings.

However, the agenda-setting role of the news media is limited neither to elections nor to the United States, nor even to the arena of political communication broadly defined. American presidential elections were just the starting point. The phenomenon of agenda setting, a continuous and inadvertent by-product of the communication process, is found in both election and non-election settings, at both the national and local levels, in a wide array of geographical settings worldwide, and increasingly for a broad array of agendas extending beyond political communication. However, for now we will focus on issue agendas, the best mapped domain of the agenda-setting role of the communication media.

National concern about civil rights

From 1954 to 1976, a 23-year span encompassing half a dozen presidential elections and all the years in between, the salience of the civil rights issue in the United States rose and fell with great regularity in response to news coverage.[18] The percentage of Americans naming civil rights as 'the most important problem' facing the country ranged from 0 to 52 per cent in the twenty-seven Gallup polls conducted during those three decades. When this continuously shifting salience of civil rights on the public agenda was compared with the news coverage on the front page of the *New York Times* for the month preceding each of the twenty-seven polls, the result was a robust correlation of +0.71. Even when the influence of news coverage in earlier months is removed, the correlation remains +0.71. This is especially compelling evidence of the media's agenda-setting role. Also note that the salience of the civil rights issue among the public primarily reflects the preceding month of news coverage, a relatively short-term response to the media agenda. Because the media agendas examined over this 23-year period were prior in time to the public agenda, this evidence on time-order further supports agenda-setting's causal assertion that the public agenda results, to a considerable degree, form the media agenda.

British and American concern about foreign affairs

Obviously, the news media are most people's primary source of information about foreign affairs. In both the United Kingdom and the United States, the salience of foreign affairs regularly rises and falls in response to media attention.[19] The salience of foreign affairs among the British public from 1990 to 2000 was significantly correlated (+0.54) with the number of foreign affairs articles in *The Times*. During an overlapping twenty-year period in the United States, 1981–2000, the salience of foreign affairs among the American public was significantly correlated (+0.38) with the number of foreign affairs articles in the *New York Times*. Beyond the sheer number of articles in each newspaper, there is an additional impact on the public agenda by news stories reporting home country involvement.

Public opinion in Germany

Weekly comparisons between the public agenda and media agenda in Germany across the entire year of 1986 revealed that television news coverage had a significant impact on public concern about five diverse issues: an adequate energy supply, East–West relations, European politics, environmental protection, and defence.[20]

The energy-supply issue illustrates these agenda-setting effects. Early in 1986 this issue had low salience on both the news agenda and the public agenda. But a rapid rise in May on the news agenda was followed within a week by a similar rise on the public agenda. News coverage catapulted from fewer than a dozen mentions per week to over a hundred per week. Concern among the public about an adequate supply of energy, which had been around 15 per cent of the population, suddenly moved into the 25 to 30 per cent range. When news coverage subsequently declined, so did the size of the constituency expressing concern about Germany's energy supply.

During this same year there were no agenda-setting effects on eleven other issues. As noted previously, the public is not a collective automaton passively waiting to be programmed by the media. The pattern of media coverage for some issues resonates with the public. For other issues, there is no resonance.

Agenda setting in a Swedish election

A panel study tracking the issue of unemployment during the 2006 Swedish national election found significant agenda-setting effects in this Northern European country.[21] When the media focused on unemployment, people also rated unemployment an important issue. These agenda-setting effects were stronger among those with higher interest in political news.

Public opinion in Louisville

All our examples of the agenda-setting influence of the news media examined to this point have been grounded in presidential elections or national portraits of public opinion. But there are also agenda-setting effects on local public issues. We begin with the long-term public opinion trends in an American city, trends that are analysed for the aggregate agenda, as well as separately for the eight individual issues on that agenda.[22] When the trends in public opinion from 1974 through 1981 in Louisville were compared to the news coverage of the *Louisville Times*, the overall correlation between the public agenda and the news agenda was +0.65. Further analysis examined the ebb and flow of concern across these eight years for each of the eight issues. Significant agenda-setting effects were found for the top four issues on the news agenda: education, crime, the local environment, and local economic development.

Despite their influence on many issues, the news media are not all-powerful dictators of public opinion. The issues ranking fifth and sixth on the *Louisville Times'* agenda – public recreation and health care, respectively – are examples of reverse agenda setting, a situation where public concern sets the media agenda. The lack of media omnipotence is also detailed in two other instances. Public concern about local government was independent of the trends in news coverage, despite the fact that local government is one of the traditional staples of daily newspaper coverage. Perhaps heavy continuing coverage of local government – or any other topic, for that matter – becomes a blur of white noise rather than a stream of information. Not only was public concern about local government immune to any agenda-setting influence of the press, the trend in news coverage was also immune to any reverse agenda setting, even though local government ranked sixth on the public agenda during those years.

Local public opinion in Spain, Japan, and Argentina

Unemployment and urban congestion, especially in the old quarter of the city during the weekends, topped the public agenda in Pamplona, Spain, during the spring of 1995.[23] Comparisons between all six major concerns on the public agenda and local news coverage in the preceding fortnight found high degrees of correspondence. The match with the dominant local daily newspaper was +0.90; with the second Pamplona daily, +0.72; and with television news, +0.66.

Agenda setting also occurred in a 1986 mayoral election in Machida City, a municipality of 320,000 residents in the Tokyo metropolitan area.[24] Comparison of the public agenda, which had seven issues in all, with the coverage of the four major newspapers serving Machida City, yielded a modest, but significant, correlation of +0.39. Although there were no significant variations in the strength of this relationship among persons differing in age, sex, or level of education, Chapter 5 will take up a psychological factor that does provide an explanation for this relatively low correlation.

Local agenda-setting effects also were found in the 1997 legislative elections in the Buenos Aires metropolitan area.[25] In September, the correlation for the top four issues of the day was +0.20 between the public agenda and the combined issue agenda of five major Buenos Aires newspapers. However, as election day approached in October, the correspondence between these agendas for the top four issues soared to +0.80, an increase that suggests considerable learning from the news media in the closing weeks of the election campaign.

Additional evidence of significant agenda-setting effects in Argentina was found during the 1998 primary election held to select the presidential candidate for a major political coalition. For the six major issues of the day, the correspondence between the public agenda at the time of the election and the newspaper agenda of the previous month was +0.60. For television news, the correspondence was even higher, +0.71.[26]

Replication with other issues

Similar evidence about the variable impact of news coverage on the trends in public opinion comes from the individual analyses of eleven different issues in the United States during a 41-month period in the 1980s.[27] In each of these eleven analyses, the media agenda is based on a mix of television, newspapers and news magazines. The public agenda is based on thirteen Gallup polls that asked Americans to name the most important problem facing the country. Two patterns are evident in these analyses. First, all except one of the correlations summarizing the match between the media agenda and the public agenda are positive. The median correspondence between these agendas is +0.45. The negative match for morality is easy to explain because morality is a topic seldom broached in the news media.

For the other ten public issues during this period in the 1980s, the positive correlations suggest some degree of agenda-setting influence. However, a pattern of considerable variability in the strength of the association between the two agendas is also apparent. This calls our attention to factors other than media coverage that influence the public's perception of what are the most important issues of the day, and Chapters 4 and 5 will discuss a variety of psychological and sociological factors that are significant in the public's daily trans-actions with the communication media and the issues of the day. These factors can enhance or constrain the degree of media influence.

Cause and effect

The evidence reviewed here, plus many other field studies conducted around the world, corroborate a cause-and-effect relationship between the media agenda and the public agenda. The initial necessary condition for demonstrating causality is a significant degree of correlation between the presumed cause and its effect, a condition met by hundreds of agenda-setting studies worldwide.

A second necessary condition for demonstrating causality is time-order. The cause must precede the effect in time. Even the initial Chapel Hill study was careful to juxtapose the results of the public opinion poll measuring public concern about the issues of the day with the content of the news media in the weeks preceding the inter-viewing as well as with the days concurrent with the interviewing.[28] Evidence of agenda-setting effects in the two subsequent US presi-dential elections was based on panel studies. There were two waves of interviewing and content analysis during June and October in Charlotte during the 1972 presidential election, plus a third wave of interviews immediately following the election.[29] During the 1976 presidential election there were nine waves of interviewing from February to December and content analyses of local newspapers and national television news across the entire year in three different communities.[30] Both of these panel designs allowed detailed tests of the time-order involved in the relationship between the media and public agendas.

Other evidence of agenda-setting effects reviewed here from a variety of non-election settings also involves longitudinal research designs that allowed tests of the time-order involved in the relationship between the media and public agendas. The examination of the civil rights issue in the United States spanned twenty-three years.[31] There are eleven replications of this type of single-issue analysis based on a 41-month period during the 1980s,[32] and an intensive week-by-week examination of five individual issues in Germany during 1986.[33] Eight local issues were analysed, both in the aggregate and individually, in Louisville during an eight-year period.[34]

All of this evidence about agenda-setting effects is grounded in the 'real world' – public opinion surveys based on random samples of the public and content analyses of actual news media. This evidence illustrates agenda-setting effects in a wide variety of situations, and it is compelling for the very reason that it portrays public opinion in the real world. But these réalité portraits of public opinion are not the best evidence for the core proposition of agenda-setting theory that the media agenda has a causal influence on the public agenda because these measures of the media and public agendas are linked with numerous uncontrolled factors.

The best, most unequivocal evidence that the news media are the cause of these kinds of effects comes from controlled experiments, a setting where the theorized cause can be systematically manipulated, subjects randomly assigned to various versions of this manipulation, and systematic comparisons made among the outcomes. Evidence from experiments provides the third and final link in the chain of causal evidence that the media agenda influences the public agenda, demonstration of a direct functional relationship between the content of the media agenda and the response of the public to that agenda.

Changes in the salience of defence preparedness, pollution, arms control, civil rights, unemployment, and a number of other issues were produced in the laboratory among subjects who viewed versions of TV news programmes that had been edited to emphasize a particular public issue.[35] A variety of controls ascertained that changes in the salience of the manipulated issue were, in fact, due to exposure to the news agenda. For example, in one experiment, subjects who viewed TV news programmes emphasizing defence preparedness were compared to subjects in a control group whose news programmes did not include defence preparedness. The change in the salience of this issue was significantly higher for the test subjects than for the subjects in the control group. In contrast, there were no significant differences between the two groups from before to after viewing the newscasts for seven other issues.

Bringing the cause-and-effect evidence of the laboratory up to date, two experiments investigated the agenda-setting effects of online news on personal agendas. One experiment compared the salience of international issues among readers of the print and online versions of the New York Times. Although there were stronger effects for the print version of the newspaper, subjects exposed to both versions were significantly different from a control group with no exposure to the *New York Times*. Opening the door to further exploration of the agenda-setting process, these experimenters argued that 'contemporary incarnations of internet news are subtly, but consequentially, altering the way that the news media set the public's agenda'.[36] Another experiment exposed participants to either a CNN newscast or the CNN news site and then measured their recall of the top stories and their rankings of issue importance.[37] The influence of television news was stronger than the impact of the web on viewers. Arguably, the format of web pages does not always contain distinctive salience cues about the media agenda.

In recent years, researchers have examined the agenda-setting effect of the news media outside of the lab, using field experiments. The advantage, in this case, is that the strong internal validity of the experimental design is matched with an equally strong level of external validity, for the results are measured in the real-world beyond the lab. The most well-known of these experiments was carried out by Gary King and his associates at Harvard University.[38] After three years of negotiations, he and his colleagues were able to recruit several news organizations to participate in the experiment, including well-known publications like *The Nation* and *Huffington Post*. Then, for a year and a half, between two and five of these outlets, in different combinations each time, volunteered to write simultaneous stories on one of eleven broad subjects, such as immigration, climate, and education. Each cluster of stories ran on these outlets in one of two consecutive weeks. The influence of these stories was measured by comparing outcomes in the 'treatment' week in which the cluster of stories ran with the 'control' week in which the cluster did not run. Each time they carried out this procedure, the researchers conducted an automated content analysis of Twitter chatter. Examination of the discussion of the chosen subject on Twitter found that there was more than a 60 per cent increase in the week after the stories ran. In his commentary on the experiment in *Science*, Matthew Gentzkow concluded that this study 'provides one of the most rigorous and convincing data points to date on the agenda-setting power of media'.[39]

While experiments are sometimes criticized as artificial situations, they provide vital complementary evidence for the agenda-setting role of the news media. A complete set of evidence for agenda-setting effects requires both the internal validity of experiments where the media and public agendas are tightly controlled and measured and the external validity of content analysis and survey research whose designs assure us that the findings can be generalized beyond the immediate observations at hand to larger settings in the real world. From both streams of evidence, a major contribution of agenda-setting theory is that it makes an explicit connection between specific media content and its effects among the public.

A new communication landscape

With the vast expansion of communication channels in recent decades, particularly the continuing proliferation of internet sites and personalized social media, we have entered a new era of agenda-setting research that is seeking answers to three key research questions.

1. Do online media have agenda-setting effects among the public?

For most of the 1990s and 2000s, attention to the agenda-setting effects of online media centred on how news websites, blogs, bulletin boards, candidate websites, and search engines influenced – or were influenced by – traditional media, a phenomenon commonly referred to as 'intermedia agenda setting'. In general, the evidence showed a two-way relationship between mainstream media and online media, where both agendas mutually reinforced each other.[40] With the arrival of social media platforms and new partisan outlets in the mid 2000s, these initial findings about the reciprocity of issue agendas largely replicated.[41]

In comparison to intermedia agenda-setting, fewer studies have documented the effect of online media agendas on the public agenda. Nevertheless, an initial overview of this research found strong support to the basic agenda-setting hypothesis.[42] For example, an analysis of candidate websites during the 2010 US Senate election found they were successful at influencing the salience of seven issues among Indianapolis voters.[43] Turning to online news media, the increased salience for an array of national issues among viewers of CNN online and for foreign affairs among participants in an experiment who viewed the *New York Times* online were noted above.[44] In South Korea, two alternative online news services, OhmyNews and PRESSian influenced the salience among the public of the deaths of two schoolgirls by a US military vehicle, an issue that resulted in massive anti-US protests.[45] The homogeneity of issue agendas between online and traditional media certainly contributes to the strong influence of digital channels on the public's priorities, a topic that we will discuss shortly.[46]

With the rise of social media over the last decades, researchers have focused on the role played by platforms such as Facebook and Twitter on influencing the public agenda. A study conducted in Spain examined whether news consumption through Facebook was associated with having an individualized agenda that diverged from the aggregated public agenda of most important problems.[47] By combining survey and web-tracking data, the authors found that the more an individual uses Facebook as a gateway for news, the less likely she will mention the top two issues in the public agenda, which at the time were unemployment and corruption. While statistically significant, the effect was small. Specifically, those who did not use Facebook for news had a 47 per cent probability of mentioning unemployment or corruption as the most important issues. This probability decreased to 35 per cent for the average Facebook user. Nevertheless, when compared to the total list of important issues mentioned by survey respondents, the influence of Facebook was not statistically significant.

Another study[48] analysed the reciprocal influence of tweets sent over two years by 36 news media and different random samples of users in the United States. First, the correlation in issue attention between media outlets and the different groups of users (namely, 'attentive' public, general public, Democratic supporters, and Republican supporters) varied from +0.55 to +0.79. These correlations suggest moderate to strong relationships between issues agendas. Second, and most importantly, the time-series analyses allowed to establish whether these correlations stem from the ability of the media to set the public agenda on Twitter, or, conversely, resulted from public discussions influencing the subsequent news agenda. The results were rather consistent:

> Notably, in each case, the power of shifts in media attention to predict subsequent shifts in attention among all audiences is greater than the reverse, confirming that media outlets play a crucial role in leading political attention.[49]

In general, then, the available studies confirm that the transfer of salience from the media agenda to the public agenda takes place not only with traditional news outlets, but also with new interactive, digital platforms.[50] That is, when people use media, the potential of that media's content to set the agenda of public concerns remains.

2. Has the proliferation of online media diminished the agenda-setting impact of the traditional media?

With the transformation of the communication landscape in recent decades – first cable television and subsequently satellite television among the traditional mass media and now the proliferation of websites and personalized social media – some observers have predicted the diminution, if not the disappearance, of agenda-setting effects on the scale that we have observed them over the past half century.[51] The argument is that the myriad content choices brought upon by interactive media has increased the competition for people's attention, thus challenging the place of traditional news in people's media diet.[52] Despite the popularity of this possibility, the overwhelming preponderance of the evidence to date suggests that the agenda-setting role of the media endures. To paraphrase Mark Twain's famous cable to the Associated Press, reports of agenda setting's death are greatly exaggerated.

An extensive longitudinal analysis of the agenda-setting effects of the *New York Times'* coverage on the public's responses to the Gallup Poll's 'most important problem facing the country' from 1956 to 2004 found variations in the strength of these effects, but no discernible trend over time.[53] This finding was replicated in a more recent time-series analysis based on media content and public opinion data collected in Sweden between 1992 and 2014. In it, the authors analysed both aggregate and individual-level agenda-setting effects on public opinion concerning twelve different political issues. Their results show that the traditional news media were as influential as an agenda setter in 2014 – an era of high-choice media – as in 1992 – an era of low choice.[54] Similarly, a longitudinal analysis[55] of broadcast television's agenda-setting power conducted in Chile between 2001 and 2016 found that the correlation between media and public agendas averaged +0.75. Furthermore, there was no downward linear trend – if in 2001 the correlation hovered at +0.90, by 2016 it was still at a strong +0.80.

Another way of tracking variation in agenda-setting effects due to the proliferation of digital channels is through cohort analysis, in which different generations of individuals are compared in their susceptibility to the media agenda. Although media-use patterns among different generations do diverge in the new communication environment, state-wide surveys in North Carolina and Louisiana found little difference in agenda-setting effects among the younger, middle, and older generations.[56] Greater attention to the internet and much less attention to traditional media among young adults had little impact on the magnitude of agenda-setting effects. Particularly compelling is the comparison in Louisiana of the issue agendas of low and high internet users to the issue agenda of the state's major newspapers. For low internet users the correlation with the newspaper agenda is +0.90. For high internet users, the correlation is +0.70.

Likewise, comparisons between the issue agendas of the *New York Times* and the younger, middle, and older generations across the election years in the US from 1976 to 2004 found no inflection points associated with these events in the long-term trends.[57] The overall pattern is one of strong agenda-setting effects across the years and no large differences among the generations despite variations in their media-use patterns. For the younger generation, the median correlation is +0.77 across these decades with a range of +0.55 to +0.93. For the 35 to 54-year-olds, the median is +0.79 with a range of +0.66 to +0.93. Among those 55-and-older, the median value is +0.77 with a range of +0.61 to +0.93.

Furthermore, the meta-analysis discussed earlier[58] showed that year of publication of the study was not a significant predictor of the strength of the agenda-setting effect, which suggests that the influence of traditional news media – which are the most studied media in the articles used in the meta-analysis – remains as strong as it used to be.

Both the strength of agenda-setting effects in past decades and their continuing strength in contemporary settings result from long-standing patterns of behaviour in the media and among the public. The high degree of homogeneity among media agendas found in the original Chapel Hill investigation continues in contemporary settings. Pablo Boczkowski not only found a high level of homogeneity among the news agendas of the major print and online newspapers in Buenos Aires, but also noted the increasing similarity of these news agendas from 1995 to 2005, a trend that he attributes to the facilitation of journalists' long-standing habit of monitoring the competition by the plethora of news now available on the internet and television.[59] Among the public, strong agenda-setting effects result from civic osmosis, the continuous exposure to a vast sea of information from many channels of communication.[60] Applying network analysis to Nielsen data on TV and internet use from March 2009 collected from over 1,000 homes, James Webster and Thomas Ksiazek noted:

> We find extremely high levels of audience duplication across 236 media outlets, suggesting overlapping patterns of public attention rather than isolated groups of audience loyalists.[61]

For most people, this exposure ranges from habitual and deliberate attention to some news channels to incidental exposure to other news channels in the course of daily life. In tandem with the homogeneity of these news channels, the outcome is a high degree of consensus among the public about the major issues of the day.

3. To what extent are there specific channel effects vs. the collective impact of a communication gestalt?

Long-standing interest in the effects of media has frequently been accompanied by a fascination with the relative power of the various communication channels to achieve those effects. Agenda setting has been no exception. Once people understand the basic idea of agenda setting, they are quick to ask which medium is more powerful in setting the public agenda. In the latter half of the twentieth century, attention was directed particularly at comparisons between newspapers and television. Now the panoply of social media has been added. The best answer to this question is: 'It depends.' Whether all these channels speak as a chorus, with little difference among them, or whether one or two channels clearly surpass the others in impact, varies considerably from one situation to another. Even where differences do exist, most of the channels contribute to these agenda-setting effects. We swim in a vast sea of news and information, a gestalt of communication channels, where the whole is far greater than the sum of its parts.

However, in the examination of media effects over the years, there has been a tendency to emphasize individual media more than the media collectively. This is particularly salient in the literature on media effects and political polarization, a body of work that has been studied in the agenda-setting literature under the rubric of 'attribute agenda setting'. For instance, a study conducted in the context of the US elections of 2012 found that the affective attributes (e.g. morality, leadership, caring, intelligence, and honesty) of the candidates emphasized by a partisan channel (Fox News) produced a different agenda-setting process when compared to more neutral networks (CNN and NBC).[62] This line of research confirms that people are influenced by the media they choose to use, such that polarization and the ensuing audience fragmentation does not weaken the existence of individual-level media effects.

In contrast, the concept of civic osmosis emphasizes this collective role of the media. And the proliferation of new media adds a rich variety of dynamic channels to this communication gestalt. Increasingly, we swim in a sea of diversity, and we need to understand the currents in this sea, both those that enhance communication and those that pollute the sea. Above all, we need to understand the sea as a whole, how it changes and shifts over time, and how it impacts the public agenda. There is abundant empirical evidence about the absorption of news and information from this communication gestalt that dates from the earliest days of our field to the present. In the benchmark 1940 Erie County study, Paul Lazarsfeld and his colleagues found substantial overlap in people's use of the various mass media:

> People highly exposed to one medium of communication also tend to be highly exposed to other media. There are relatively few who are highly exposed to one medium and little exposed to the other.[63]

Although, in response to survey questions, people can name a particular news medium as their primary source – the newspaper that they read most mornings, the radio or TV news that they tune to with some regularity – people are far from immune to the larger news environment. In the 1996 Spanish national election, there was considerable similarity between people's level of agreement with their primary medium's agenda in comparison to their level of agreement with the agenda of the primary medium's principal competitor.[64] For example, among voters who identified *Diario de Navarra* as their primary news source, the agenda-setting correlation was +0.62. Their level of agreement with the competing local newspaper was +0.57. Across eighteen comparisons, the median difference in the correlations is only 0.09.

Returning to the previous comparisons between agenda-setting effects of daily newspapers among contemporary generations:

> despite evidence that the youngest generation is not exposed to tradi-tional media as frequently as the older generations, and does use the Internet significantly more, there is little support for the intuitive idea that diversity of media will lead to the end of a common public agenda as we have known it. Rather, different media use among the young did not seem to influence the agenda-setting effect much at all.[65]

During the 2006 Swedish national election, Jesper Stromback and Spiro Kiousis measured the impact of daily news use across nine major news media – a mix of newspapers, television, and radio – and found that:

> attention to political news exerts a significant and rather strong influence on perceived issue salience and that attention to political news matters more than attention to various specific news shows on television and in radio, or to different newspapers.[66]

This finding does not deny that there are powerful and influential newspapers, broadcast stations, and websites. However, zooming out for a broader look, it is the vast gestalt of communication voices that defines our social fabric. Often, the major effects of communication result from the collective impact of the media and a continuous process of civic osmosis. An important aspect of civic osmosis is the sheer number of news channels available to the public. At the individual level, the number of different problems mentioned by respondents when asked to name the most important problems facing the local community or the nation is significantly related to the number of media voices in the community.[67]

Summing up

This is far from all the accumulated evidence that the news media exercise an agenda-setting influence on the public, but it is a wide-ranging sample of that evidence. The examples presented here describe agenda-setting effects by a wide array of media on numerous national and local issues, during elections and more quiescent political times, in a variety of national and local settings in the United States, Britain, Spain, Germany, Japan, and Argentina, from 1968 to the present. Recent research also has documented the agenda-setting effects of entertainment media, such as Oprah Winfrey's daytime TV show.[68]

There are, of course, several other significant influences that shape individual attitudes and public opinion. How we feel about a particular issue may be rooted in our personal experience, the general culture or our exposure to the media.[69] Trends in public opinion are shaped over time by new generations, external events, and the communication media.[70] Nonetheless, the general proposition supported by this accumulation of evidence about agenda-setting effects is that journalists do significantly influence their audience's picture of the world.

For the most part, this agenda-setting influence is an inadvertent by-product of the media's necessity to focus on a few topics in the news each day. And a tight focus on a handful of issues by numerous media conveys a strong message to the audience about what are the most important topics of the moment. Agenda setting directs our attention to the early formative stages of public opinion, when issues emerge and first engage public attention, a situation that confronts journalists with a strong ethical responsibility to select carefully the issues on their agenda.

In theoretical terms, this chapter's examples of agenda setting illustrate the transmission of issue salience from the media agenda to the public agenda. As we shall see in subsequent chapters, agenda setting as a theory about the transmission of salience is not limited to the influence of the media agenda on the public agenda, or even to an agenda of public issues. There are many agendas in contemporary society. Beyond the various agendas that define the context in which public opinion takes shape, this idea about the transmission of salience has been applied to a variety of other settings. Chapter 8 discusses some of these new, broader applications, that extend agenda-setting theory beyond political communication. But, first, we will add further detail to our theoretical map of the causal influence that the media agenda has on the public agenda.

2 Reality and the News

Some journalists disclaim any agenda-setting influence on the public. 'We just report the news about what is happening in the world', they say. Making a similar assumption, some critics of the idea of agenda setting have asserted that public and media alike are just responding to their surrounding environment – that is, that the correlation between media and public agendas is spurious. However, in his discussion of the role of the news media as a bridge between 'the world outside and the pictures in our heads', Walter Lippmann introduced the idea of the pseudo-environment, the view of the world that exists in our mind – a view that is always incomplete vis-à-vis reality and frequently inaccurate. Our behaviour is a response to this pseudo-environment, not the actual environment, asserted Lippmann. Now the accumulated evidence from decades of research on the agenda-setting role of the communication media further underscores the importance of Lippmann's distinction between the environment and the pseudo-environment.

This is not to assert that the news is made from whole cloth. Far from it. Journalism is an empirical activity grounded in verifiable observations, and the failure to observe this professional ethic has been the basis of prominent scandals in journalism across the world over the years. But when the events and situations of each day are refracted through the professional lens of news organizations, the result often is a picture of the world, a pseudo-environment that is far from isomorphic with more systematic assessments of that environment. Many events and situations vie for the attention of journalists. Because there is neither the capacity to gather information about all these events nor to tell the public about them, journalists rely upon a traditional set of professional norms to guide their daily sampling of the environment. The result is that the news media present a limited view of the larger environment, something like the highly limited view of the outside world available through the narrow slit windows of some contemporary buildings. This metaphor is even more apt if the windowpane is a bit opaque and has an uneven surface.

Idiosyncratic pictures

There is a famous New Yorker magazine cover parodying Manhattan residents' view of the United States. This drawing is dominated by a very large New York City and a rather large California on the other side of the country. All the states in between are squeezed tightly together and barely exist. There is a similar drawing of the Texan's view of the United States, which, of course, is dominated by a huge Texas with forty-seven tiny states squeezed around the edges. Neither of these psychological maps of the United States bears much resemblance to the geographer's map studied in school, but both – albeit exaggerated – are viable psychological maps of the United States. Here, we shall consider several empirical examples in which the news media's 'maps' of the world – and subsequent perspectives among the public – resemble those famous drawings that satirize New Yorkers and Texans.

A decade of American public opinion

Repeating a pattern with which we are now very familiar, national public opinion in the United States on a wide variety of issues evidenced major agenda-setting effects by the news media across the entire decade of the turbulent 1960s.[1] When the Gallup Poll, in its surveys during that decade, asked Americans to name 'the most important problem' facing the country, Vietnam, race relations and urban riots, campus unrest, and inflation topped the public agenda. Comparing the salience of all fourteen major issues on the public agenda during the 1960s with the coverage of those same issues in *Time*, *Newsweek*, and *US News and World Report* revealed a high degree of correspondence, a correlation of +0.78.

To counter the criticism that this strong correlation between the media agenda and the public agenda is spurious because both the media and the public were simply responding to 'the world outside', Ray Funkhouser also constructed an historical agenda, primarily from Statistical Abstracts of the United States. For example, the salience of Vietnam was measured by the highly variable number of American troops committed during the 1960s to the war there. This 'control for reality' introduced into the analysis dramatically underscores the strength of the agenda-setting process. Coverage of the Vietnam War, campus unrest and urban riots peaked a year or two earlier than those events reached their historical climaxes. For all the issues, peaks in coverage frequently appeared during years in which the situation was no different from other years. In some cases, coverage increased while the problem showed improvement or dropped while the problem increased. Funkhouser noted that 'the patterns of media coverage did not have a one-to-one relationship to the realities of any of the issues'.[2] In short, at the same time that the media agenda and the public agenda of the 1960s were strongly related to each other, both maintained an arm's length relationship and minimal correlation with historical trends of the period.

The inclusion of 'reality' here is a particularly significant contribution to the causal evidence of an agenda-setting effect upon the public by the media because it rebuts the contention that both news coverage and audience concerns are simply reflections of events in the real world. The media construct and present to the public a pseudo-environment that significantly shapes how the public views the world.

Creating a crisis

Idiosyncratic pictures of the larger environment beyond personal experience were present in the German press during the autumn of 1973.[3] In every week from early September until late December, negative statements outnumbered positive statements about the available supply of petroleum in the country. Moreover, during October and November, the description of the situation as a 'crisis' steadily increased. Only in January and February of 1974 did discussion of a crisis abate, and the news coverage reflect a balance between positive and negative assessments of the situation.

Was there really an energy crisis in Germany that autumn and winter? The impetus for this news coverage was a series of Arab price increases and boycotts in the early autumn directed primarily at the United States and The Netherlands. German oil imports during September and October were significantly higher than in those months the previous year and, in November, imports were about the same. Although there was little factual basis for asserting the existence of an energy crisis, major German newspapers – three national quality papers covering the political spectrum and two tabloids – published more than 1,400 articles about the availability of petroleum and petroleum products from September through February; enough to place this situation high on the public agenda.

In a series of polls taken during November, more than two-thirds of the vehicle owners interviewed feared that there would be serious shortages of fuel. In December, as the number of negative statements about the situation began to diminish, the percentage who feared shortages dropped to about half of the vehicle owners and then to about one-third.

The salience of the energy situation – as depicted in the newspapers – produced a strong behavioural reaction among the German public. Purchases of petroleum products in October skyrocketed. Sales of petrol and diesel fuel increased 7 per cent over the previous year, heavy fuel oil by 15 per cent and light fuel oil by 31 per cent. Even though the October petroleum imports exceeded those of the previous year and the November imports were about the same, scattered spot shortages did occur because of the unusually high demand. Needless to say, sales were sharply lower in subsequent months due, in large measure, to the considerable reserves already held by consumers.

This 1973 oil 'crisis' in Germany resulted from a sharp rise in demand stimulated by intense press coverage, not from any critical decrease in supply. In this instance, the agenda-setting effects of the newspapers extended beyond the creation of salience and concern among the public – the usual cognitive effect demonstrated in hundreds of studies – to include a behavioural effect, the individual reactions of consumers to their picture of the situation at hand.

National concern about drugs

A similar situation arose during the 1980s in the United States. Public concern about drugs began to build after the *New York Times* 'discovered' the drug problem in late 1985 and published the first of more than one hundred stories.[4] Following the *NY Times'* lead on this issue, the next year there was a *Newsweek* cover story, specials on two of the national television networks, a surge in coverage of drugs in newspapers across the United States and, predictably, a rise in public concern about the drug problem.

This agenda-setting influence of the *New York Times* – on other news media, on the public and on the federal government – was sustained by the drug-related deaths of sports celebrities in mid 1986, such as the all-American basketball player Len Bias and the professional football player Don Rogers. But these dramatic events did no more than sustain a media agenda that was already in place. The increasing salience of the drug issue in the news media and subsequently among the public is a dramatic case of 'pure' agenda setting because there was no change at all in the actual incidence of drug use across all those months. Putting drugs on the national agenda resulted from the intellectual discovery of a situation by journalists, not from any response to a change in the reality of the situation.

But national attention is volatile. Both the *New York Times'* coverage and public opinion peaked during 1989 in response to a major media campaign by the Bush administration. In September 1989, an astronomical 63 per cent of the public considered drugs the most important problem facing the country. A year later, 9 per cent regarded it so. The agenda-setting triad composed of the news media, the president and the general public is a complex and continually changing set of relationships.[5] In turn, this triad's relationship with the world outside is frequently tenuous and its attention span for public issues uncertain.[6]

Fear of crime

In the 1990s there was another occasion on which the process of agenda setting for a public issue operated with extreme independence of any underlying reality. In 1992, when the Texas Poll asked what was the most important problem facing the country, we see in Box 2.1 that only two per cent named crime. By the autumn of 1993, 15 per cent named crime, and in two subsequent polls during the first six months of 1994 more than one-third of the Texas Poll respondents named crime. This is an unusually high level of concern. Although this question, originated by the Gallup Poll in the 1930s, has been asked dozens and dozens of times since then, few polls have found these levels of concern about any problem. Concern about crime abated somewhat during 1995 and early 1996, but even then about 20 per cent of Texans still designated crime as the most important problem.

Ironically, during that same time period, when public concern over crime rose to unusually high levels, statistical measures of the reality of crime indicated that the rate of crime was actually declining. Of course, a likely source of rising public concern in the face of these declining crime rates was crime coverage in the news media. Box 2.1 also documents a pattern of intense crime coverage during late 1993, 1994, and 1995 in two major Texas newspapers, the *Dallas Morning News* and the *Houston Chronicle*. In all nine periods of time there

Box 2.1   Newspaper coverage and public concern about crime

Time Period	Texas Poll* %	Crime articles in Dallas and Houston newspapers	
		Total number	Excluding Simpson and Selena
Summer, 1992	2	173	173
Autumn, 1993	15	228	228
Winter, 1994	37	292	292
Spring, 1994	36	246	246
Summer, 1994	29	242	216
Autumn, 1994	22	220	205
Winter, 1995	24	233	207
Spring, 1995	21	248	211
Summer, 1995	19	212	200
Autumn, 1995	15	236	126

* This is the percentage of Texas Poll respondents citing crime as the most important problem facing the country.
Source: Salma Ghanem, 'Media coverage of crime and public opinion: an exploration of the second level of agenda setting'. Unpublished doctoral dissertation, University of Texas at Austin, 1996.

are more crime stories than during the summer of 1992, when few members of the public expressed concern about crime.

Detailed analysis of these trends in Box 2.1 documented that this pattern of increased crime coverage was mirrored in subsequent public opinion.[7] Across two and a half years the match between the trend in public concern about crime as a major social problem and the pattern of crime coverage was +0.70. This high degree of correspondence persists even when two sensational crimes occurring during this period are taken into account. During the summer of 1994 the news media began to flood the public worldwide with coverage of the O. J. Simpson murder case. Simpson, a popular football hero and subsequent sports commentator, was accused of stabbing his wife and a friend to death on a Los Angeles sidewalk. In the spring of 1995 a popular Hispanic singer in Texas, Selena, was murdered. Altogether these two murder cases account for nearly one-sixth of the crime coverage from the summer of 1994 through the autumn of the next year. One could argue that the coverage of these two spectacular murder cases, one actually occurring in Texas, accounts for much of the concern about crime among the Texas public. However, even when all the news stories about the Simpson and Selena murder cases are excluded from the analysis, the high degree of correspondence between the media agenda and the public agenda remains +0.73.

This same pattern of public response to newspaper crime coverage also has been found among daily newspaper readers in Chicago, Philadelphia, and San Francisco. In each of these cities the competing newspapers had very different styles and approaches to crime, one fairly conservative, the other more flamboyant. In all three cities, readers of the newspaper that devoted the largest proportion of its space to stories about crime exhibited higher levels of fear about crime than did the readers of the other newspaper.[8]

Newspapers are not the only culprit here. Television, perhaps even more through entertainment programming than through news stories, can foster a fear of crime and violence among its viewers. George Gerbner and his colleagues, who named this worldview 'the mean world syndrome', concluded on the basis of extensive examination of television audiences over many years that 'long-term exposure to television, in which frequent violence is virtually inescapable, tends to cultivate the image of a relatively mean and dangerous world'.[9] This is an assertion, backed by considerable evidence, about entertainment television setting a long-term agenda.

A comprehensive look at the effects of local television crime news in Washington, DC,[10] complements both the investigations of crime news in local US newspapers and the cultivation effects of crime and violence in entertainment television. Outcomes commonly associated with agenda-setting theory – naming crime as the most important problem – and cultivation analysis – the risk of being a crime victim and fear of walking alone at night – were all measured simultaneously. In addition to exposure to local TV news with its heavy diet of crime, three sets of reality measures were examined as predictors of these outcomes – direct experience as a victim of crime, local neighbourhood crime rates, and being the friend, neighbour, or relative of a crime victim. Exposure to local TV news was strongly linked with naming crime as an important problem facing the Washington metropolitan area, but only one of the reality measures – neighbourhood violent crime rates – impacted the salience of crime in Washington. In contrast, exposure to local TV news was not linked to any of the outcomes predicted by cultivation analysis, but nearly half of the reality measures were significantly linked with the fear of crime.

A similar analysis of agenda-setting and cultivation effects of television coverage of the crime issue was conducted in Chile, the results of which were largely comparable to the findings from the United States.[11] Specifically, a time-series analysis of public opinion data, television news, and crime rates collected between 2001 and 2012 found that the volume of crime news in the four main broadcast networks had an independent effect on the proportion of people fearing crime and naming crime as Chile's most important problem – effects that were above and beyond the influence of victimization rates and trends in economic insecurity. Furthermore, between 2001 and 2006, while crime victimization rates were practically stable, the time spent by primetime newscasts on crime doubled, and so did the number of people naming crime as the MIP. This aggregate-level analysis was replicated with individual-level data. Again, these relationships held true in the presence of several statistical controls, such as being a crime victim.

Long before contemporary mass media stimulated concern over crime in the minds of the public, an axiom of early twentieth-century tabloid journalism was 'Give me thirty minutes at the police station to browse the crime reports, and I'll give you a crime wave.' In short, the public's fear of crime and concerns about crime as a social problem have as much to do with the media agenda as with the realities of crime – if not more.

As observed in a *New York Times* editorial, 'A simple truth of human existence is that it is vastly easier to amplify fear than it is to assuage it.'[12] In this case, the editorial was commenting on a flurry of news reports during the summer of 2001, including a dramatic *Time* magazine cover, about shark attacks on humans. Marine scientists quickly pointed out there was nothing unusual at all in the number of attacks that summer other than concerted media attention to scattered incidents. In comparison, *The Times* editorial noted that 28 children in the United States were killed by falling television sets between 1990 and 1997, four times as many people as were killed by great white shark attacks in the entire twentieth century. Watching *Jaws* or *Sharknado* on TV may be even more dangerous than swimming in the ocean.

Discovering the environment

An extensive examination of US public opinion about environmental problems from 1970 to 1990 found no relationship between the salience of these problems on the public agenda and the statistical trends for three different 'reality' measures of air and water pollution.[13] In contrast, there was a substantial relationship between the public agenda – measured by MIP questions from sixty-six Gallup polls – and both the length and the prominence of environmental stories in the *New York Times*. With the reality measures partialled out, the correlations with the public concern were +0.93 with the length of the stories and +0.92 with their prominence in

The Times. Both the length and prominence of these stories increased substantially from 1970 to 1990, while statistical measures of 'reality' indicated a downward trend in total pollution.

The environment was also one of the focal issues tracked in Stuart Soroka's ground-breaking analysis of agenda-setting dynamics in Canada between 1985 and 1995.[14] In addition to measuring news coverage, public opinion, and real-world indicators such as CO_2 emissions, the study included policymakers' attention to environmental topics. This sets an even more stringent test of media's power to set the public agenda. The statistical results paint a complex picture of influences between all the agendas, but a consistent result is that controlling for real-world trends, media attention to the environment leads both public and policy attention to this issue. This was particularly evident in the late 1980s, when environmental concerns rose quickly in the media, public, and policy agendas before levelling out in the 1990s.

Alarmed discovery

Collectively, these portraits of public opinion tell us a great deal about both the discretion of journalists and the discrepancies that are sometimes found in media portrayals of reality. These examples cover a diversity of situations. From 1970 to 1990, the American public responded to the increasing coverage of environmental problems in the face of decreasing air and water pollution. In the 1990s there was a similar response to an increase in news coverage of crime at a time when there was a decreasing trend in the reality of crime. A similar trend was manifest in Chile during the 2000s. In the 1980s public opinion in the US responded to the increasing news coverage of drugs at a time that there was no change at all in the reality of the drug problem. This was also true for the news coverage of shark attacks and the availability of petroleum in Germany. In the 1960s there was no correlation at all between the trends in news coverage or public concern about major issues and the reality of these issues.

The public's response in all these situations is reminiscent of the phenomenon of 'alarmed discovery', the initial stage of public response to a new issue on the agenda that is described in Anthony Downs' theory of the 'issue attention cycle'.[15] The news media's presentation of the issues just discussed can be characterized as 'alarmed discovery' because the news began to emphasize each of these issues at a time that nothing out of the ordinary was occurring in the real world. In effect, these were natural experiments in a real-world setting that yield especially compelling causal evidence of the agenda-setting influence of the news media on the public.

Perspectives on agenda-setting effects

Explorations of agenda-setting effects around the world have observed this communication phenomenon from a variety of perspectives. A four-part typology describing these perspectives is frequently referred to as the Acapulco typology because it was initially presented in Acapulco, Mexico, at the invitation of International Communication Association president Everett Rogers. This typology is defined by two dichotomous dimensions. The first dimension distinguishes between two ways of looking at agendas. The focus of attention can either be on the entire set of items that define the agenda or be narrowed to a single item on the agenda. The second dimension distinguishes between two ways of measuring the public salience of items on the agenda, aggregate measures describing an entire group or population versus measures that describe individual responses. The combination of these two dimensions describes the four distinct perspectives on agenda setting outlined in Box 2.2.

Perspective I encompasses the entire agenda and uses aggregate measures of the population to establish the salience of these items. The original Chapel Hill study of agenda setting took this perspective. Recall that the media and public agendas consisted of the five major issues in that US presidential election. The relative salience of those issues was determined by two aggregate measures. For the media agenda, the salience of the issues was determined by the number of news articles on each issue; and for the public agenda,

---

Box 2.2   The Acapulco typology: four perspectives on agenda setting

	Measure of Public Salience	
Focus of attention	Aggregate data	Individual data
Entire agenda	Perspective I	Perspective II
	Competition	*Automaton*
Single item on agenda	Perspective III	Perspective IV
	Natural History	*Cognitive Portrait*

by the percentage of voters who thought the government should do something about each issue. This perspective is named competition because it examines an array of issues competing for positions on the agenda. Other examples of agenda setting where the full array of competing issues has been examined include the two subsequent US presidential elections, local public opinion in Japan, Argentina, and Spain, and the trend in US public opinion across the entire decade of the 1960s.

Perspective II is similar to the early agenda-setting studies with their focus on the entire agenda of issues, but shifts the focus to the agenda of each individual. Whereas perspective I is at the system level, perspective II is at the individual level. However, when individuals are asked to rank order a series of issues, there is little evidence of any correspondence between those individual rankings and the emphasis on those issues in the news media.[16] This perspective is called automaton because of its unflattering view of human behaviour, essentially a return to the hypodermic theory of mass media effects. Although the media can influence the views of individuals regarding the salience of some issues, the entire agenda of the media is seldom, if ever, reproduced to any substantial degree by an individual.

Perspective III narrows the focus to a single issue on the agenda, but like perspective I uses aggregate measures to establish the salience of this issue. Commonly, the measures of salience are the total number of news stories about the issue and the percentage of the public citing an issue as the most important problem facing the country. This perspective is named natural history because the focus is on the degree of correspondence between the media agenda and the public agenda in the shifting salience of a single issue over time. Examples of this perspective already discussed include a 23-year look at the civil rights issue in the United States, an eight-year look at eight different issues in the city of Louisville, and an intensive year-long look at sixteen individual issues in Germany.

Perspective IV again focuses on the individual, but narrows its observations to the salience of a single agenda item. This perspective, called cognitive portrait, is illustrated by the experimental studies of agenda setting in which the salience of a single issue for an individual is measured before and after exposure to news programmes where the amount of exposure to various issues is controlled.

The existence of these varied perspectives on the agenda-setting phenomenon strengthens the degree of confidence that we can have in our knowledge about this media effect. Perspective I provides useful, comprehensive descriptions of the rich, ever-changing mix of news media content and public opinion at particular points in time.

This perspective strives to describe the world as it is. Perspective III provides useful descriptions of the natural history of a single issue, but at the expense of the larger social context in which this issue exists. Nevertheless, knowledge about the dynamics of a single issue over an extended period of time is highly useful for understanding how the process of agenda setting works. Perspective IV also makes a valuable contribution to our understanding of the dynamics of agenda setting. From a theoretical viewpoint, evidence generated by perspectives III and IV is absolutely necessary to the detailed explication of agenda-setting theory that will explain how and why this phenomenon occurs. But the ultimate goal of agenda-setting theory returns us to perspective I, a comprehensive view of communication and public opinion in the life of each community and nation.

Content versus exposure

Agenda-setting research focuses on the transfer of salience from one agenda to another, usually the media agenda to the public agenda. The Acapulco typology identifies the variety of research designs that have been employed to measure this transfer of salience. Note that these designs and the examples that we have reviewed emphasize comparing the content of the media agenda to the content of the public agenda. In the majority of agenda-setting studies, exposure to the news media is assumed, not measured. However, these content-based studies of agenda setting are complemented by a small body of attention-based studies documenting explicit links between level of attention to the news media and the strength of agenda-setting effects.[17]

Expanding upon this attention-based perspective, an investigation of the 2006 Swedish national election, which measured the impact of daily news use across nine major news media, found that 'attention to political news exerts a significant and rather strong influence on perceived issue salience and that attention to political news matters more than attention to various specific news shows on television and in radio, or to different newspapers'.[18] Likewise, the study on media use and crime perceptions in Chile discussed earlier, found that the more attention to television news was paid, the more likely it was for viewers to name crime as the country's MIP.[19]

Agenda setting in past centuries

Although the term 'agenda setting' was not coined until 1968, there is historical evidence of this phenomenon in much earlier times. In the British colonies that became the United States, the focus of geographical attention and the salience of place names in the American colonial press changed dramatically in the forty years preceding the Declaration of Independence in 1776.[20] About a third of the place names in the earliest of these decades, the period 1735 to 1744, referred to a location in the larger Anglo-American community, that is either Great Britain or North America. But, in the decade immediately prior to the Declaration of Independence, a third of the names referred to North America alone. In the final two years, 1774 and 1775, fully half of the place names referred to North America alone. Even more pertinent to the idea of an agenda-setting role of the press in achieving political consensus, symbols referring to the American colonies as a single unit increased significantly after 1763. After that date, about a quarter of all the American symbols in the newspapers referred to the colonies as a single, common unit. The geographical agenda of the eighteenth-century colonial press helped build the cultural and political identity of a new nation.

Moving to the late nineteenth century, progressive-era reformers strongly believed in this agenda-setting role of the news media as an exercise of power that lies at the heart of democratic politics. Municipal reformers learned this lesson in the 1890s, not only in Chicago and St Louis, but in other large American cities as well.[21] In Chicago, for example, all the public issues that exploded in the late 1890s had been prominent on the newspapers' agendas for much of the decade. The intense and continuing coverage of one issue, street railway regulation, resulted in that issue dominating local elections for years, so much so that by 1899 all the candidates for mayor felt compelled to make street railway regulation the chief issue of their campaigns.[22]

Elsewhere in turn-of-the-century American politics, the famous Kansas editor William Allen White used his newspaper, the *Emporia Gazette*, to articulate an anti-populist agenda. Although it is difficult to ascertain the precise effects of this newspaper's agenda on the local public agenda of that time, Jean Lange Folkerts concluded that:

> White set an agenda for his readers that denied the economic hardship of farmers from 1895–1900 because he disliked the institutional

remedies they proposed, and he feared loss of control by businessmen and loss of Eastern capital.²³

At the beginning of this chapter, the evidence of news media influence on the focus of public opinion included a look at the entire decade of the turbulent 1960s.²⁴ Chapter 1 reviewed the evolution of the civil rights issue in the United States from 1954 to 1976.²⁵ Although these two twentieth-century examples are attenuated bits of history, they are useful benchmarks because they have the advantage of comparing the content of the news media with a systematic assessment of public opinion over a substantial period of time. Most historical research, which is to say, all research on periods of time prior to the development of public opinion polling in the 1930s, does not have this advantage. But drawing upon the array of contemporary evidence that defines agenda-setting theory, Edward Caudill concluded: 'the historical ramification is that the press agenda might be a reasonable guide to opinion beyond the immediate audience of the newspaper or magazine'.²⁶ Of course, he noted, there are limits and constraints, notably the requirement that widespread mass communication existed and enjoyed meaningful links to the populace whose opinions are of interest.²⁷

Summing up

The pictures in our heads have many origins. Among the various sources of our knowledge about the world around us, the news media are especially prominent. Agenda-setting theory describes and explains the role of the news media in building a consensus about the most important issues of the day. Chapter 1 reviewed a considerable body of evidence demonstrating a high degree of correspondence between the priorities of the media agenda and the subsequent priorities of the public agenda. To remove any doubt about this causal relationship between the media agenda and the public agenda, agenda setting was taken into the experimental laboratory. Further solidifying the proposition that the media agenda sets the public agenda, this chapter reviewed additional evidence demonstrating a considerable degree of independence between the events of the world and the portrayal of those events in the news media and the public mind. For a wide array of issues in the 1960s, for the availability of petroleum in the 1970s, for drugs in the 1980s, for environmental problems from the 1970s to the 1990s, for crime in the 1990s and 2000s, and for both crime and shark attacks at the beginning of this century, the media agenda bore little resemblance to the historical agenda of events. More recently, this list includes so-called 'fake' news – verifiably false news reports that are premeditated efforts to achieve a political or other self-interested goal. This is a major new area of agenda-setting research, as there is evidence that the professional news media are susceptible to reflecting the agenda of fake news sites.[28] In all these situations, there is strong evidence that it is the media and its portrayals of the world that set the public agenda.

The knowledge that we have gained in recent times about the agenda-setting role of the news media has been used, in turn, to organize our understanding of the historical past. If the contemporary dynamics of public opinion described by agenda-setting theory can be extrapolated to the past, scholars have used content analyses of newspapers and magazines to write the history of past public opinion. This merger of historical analysis with contemporary explications of public opinion offers rich theoretical promise for understanding the rapid evolution of new political practices that are linked with new communication technologies and global media.

Important conceptual adjuncts of this theoretical promise are two of the perspectives identified by the Acapulco typology, the natural history perspective at the system level and the cognitive portrait perspective at the individual level. Both offer a close-up view of how the process of agenda setting works. Insights gleaned from these perspectives can be incorporated into a more finely tuned theoretical picture of the complex interactions of media and public for the continuously changing mix of issues. This broader perspective with its focus on an array of issues is labelled competition in the Acapulco typology. Agenda-setting research began in Chapel Hill with this 'real-world' situation, which remains the ultimate perspective for both scholars and citizens seeking to understand public opinion.

Finally, echoing Lippmann's idea of the pseudo-environment in this new century, New York Times columnist William Safire provided this succinct summary of reality and the news: 'And in politics, what is widely perceived by the press and public is what is.'[29]

3 The Pictures in our Heads

Walter Lippmann's eloquently argued thesis that the news media are a primary source of the 'pictures in our heads'[1] has produced a hardy intellectual offspring, agenda setting, a social-science theory that maps in considerable detail the contribution of communication media to our pictures of politics and public affairs. The core theoretical idea is that elements prominent in the media pictures not only become prominent in the public's pictures, but also come to be regarded as especially important.

In the previous chapters the focus was on agendas of public issues. Theoretically, however, these agendas can be composed of any set of elements, issues, political candidates, competing institutions, or whatever. In practice, the primary focus of the vast majority of the hundreds of studies around the world to date has been on an agenda composed of public issues. In these investigations of agenda setting, the core finding is that the degree of emphasis placed on issues in the news influences the priority accorded those issues by the public. But even the original agenda-setting study in Chapel Hill during the 1968 US presidential election found that only about one-third of the news coverage concerned issues. The remainder emphasized the events and political strategies of the campaign and information about the candidates.[2]

There are compelling reasons why public issues have prevailed for decades as the major focus of agenda-setting theory. First, the easy fit of the metaphor to an agenda composed of public issues provided a strong, explicit theoretical link between the news media and public opinion, a link that is obvious to anyone interested in journalism, politics, and public opinion. Second, there exists a strong normative tradition in social science research on elections that places great emphasis on the importance of issues to an informed public opinion. Finally, the well-established practices of public opinion polling, with its emphasis on societal issues, provided the methodology that has most commonly been used to measure the public agenda.

Although agenda setting is concerned with the salience of issues rather than the distribution of pro and con opinions, which has been the traditional focus of public opinion research, the core domain is the same – the important issues of the moment. Walter Lippmann's quest to link the world outside to the pictures in our heads via the news media was brought to quantitative, empirical fruition by agenda-setting research.[3]

When the key term of this theoretical metaphor, the agenda, is considered in totally abstract terms, the potential for expanding beyond an agenda of issues becomes clear. In most discussions of the agenda-setting role of the mass media the unit of analysis on each agenda is an object, a public issue. However, public issues are not the only objects that can be analysed from the agenda-setting perspective. In the party primaries that precede national elections in the United States and other countries around the world, the objects of interest are the candidates vying for the presidential nomination of their political party. In that situation, the agenda is an agenda of candidates whose prominence on both the news agenda and the public agenda varies considerably during the political season. In the Canadian parliament, another agenda, the agenda of questions posed to government ministers by members of the House of Commons, also reflects the agenda-setting influence of newspapers, especially in sensible issues such as national unity.[4] There are many objects competing for attention among journalists and various audiences that can define an agenda.

Whether public issues, political candidates, or other items define the agenda, the term object is used here in the same sense that social psychologists use the term attitude object. The object is that thing towards which our attention is directed or the thing about which we hold an opinion. Traditionally in discussions of agenda setting that object has been a public issue. But the kinds of objects that can define an agenda in the media and among the public are virtually limitless, from corporations to countries to other phenomena.

Beyond the agenda of objects there is another level of agenda setting to consider. Each of these objects on the agenda has numerous attributes, those characteristics and properties that fill out the picture of each object. Just as objects vary in salience, so do the attributes of each object. These attributes, of course, can vary widely in their scope, from such narrow descriptions as 'left-handed' to such broad descriptions as 'literary genius'. In agenda-setting theory, attribute is a generic term encompassing the full range of properties and traits that characterize an object.

Both the selection of objects for attention and the selection of attributes for picturing those objects are powerful agenda-setting roles. An important part of the news agenda and its set of objects are the attributes that journalists and, subsequently, members of the public have in mind when they think and talk about each object.

How these news agendas of attributes influence the public agenda is the second level of agenda setting. The first level is, of course, the transmission of object salience. The second level is the transmission of attribute salience. These two aspects of the agenda-setting role of the news media are shown in Box 3.1.

In the theoretical context of the larger communication process traditional agenda setting is focused on a key early step in communication, gaining attention.[5] Appearance of an issue, political candidate or other topic on the public agenda means that it has gained substantial public exposure and attention. Attribute agenda setting is focused on a subsequent step in the communication process, comprehension, the step that Lippmann described as the pictures in our heads. The focus here is on which aspects of the issue, political candidate or topic are salient for members of the public.

The theoretical distinction between attention and comprehension is important. Although media messages usually contain information that is simultaneously relevant to both the first and the second level of the agenda-setting process, the nature of the influence

---

Box 3.1   First- and second-level agenda setting

| MEDIA | PUBLIC |
| AGENDA | AGENDA |

Transfer of salience

Objects ======> Salience of Objects

First-level effects: Traditional agenda setting

Attributes ======> Salience of Attributes

Second-level effects: Attribute agenda setting

is distinct – the salience of objects versus the salience of specific attributes. Furthermore, these two aspects of agenda-setting effects are not always coincidental. Commenting on the candidacy of veteran politician H. Carl McCall in the 2002 New York governor's race, the *New York Times* observed:

> But despite 30 years on the political scene, Mr McCall, 67, the Democratic candidate, is barely known by voters, who, according to polls, may recognize his name but do not have an impression of him.[6]

With this expanded perspective on agenda setting, it is necessary to revise Bernard Cohen's famous dictum about the influence of the communication media. Recall that in a succinct summary statement distinguishing agenda setting from earlier research on media effects, Cohen noted that, while the media may not tell us what to think, they are stunningly successful in telling us what to think about.[7] Explicit attention to the second level of agenda setting further suggests that the media not only tell us what to think about, but that they also tell us how to think about some objects. Could the consequences of this be that the media sometimes do tell us what to think? As we shall see, the evidence suggests a resounding positive answer.

Pictures of political candidates

Although popular images of science centre on dramatic discoveries, most social science is better described as an evolutionary process in which the implicit gradually becomes explicit. This evolutionary process is illustrated particularly well by the gradual translation and expansion of Walter Lippmann's phrase 'the pictures in our heads' into a social science theory backed by precise, rigorous evidence. Beginning with the 1968 Chapel Hill study, the vast majority of this evidence concerns which public issues are on the agenda. In Lippmann's language, this evidence focuses on what these pictures in our heads are about. Over time, attention shifted to attribute agenda setting as an additional influence where the focus is on the actual details of these pictures.

This theoretical distinction between agendas of objects and agendas of attributes, the first and second levels of agenda setting shown in Box 3.1, is especially clear in an election setting where the ballot lists the agenda of candidates. Candidates vying for a political office are – in agenda-setting terms – a set of objects whose salience among the public can be influenced by news coverage and by political advertising. Campaign research on 'name recognition' and other measures of object salience describe the relative prominence of these candidates in the public mind. Increasingly, the task of campaign managers is to secure the news coverage and to design the political advertising that will increase the salience of their candidates among the voters.[8] However, the goals of these media campaigns extend considerably beyond object salience and usually include building an image of the candidate in which specific attributes are particularly salient. In fact, most political strategists assume that voters elect candidates based on these specific images rather than on the issue stances promoted by them.

Several of these pictures in our heads about political candidates – and their origins in the news media – were sketched during the 1970s. However, they remained isolated, idiosyncratic pieces of evidence about agenda setting until renewed theoretical discussions at the end of the last century prompted a new look at those sketches as well as the production of new sketches.[9]

Candidate images in national elections

The pictures in voters' heads of the 1976 US presidential candidates illustrate concisely this second level of agenda setting and its attention to an agenda of attributes. The Republicans had an incumbent president, Gerald Ford, to head their ticket that year, while the Democrats had eleven aspiring presidential candidates competing for their party's presidential nomination during the spring primaries. This was an extraordinarily large group of candidates to learn about and, because most American voters are not avid students of politics, raises an obvious question about the extent to which voters' images of them were shaped by the news coverage. Comparison of descriptions of these candidates by upstate New York Democrats with the agenda of attributes presented in *Newsweek*'s early January sketches of the eleven contenders found significant evidence of media influence.[10]

Especially compelling in this evidence is the increased correspondence between the news agenda of candidate attributes and the voter agenda of candidate attributes from +0.64 in mid February to +0.83 in late March. Voters not only learned the media's agenda, but with some additional exposure over the weeks of the primaries, they learned it even better.

Jimmy Carter emerged from those primaries as the Democratic challenger to incumbent Republican president Gerald Ford, and there is additional evidence of voter learning from the news media about these two men among a general sample of Illinois voters.[11] A striking degree of correspondence was found between the agenda of attributes presented in the election coverage of the *Chicago Tribune* and the agenda of attributes in those Illinois voters' descriptions of Carter and Ford.

Across the entire election year, the median value of the cross-lagged correlations between the media attribute agenda and the subsequent public attribute agenda was +0.70. Defined in terms of fourteen different traits, these attribute agendas included such wide-ranging traits as competency, compassion, and political beliefs. Because these cross-lagged correlations simultaneously take into account the influence of the news media on the voters and the influence of voters on the news media, the evidence is especially clear that the direction of influence was from the media agenda to the public agenda.

As more and more evidence accumulates, it is clear that the attribute agenda-setting influence of the media occurs in elections worldwide, wherever both the political system and the news media are reasonably open and free. The existence of these media effects in diverse cultural settings is well illustrated by the extensive evidence gathered during the 1996 Spanish general election.[12]

In 1996 José María Aznar, the conservative Popular Party's candidate, successfully challenged Spain's twelve-year incumbent Socialist prime minister, Felipe González. A third candidate, Julio Anguita, represented a coalition of far-left parties. Among voters in Pamplona, Spain, there was evidence of significant influence by the major news and advertising media on the images of these three candidates.

The five substantive attributes in the descriptions of the candidates by the news media and by the voters were issue positions and political ideology; formal qualifications and biographical data; personality; perceived qualifications and evaluative judgements; and integrity, which was based on statements explicitly describing a candidate as 'corrupt' or 'not corrupt'. This last attribute was noted in the descriptions of the candidates in order to capture a major issue in the national election, corruption in the government and the related controversy over whether the incumbent prime minister, González, was personally involved in the corruption.

Going beyond previous examinations of attribute agenda setting in US elections, this investigation expanded the scope of the attribute agenda to include both substantive attributes and a second dimension of these attributes, their affective tone. The tone of these candidate descriptions in the news media and by voters was noted as positive, negative or neutral. Tone, of course, is a particularly important aspect of political communication.

In a demanding test of second-level agenda-setting effects, the substantive categories and the affective tone of these descriptions were combined to create a set of 5 by 3 descriptive matrices (5 substantive categories × 3 categories of tone). First, a descriptive matrix was prepared from a post-election survey of Pamplona voters for each of the three candidates. Twenty-one additional descriptive matrices were prepared from the content analyses of two local newspapers, two national newspapers, two national TV news services and the TV political ads (7 media × 3 candidates). The addition of political ads to the mix of news media is another new feature of this evidence from Spain.

Comparisons between the voters' pictures of the candidates with these twenty-one descriptions of the candidates in the various communication media yielded striking results. First, all twenty-one correlations were positive. Comparisons between the voters with the newspapers, both local and national, are especially impressive. For example, the correlations between the voters' agenda of attributes and the attribute agenda of a local newspaper, *Diario de Navarra*, were +0.87 for González, +0.82 for Aznar and +0.60 for Anguita. For *El País*, a national newspaper, the correlations were +0.84, +0.83, and +0.86, respectively.

For all six comparisons between the voters' descriptions and the two local newspapers, the median correlation was +0.70. For all six comparisons with two national newspapers, the median correlation was +0.81. For the six comparisons with the two national TV news services, the median correlation was +0.52. For the three comparisons with the political ads appearing in the public television service, the median correlation was +0.44.

Additional analyses found that these mass media messages overcame selective perception, the tendency to emphasize the positive attributes of one's preferred candidate, and the negative attributes of the competing candidates. With increased exposure to newspapers, television news, and political advertising, there were increases both in positive appraisals of other candidates and in negative appraisals of one's preferred candidate.[13] Voters do learn from the media. This evidence for attribute agenda setting by the media is especially impressive because it combines a large, diverse set of news channels with rich substantive and affective descriptions of three national candidates in the political setting of a democracy.

Candidate images in local elections

Extending our view to both an Asian setting and a local election, there is further evidence of attribute agenda setting from the 1994 mayoral election in Taipei, Taiwan.[14] Voters' images of the three candidates for mayor were compared with the descriptions of these men by the Taipei newspapers and TV stations. The agenda of attributes consisted of twelve categories representing a broad variety of personal and political characteristics. Comparisons between the voters' images and the agenda of attributes in the *China Times* and *United Daily News* ranged from +0.59 to +0.75. The median value of these six comparisons was +0.68. None of the comparisons with the opposition newspaper, *Liberty Times*, was significant, nor were any of the comparisons with TV news significant. In the case of Taipei television, voters were well aware that all three television stations at that time were under the domination of the government and long-ruling KMT political party. In one instance, 40 per cent of the shares in the television station was held by the Department of the Navy. The lack of attribute agenda setting in these instances further confirms our previous observation that the appearance of these effects requires the existence of a free and open media system.

Returning to the Spanish political setting, the images of five political parties' candidates in the 1995 local elections in Pamplona were examined in terms of substantive attributes and, separately, affective tone.[15] Images among members of the public at three levels of media exposure were compared with candidate descriptions in local television news and news stories in two Pamplona newspapers. Like the earlier evidence from the United States on images of the 1976 contenders for the Democrat Party's presidential nomination, each of these comparisons was made for the candidates taken as a group. In Box 3.2, for substantive attributes – descriptions of political candidates in terms of ideology, qualifications, personality, etc. – the match between the media agenda and the public agenda increases monotonically with greater exposure to political information both in the newspapers and on television. Although the pattern is perfectly monotonic across the three levels of exposure, the critical distinction is between exposure to none and at least some of the political information in the media. This same pattern is found in Box 3.2 for affective descriptions of the candidates. Persons making at least some use of the political information in the newspapers and on television describe the candidates in a manner very similar to the news media. The match between the affective descriptions of the news media and

Box 3.2   Attribute agenda setting in Spanish local elections

Substantive attributes

Level of exposure to political information in each medium	Newspapers	TV news
None	+0.74	+0.81
Some	+0.90	+0.91
All	+0.92	+0.92

Affective attributes

Level of exposure to political information in each medium	Newspapers	TV news
None	+0.49	+0.56
Some	+0.88	+0.86
All	+0.79	+0.83

Source: Esteban López-Escobar, Juan Pablo Llamas and Maxwell McCombs, 'Una dimensión social de los efectos do los medios de difusión: agenda-setting y consenso', *Comunicación y Sociedad* IX (1996):91–125.

members of the public making no use of political information in the media is much weaker.

Parallel to the accumulated evidence for traditional agenda-setting effects on the salience of public issues, this evidence about attribute agenda setting and the images of political candidates among the public is grounded primarily in comparisons between public opinion polls and content analyses of the news media and political advertising.[16] Both the advantages of this kind of evidence in presenting a representative picture of political communication and its limitations in terms of definitively proving a cause-and-effect relationship between the media agenda and the public agenda were noted in Chapter 1's discussion of the importance of laboratory experiments as complementary evidence for the existence of a causal relationship between the media agenda and the public agenda. Fortunately, experimental evidence on causality also exists for attribute agenda setting and the images of political candidates among the public.

In a laboratory experiment, half of the subjects read a newspaper article in which a fictitious political candidate was presented as highly corrupt. The other half of the subjects read a newspaper article presenting the candidate as a moral person. Subsequent descriptions of the candidate by individuals exposed to these contrasting characterizations revealed major differences in responses both to an open-ended question and to closed-end rating scales. Even brief exposure to a news article resulted in significant differences between the two groups' responses to the question, 'Suppose that your friend came to see you from another state, and he doesn't know about the candidate. How would you describe the candidate to your friend?' Similar differences also were found between the two groups of subjects in rating how honest, sincere and trustworthy the candidate was perceived to be. Both the rating scales and the open-ended question documented the appearance of second-level agenda-setting effects under the controlled conditions of the laboratory.[17]

Visual images and attributes

Although many agenda-setting studies have included television news, the actual visual content of this news has received little attention. In an innovative study, Renita Coleman and Stephen Banning[18] examined the affective agenda of television news in its visual portrayals of George Bush and Al Gore during the 2000 US presidential election. Their content analysis of the two candidates' nonverbal behaviour – facial expressions, posture, and gestures – found more shots showing positive behaviour by Gore than by Bush and more shots showing negative behaviour by Bush than by Gore.

These images were compared with the results of the 2000 National Election Study. One set of the American National Election Study (ANES) survey questions for each candidate asked if he had ever made the respondent feel 'angry', 'hopeful', 'afraid', and 'proud'. Another set of questions asked respondents to what extent seven positive and negative words and phrases described Bush and Gore. Scores on these questions were summed to form a positive and a negative affective attribute index for each candidate.

Comparisons between the media attribute agendas and the public's attribute agendas found modest evidence for the impact of visual messages. For Bush, there were significant correlations between the media and the public for both the positive and negative attribute agendas (+0.13 for each). For Gore there was a significant correlation between the media and public only for the positive attribute agenda (+0.20). As the authors concluded:

> While the effect of nonverbal cues may be less than the effects reported for some verbal cues, the effect is nevertheless significant [...] Visuals can play an important albeit modest role in facilitating impression formation in the political process.[19]

In the polarized environment that characterizes many advanced democracies, the second level of agenda setting has become a useful explanation to understand the influence of the partisan media. Compared to traditional news, partisan outlets exacerbate coverage of the positive attributes of the preferred candidate and the negative attributes of oppositional candidates. Thus, partisan media tend to reinforce a polarized agenda of attributes among audience members. For instance, in an analysis of the 2012 US election, the frequency with which NBC's Nightly News, CNN's Anderson Cooper 360, and Fox News' Special Report with Bret Baier mentioned five traits of candidates Barack Obama and Mitt Romney were compared to viewers' thoughts along those same traits, using the ANES survey.[20] These traits included aspects such as morality, leadership, and intelligence. Three results were noteworthy. First, a content analysis showed there was a strong imbalance of positive and negative attributes given to the two candidates among the three programmes. As could be expected, Fox had a clear tilt in favour of Romney and against Obama, while CNN had a slight tilt against Romney. NBC, in contrast, had the most balanced attribute agenda. Second, these imbalanced media agendas were strongly correlated with viewers' attribute agendas towards the two candidates. This was particularly true for viewers of Fox's Special Report. Last, attribute agenda-setting effects of Fox were predictive of having positive attitude towards Romney and negative attitudes towards Obama – a polarizing effect that is partially explained by attribute agenda setting. NBC's Nightly News, in contrast, was found to have a depolarizing effect – the more its viewers adopted the programme's attribute agenda, the less likely they were to have extreme opinions about either candidate. Because all these relationships were found when controlling for the effects of party identification, political interest, and other variables, the findings are quite robust.

The influence of the media on the public's images of political candidates is a straightforward instance of attribute agenda setting. Most of our knowledge about the attributes of political candidates – everything from their political ideology to their personality – comes from the news stories and the advertising content of the media. The existence of these attribute agenda-setting effects has been replicated across a variety of geographical and political settings. For national candidates, we have evidence from the United States and Spain. For local candidates, we have additional evidence from Spain and Taiwan. The evidence from actual elections is complemented by an experiment in the United States.

Attributes of issues

Issue salience, which has been the traditional centre of attention for agenda-setting theory, can also be extended to the second level. Public issues, like all other objects, have attributes. Some aspects of issues, which is to say, some attributes, are emphasized in the news and in how people think and talk about these issues. Moreover, the salient attributes of a particular issue often change over time. As we shall see, this is especially true for the economy, a recurring major issue for many countries in recent decades. Sometimes the prominent attribute of the economy is inflation; at other times it is unemployment or budget deficits. Attribute agenda setting extends our understanding of how the news media shape public opinion on the issues of the day.

Demonstrating the validity of agenda-setting theory across cultures as well as at two distinct levels of cognition, attention to an object and comprehension of its attributes, both the first and second levels of agenda setting, were simultaneously examined during the 1993 Japanese general election.[21] Beginning with traditional agenda setting, the impact of intensive news coverage was examined on the salience of political reform, an issue that accounted for more than 80 per cent of the issue coverage in two major national newspapers and three TV networks. Because the issue of political reform had a near-monopoly on the news agenda, the usual comparison of the rank order of issues on the media agenda with their ranking on the public agenda was not feasible in this situation.

Of course, the assumption behind such comparisons is that the high degree of correspondence between these agendas results from exposure to the media. In this Japanese election, the behaviour linking these two agendas – exposure to the media – was explicitly measured. Combining measures of exposure and political interest to yield an index of attentiveness to political news, support was found for the proposition that the salience of a prominent media issue among members of the public is positively correlated with their level of attentiveness to political news. For attentiveness to TV news, the correlation with the salience of political reform was +0.24. For attentiveness to newspapers, the correlation was +0.27.

At the second level of agenda setting, the fact that both TV news and the newspapers mentioned system-related aspects of reform twice as often as ethics-related aspects created counterbalanced expectations about the attribute agenda-setting roles of the news media. First, the salience of system-related aspects of reform on the public agenda should be positively related with attentiveness to political news. This was the aspect of the issue, its attribute, emphasized in the news. In contrast, there was little reason to expect any significant relationship between the salience of the ethics-related aspects of reform on the public agenda and attentiveness to political news. This attribute of political reform received minor attention in the news.

Both hypotheses were supported. For the ethics-related aspect of political reform, the correlations were nearly zero (+0.05 for TV and +0.09 for newspapers). For the system-related aspect of political reform, the correlations were +0.20 for TV news and +0.26 for newspapers. Note that all of these correlations are virtually identical for both first and second-level agenda-setting effects as well as for newspapers and TV news.

Beyond an election setting, news coverage and people's ideas about a complex issue such as the economy can involve many different aspects or attributes. One set of attributes associated with the general topic of the economy consists of the specific problems of the moment, their perceived causes and the proposed solutions to these problems. Another, narrower, set of attributes consists of the pro and con arguments for the proposed solutions to these economic problems. For both of these sets of attributes, agenda-setting effects were found among the general public in Minneapolis for newspapers, but not for television news.[22] For the specific problems, causes and proposed solutions associated with the general topic of the economy, the correspondence between the newspaper agenda and the public agenda was especially high (+0.81). The degree of correspondence was only slightly less for the pro and con arguments about economic solutions (+0.68). The focus in the newspapers on specific aspects of the economy influenced how members of the public thought about the economy.

The environment is another contemporary issue that is equal in breadth and complexity to the economy. As a public issue, the environment can range from international to very local concerns and from rather abstract to very concrete concerns. The influence of news coverage in two major Japanese daily newspapers was apparent in the pattern of concerns among residents of Tokyo about global environmental problems.[23] During the four months leading up to the June 1992 United Nations Conference on Environment and Development, both *Asahi* and *Yomiuri* steadily increased their coverage on eight aspects of the global environment. These aspects ranged from acid rain and preservation of wildlife to the population explosion and global warming.

Among Tokyo residents, this news coverage resulted in significant agenda-setting effects. As early as February, the match between the newspapers' attribute agenda and the subsequent public agenda of attributes was +0.68. By early April, the correspondence had increased to +0.78, its highest point, and it remained there through mid May. The lower degree of correspondence with the newspapers' agenda in the weeks immediately preceding and including the conference reflects the time lag that is part of the learning process involved in agenda setting. The time lag found in Japan is similar to that found for aspects of the global environment issue in the United States.[24] Additional details of the time lag for agenda-setting effects are discussed in Chapter 6.

Evidence continues to accumulate that the ways we think and talk about public issues are influenced by the pictures of those issues presented by the news media. The attributes of issues that are prominent in media presentations become prominent in the public mind. This is a significant extension of the original idea of agenda setting about the ability of the news media to shape the agenda of issues that are considered important by the public. It is the agenda of attributes that define an issue and, in some instances, tilt public opinion towards a particular perspective or preferred solution. Setting the agenda of attributes for an issue is the epitome of political power. Controlling the perspective of the political debate on any issue is the ultimate influence on public opinion.

Compelling arguments

As with the inhabitants of George Orwell's *Animal Farm*, some attributes are more equal than others. Some are more likely than others to be regularly included in media messages, and some are more likely than others to be noticed and remembered.[25] In the interpretation of a message, some attributes will also be considered more pertinent than others. Certain characteristics of an object may resonate with the public in such a way that they become especially compelling arguments for the salience of the issue, person, or topic under consideration.

The idea that certain attributes of an object function as compelling arguments for their salience adds a new link to the theoretical map of agenda setting. Earlier in this chapter, Box 3.1 illustrated the first and second levels of agenda setting, with two horizontal arrows connecting the media agenda and the public agenda. Object salience on the media agenda influences object salience on the public agenda. Attribute salience on the media agenda influences attribute salience on the public agenda. Box 3.3 adds an additional link to this diagram, a diagonal arrow connecting attribute salience on the media agenda with object salience on the public agenda. In other words, when a particular attribute of an object is emphasized on the media agenda, there may be a direct impact on the salience of that object among the public. Certain ways of describing an object may be more compelling than other ways in creating object salience among the public. Up to this point, the salience of an object among the public has been explained primarily by how frequently the object appeared on the media agenda. Mentions of the object on the media agenda have not been stratified according to the kinds of attributes ascribed to the object by the media.

There is now evidence in hand that the diagonal arrow in Box 3.3, a relationship called compelling arguments, is an important aspect of the agenda-setting process.[26] Chapter 2 discussed a situation in Texas during the early 1990s when intensive crime coverage in the news generated astoundingly high levels of public concern about crime as the most important problem facing the country. Box 2.1 detailed those parallel trends in news coverage and public concern.

Ironically, during this time when public concern about crime rose to unusually high levels, the actual rate of crime in Texas was declining, and had been doing so for several years. Is crime a 'hot button' issue to which the public responds in a particularly volatile way when it is emphasized in news coverage? Or did the news coverage include especially compelling arguments about the salience of crime as a social issue? Was there more to this situation than traditional agenda-setting effects?

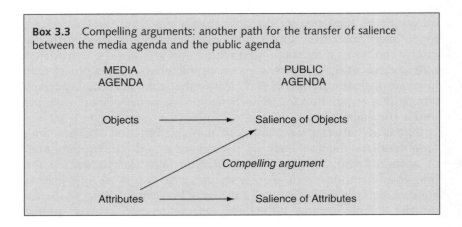

Box 3.3 Compelling arguments: another path for the transfer of salience between the media agenda and the public agenda

MEDIA AGENDA   PUBLIC AGENDA

Objects   ⟶   Salience of Objects

Compelling argument

Attributes   ⟶   Salience of Attributes

Examination of the various ways in which crime was presented in the news revealed that two perspectives had especially strong links with public concern, links whose strength actually exceeded the total impact of crime coverage on the public.[27] Both of these were aspects of crime in which the psychological distance is small between the average person and the criminal activity described in the news story. While Texans were not anxious about distant murders and the traditional array of crimes that are a staple of the news, they were anxious about drive-by shootings, robberies of individuals in broad daylight, and local crime. Specifically, the salience of crime among Texans as the most important problem facing the country was strongly related to the frequency of newspaper stories about crime in which the average person would feel personally threatened by that kind of crime (+0.78) or where the crime actually occurred in Texas (+0.73). Each of these attributes explained the salience of crime as well as or even somewhat better than the total barrage of crime coverage during this time (+0.70). These attributes were compelling arguments for the salience of crime.

There is other evidence in hand as well about the impact of compelling arguments, specific attributes in the news coverage that have an impact on the salience of an object among the public. An analysis of US public opinion during the 1990s about the salience of the federal budget deficit found substantial agenda-setting effects.[28] The frequency of news coverage in nineteen daily newspapers across the country explained 85 per cent of the variance in the salience of this issue during an eighteen-month period from 1994 to 1996. Additional analysis of four specific aspects found that two of them (non-confrontational talks among political leaders and political conflicts over the deficit) were compelling arguments for public concern about the budget deficit. Adding this pair of attributes to the analysis accounted for 92 per cent of the variance in the salience of the federal budget deficit among the US public. Although these compelling arguments, the salience of two aspects of the federal budget deficit, made only a minor contribution to the overall salience of this issue, this is a rare opportunity to observe simultaneously the distinct effects of first and second-level agenda setting. In media messages and in the communications of the public, these two components of the agenda-setting process are bundled together and largely inseparable in practice.

A dramatically different result of a compelling argument was found during the 1990 German national election, where the salience of problems in the former East Germany significantly declined among voters, despite intensive news coverage.[29] The decline – an agenda-deflating effect – was especially apparent among readers of the large circulation tabloid *Bild*, whose coverage of the integration of Germany was framed in highly optimistic terms. In this case, the compelling argument was the positive tone of the news coverage on the issue of German integration, an attribute that reduced the salience of the issue on the public agenda.

Theoretically, a focusing event[30] can be regarded as a dramatic version of a compelling argument, an aspect or attribute of a public issue that can have dramatic effects on the public and policy agendas. For example, the devastating effects of the 2011 earthquake and tsunami on nuclear reactors in Japan was a factor in Germany's decision to immediately shut down eight of its seventeen nuclear reactors, the source of a quarter of the country's electricity. A study in the Czech Republic explored this role of focusing events in regard to the issue of the restitution of church property that had been seized during the years of Communist rule.[31] The focusing event was a trial regarding a specific property, the St Vitus Cathedral, an event that received extensive news coverage. For the analysis, the media agenda was divided into three segments, coverage of the restitution issue alone, coverage of the cathedral trial alone, and a combination of the restitution issue and the trial. The agenda-setting effect on the salience of the restitution issue among the public was much stronger for the combined news coverage than just the coverage of the restitution issue alone. The coverage of the cathedral trial alone did not impact the salience of the restitution issue among the public.

Shifting from issue salience to candidate salience, an extensive set of replications identified two attributes, the moral quality and leadership of the Democratic and Republican US presidential candidates from 1980 to 1996, as compelling arguments for the salience of these men among the public.[32] The salience of these attributes was examined in four news media, the *New York Times*, the *Washington Post*, *Newsweek*, and *US News and World Report*. For moral quality, six of the eight correlations between the salience of the attribute and the salience of the party's presidential candidate among the public were significant, ranging from +0.66 to +0.98. For leadership, four of the eight correlations were significant, ranging from +0.80 to +0.87.

In many instances, these worldviews of journalism substantially influence the pictures of the world held by the public. But not always! Although an extensive examination of how the American media and public view public affairs identified five major aspects – conflict, economics, human interest, powerlessness, and morality – the level of agreement between media and public regarding their salience was only +0.20.[33] However, the lack of media agenda setting in this situation is not nearly as great as this summary index of +0.20 might appear to indicate. When conflict, which ranked second in the media but last among the public, is removed from the agenda, the level of agreement between the media and the public on the remaining four is +0.80.[34] The news media are the public's major source of information about public affairs, but the public is not an automaton passively waiting to be programmed by the media.

Attention to this impact on the public resulting from an emphasis on various attributes in news stories is the basis of a new approach to media criticism. Traditional criticism of the media examined whether the content of news stories was accurate and balanced. This new approach, grounded theoretically in attribute agenda setting, examines the patterns of emphasis and tone in media messages and the resonance of these attribute agendas for public thought and behaviour.

Agenda setting and other communication theories

Agenda setting theory has continued to evolve for more than fifty years because it complements a variety of other ideas in the social sciences. As scholars have constructed an increasingly detailed intellectual map of communication's influence on the public, the theory of agenda setting has incorporated or converged with a number of other communication concepts and theories.

Incorporated concepts include status conferral, stereotyping, image building, and gatekeeping. Status conferral refers to the increased salience of a person who receives intensive media attention.[35] This conceptualization of celebrity identifies an instance of first-level agenda-setting in which the object is a person. Stereotyping and image building, which involve the salience of attributes, are instances of second-level agenda-setting.[36] Gatekeeping, which describes and explains the flow of news from one media organization to another, was linked with agenda-setting theory in the early 1980s, when scholars opened a new aspect of intellectual map-making by asking 'Who sets the media's agenda?'[37] Responses to this question have identified a vast web of relationships and influences, which will be detailed in Chapter 7.

Theoretical complements to agenda setting include cultivation analysis and the spiral of silence. Taking a long-range view of the cognitive effects of mass communication, cultivation analysis examines the salience of various perspectives engendered by the media, especially by entertainment programming on television.[38]

One of the best known of these perspectives, 'the mean world syndrome', is a pessimistic picture of the world around us, stemming from the abundance of crime shows on television.[39] The theories of agenda setting and the spiral of silence[40] appear to examine very different kinds of behaviour among mass media audiences, cognitive representations of the world versus a willingness to engage in conversation on public issues. However, there is a common psychological basis for both ideas in an individual's surveillance of his or her social surroundings.[41] One consequence of this surveillance is the public agenda of issues; another consequence is the frequency of conversations with others about the issues of the day.

These links between agenda setting and a variety of other communication concepts are analogous to the One World, SkyTeam, and Star Alliance links in aviation, an integration of independent airlines to achieve comprehensiveness. This evolving integration of theoretical concepts reflects maturation in the field of communication.

Attribute agenda setting and framing

Explication of a second level of agenda setting, attribute agenda setting, also links the theory with another major contemporary concept, framing. Attribute agenda setting and framing focus on how the objects of attention in messages – issues, political figures, or other topics – are presented. Both attribute agenda setting and framing explore the extent to which an emphasis on certain aspects and details of these objects influence our thoughts and feelings about them. Moving beyond this general statement about their convergence is difficult, due to considerable divergence among the definitions of framing. As a consequence, sometimes attributes and frames are synonymous concepts. At other times, attributes and frames are overlapping concepts, or entirely distinct concepts.

Beginning with their synonymous use, computerized content analysis of four Republican candidates' campaigns for their party's 1996 US presidential nomination identified twenty-eight attributes in campaign press releases and news about the campaign in the *New York Times*, *Washington Post*, and *Los Angeles Times*.[42] Although the focus of the study from an agenda-setting perspective was the attribute agendas of the press releases and news coverage, the focus was described in the article's title as 'framing the candidates'. In contrast to an agenda-setting research design, the published article did not compare the descriptions advanced by the candidates' campaigns and the descriptions presented by journalists.

Agenda-setting theory suggests taking the additional step of making these comparisons in order to determine the attribute agenda-setting effect of the candidates' press releases on the news agenda. Calculated in a seminar on agenda-setting theory at the University of Texas, the evidence from this framing study for attribute agenda-setting effects was substantial: +0.74, +0.75, and +0.78 for three of the candidates, and a slightly lower, but still robust +0.62 for Robert Dole, the front runner and eventual party nominee.

A creative look at the overlap – theoretical linkage – between frames and attributes comes from an investigation of public opinion about difficulties in the Japanese economy.[43] Grounded in the idea that frames are bundling devices for lower-order attributes, this analysis also drew upon the concept of problematic situations, a perspective that translates specific social issues and concerns into a set of broader cognitive categories.[44] A content analysis of the *Mainichi Shimbun* during a 52-week period identified twelve distinct aspects or attributes of the country's economic difficulties in the news coverage. Placing these attributes of Japan's economic difficulties in the context of problematic situations, a survey of the public asked how problematic they regarded each of the twelve aspects. A factor analysis of these items found that four macro-frames previously identified theoretically as problematic situations – breakdowns in institutional values, loss of individual value, ambiguous and confusing situations, and social conflicts – subsumed all twelve items.

The attribute agenda-setting effects of *Mainichi Shimbun's* coverage of the economy were tested both at the level of lower-order attributes, the twelve aspects of the issue, and at the macro-level of frames, the four problematic situations. At both levels, the degree of correspondence between the newspaper's agenda and the public's agenda tended to increase with greater exposure to the news. For lower-order attributes, the correlations for low, moderate, and high exposure to the news are +0.54, +0.55, and +0.64, respectively. For the frames, the correlations for these three levels of exposure are +1.00, +0.80, and +1.00. Although the differences in the values of these two sets of correlations are undoubtedly due to the difference in the number of categories, twelve versus four, there are agenda-setting effects for both micro- and macro-attributes.

A recent review of framing concluded that 'media effects research should abandon the general term "framing" as a catch-all phrase for a number of distinct media effects models and replace it with the more precise terminological distinction between *equivalence* and *emphasis* framing'.[45] Although the focus of the review is on framing, this distinction reveals both the similarity and dissimilarity between framing and agenda setting. Emphasis frames are similar to salient attributes in agenda-setting theory. For example, the issue of global warming can be framed in economic, political, or personal lifestyle terms, depending on the emphasis given to these angles in the news. In agenda setting, these frames would be conceptualized as issue attributes. Equivalence frames, however, are totally different from any aspects of agenda-setting theory. What the review terms 'equivalence frames' can also be referred to as 'rhetorical frames', two ways of saying the same thing that produce different outcomes.

A classic example of how different point-of-view perspectives – two different ways of presenting the same situation – result in vastly different responses is Daniel Kahneman and Amos Tversky's experiment, in which alternative messages were cast in terms of saving lives versus causing death.[46] Another example is the familiar 'the glass is half full' versus 'the glass is half empty'. In terms of an attribute, of course, the two phrases are equivalent descriptions of the contents of the glass. Apart from the overlap between attributes and emphasis frames, agenda setting and framing are distinct theoretical approaches to the study of communication.

Summing up

Elements prominent in the media's presentation of the vast world of public affairs frequently become prominent elements in our individual pictures of that world. This general proposition of agenda-setting theory was tested originally in terms of attention to the issues of the day, comparisons between the issues emphasized on the media agenda and those issues that became prominent on the public agenda. Time after time, these comparisons showed a high degree of correspondence between the media and the public in their ranking of issues. To borrow Lippmann's phrase, there is a high degree of correspondence in what these pictures were about. This is the first level of agenda setting.

There also is a high degree of correspondence in the actual details of these pictures. Comparing descriptions of political candidates and of public issues in the mass media with descriptions of these same objects by the public reveals a high degree of correspondence in the content of these pictures. Attributes that are prominent in the mass media also tend to become prominent in the public mind. This is the second level of agenda setting, where specific aspects of media content about public affairs are explicitly linked to the shape of public opinion. Both levels of agenda-setting reflect a major media role in the formation of public opinion, effects in the early stages of the communication process that encompass both the audience's initial level of attention and its subsequent understanding about a message's subject.[47]

How the public thinks about these matters, which typically embrace both cognitive and affective elements, is intertwined with what the public thinks, their attitudes and opinions. In *Agendas and Instability in American Politics*, Frank Baumgartner and Bryan Jones found that major shifts in public opinion and public policy were frequently preceded by significant shifts in the salient aspects of these issues among the public. Their case studies included nuclear power, tobacco, pesticides and auto safety.[48]

It is ironic that these consequences of attribute agenda setting bring us back to media influences on attitudes and opinions. That is where the empirical study of mass communication started in the 1940s and 1950s, and that is the area that was largely abandoned after a generation of scholars reported that there were few, if any, significant effects. The theory of agenda setting emerged as a response to that narrow judgement, and Chapter 8 will revisit that judgement in light of recent theoretical developments.

4 Networks of Issues and Attributes

In agenda-setting research, an agenda is usually conceived as a list of discrete issues (or other objects) and their attributes rank-ordered by the frequency with which they are covered by the media or mentioned by the public in opinion polls. In the news, however, issues and attributes are bundled together. In the homepage of a news website, a story about a major scientific breakthrough may compete for space and attention with a feature on healthy lifestyles. Important events and 'soft news' are displayed side to side, without any explicit cue to determine which one is more important. At the same time, a political journalist can highlight many different attributes about a candidate in the same story. In all these examples, determining which issues or attributes are higher up in the news agenda can only be done through systemic analysis over time. Basic agenda setting provided a straightforward methodology for doing this – count how many times a topic is covered in the news. Attribute agenda setting heeded the call for more fine-grained analyses of how media influence public opinion by exploring the exact attributes of those issues highlighted in the news. Still, basic and attribute agenda setting take a discrete view of issues and attributes. A subsequent step in the same direction is what we now call network agenda setting, which studies the specific issue and attribute 'bundles' that make up the news and show up in public thought and conversation.

The concept of compelling arguments, reviewed in Chapter 3, is the first theoretical recognition of the ability of the media to transfer the relationships among the elements of the media agenda to the public agenda. The concept of compelling arguments holds that news media can bundle an object with an attribute and make them salient in the public's mind simultaneously. A number of other bundles also can be considered.

Son and Weaver's expansion of the media's object and attribute agendas takes into account journalistic aspects of the context in which the news media present the candidates and their affective attributes to the public.[1] Their 2000 US presidential election study investigated which news sources of candidate salience and which news sources of candidate affective attribute salience predicted changes in public opinion about each of the candidates, either immediately or cumulatively. The effects at both the first and second levels of agenda setting on the standings of the candidates in national public opinion polls were primarily cumulative, rather than immediate, and different news sources had very different effects. For candidate salience, reporters' analysis and polls had strong cumulative effects on the poll standings. For candidate attribute salience, statements by both the candidate himself and by members of the competing party had strong cumulative effects on the poll standings. Other news sources had little or no impact.

This expanded perspective suggests integrating traditional measures of object and attribute salience with journalistic elements, such as sources or perhaps the style of writing, that characterize news stories. In terms of Lippmann's 'pictures in our heads', both the concept of compelling arguments and the integration of the attributes of news stories with traditional measures of object and attribute salience raises the question: 'To what extent are the media able to transfer the salience of an integrated picture?'

Some psychologists and philosophers hold that people's mental representations operate pictorially, diagrammatically, or cartographically. In other words, audiences map out objects and attributes as network-like pictures according to the interrelationships among these elements. From this perspective, the news media transfer the salience of relationships among a set of elements to the public. These sets could be the objects on the media or public agendas, the attributes on the media or public agendas, or a combination of objects and attributes, which is to say, a fully integrated set of objects and attributes (including attributes of the media message). These sets of relationships among elements of the media and public agendas are the third level of agenda setting.[2] Here the focus is on the transfer of the salience of entire networks of objects and/or attributes, not just the salience of the discrete elements examined at the first and second levels of agenda setting.

Associative memory

Theoretically central to network agenda setting is an associative network model of memory. Scholars in various disciplines – cognitive psychology, philosophy, geography, and communication – have theorized this associative memory model in similar ways, yet under different names. Examples include the associative network model,[3] cognitive mapping,[4] and the spreading activation model.[5] Rather than conceptualizing our mental representations as hierarchical or linear structures – as implied in first and second-level agenda-setting theory – these associative models hold that representation operates as a network of elements.[6] In a network model of the public agenda, individuals' cognitive representations are a network-like structure where each particular node typically will be connected to numerous other nodes. Here a node in the network can refer to any unit of information: objects and their attributes; goals, values, and motivation; affective or emotional state; and even macro units like schema or frame.[7]

Take political communication as an example. When an individual considers a political candidate and cites certain attributes to describe that candidate, it is not necessary for the individual to articulate a hierarchy of attributes ranked by their salience. Instead, an assortment of attributes can constitute a network-shaped picture describing that candidate in the individual's mind. And the news media are a major source of information for these cognitive networks. As we noted in Chapter 1, the news media can determine our cognitive maps of the world.

Networks of candidates and attributes

The initial exploration[8] regarding whether the media can bundle a variety of elements and make them salient in the public's mind used data from an earlier study, which found strong attribute agenda-setting effects based on a traditional analysis of discrete sets of political candidates' attributes. In the original study of the images held by voters of four state-wide political candidates in Texas,[9] the overall correspondence between the media attribute agenda and the public attribute agenda was +0.65. Using the statistical technique of network analysis to analyse the pattern of bundled attributes on the media agenda and the public agenda – that is, an investigation of third-level agenda-setting effects – the correlation was +0.67, a result that is statistically very similar to the original analysis. Of course, the networked representations of these agendas are a much richer picture of these attributes. These results from the bundled election data were replicated with new data, collected during the 2010 gubernatorial election,[10] and yielded a correlation of +0.71.

For these third-level agenda-setting studies, the initial step was to array the data in a matrix, indicating how often each pair of attributes occurred in the same news article (the media network attribute agenda) and how often each pair of attributes occurred in survey respondents' descriptions of the candidates (the public network attribute agenda). The matrix displaying the co-occurrence of the ten attributes found in the content analysis of the media is in Box 4.1. A similar matrix for the co-occurrence of these same ten attributes was constructed from survey respondents' descriptions of the candidates.

These matrices are the input for network analysis of the data – UCINET for this study, other studies have used R or similar software.

Box 4.1   Matrix of candidate attributes

	A	B	C	D	E	F	G	H	I	J
A		4	2	3	3	0	1	2	0	3
B	4		9	11	7	5	7	2	4	17
C	2	9		7	6	3	4	1	2	8
D	3	11	7		6	4	3	1	1	12
E	3	7	6	6		1	1	1	1	8
F	0	5	3	4	1		3	0	2	6
G	1	7	4	3	1	3		1	2	5
H	2	2	1	1	1	0	1		0	1
I	0	4	2	1	1	2	2	0		2
J	3	17	8	12	8	6	5	1	2	

(A= Leadership; B= Experience; C= Competence; D= Credibility; E= Morality; F= Caring about people; G= Communication Skills; H= Pride in family/backgrounds, roots, and race/ethnicity; I= Non-politician; J= 'Other' comments about the candidates' personal qualification and character.)

Source: Lei Guo and Maxwell McCombs, 'Network agenda setting: A third level of media effects', Paper presented to the International Communication Association, Boston, 2011.

Box 4.2   Media and public attribute agenda networks

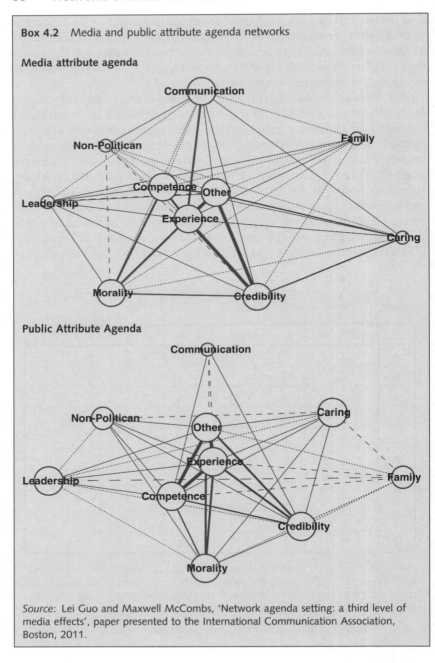

Source: Lei Guo and Maxwell McCombs, 'Network agenda setting: a third level of media effects', paper presented to the International Communication Association, Boston, 2011.

This software calculates the correlation between the two matrices and also diagrams the underlying networks. Both the media network attribute agenda and the public network attribute agenda examined in the first network agenda-setting study[11] are presented in Box 4.2.

In addition to calculating the correlation measuring the degree of correspondence between the media network attribute agenda and the public network attribute agenda, network analysis also details the degree centrality of each attribute in the media and the public attribute agenda networks. In the case of networks composed of objects, such as issues, network analysis details the degree centrality of each object in the media and the public agenda networks. Specifically, degree centrality refers to the number of links (ties) that a node in the network (a specific attribute or object) has with all the other elements in the network. In the context of a network, degree centrality is a measure of the salience of each element in the network.

In Box 4.2, the attributes Competence and Experience have many ties to other attributes in the networks and consequently high degree centrality scores. In contrast, the attribute Non-politician has a low degree centrality score. Also note that the thickness of the lines connecting the nodes in the diagrams indicates the number of links between elements.

Accumulated evidence on network agenda setting

Moving beyond a tight focus on network attribute agendas during political campaigns, a subsequent study examined network issue agendas across a five-year period.[12] For each of five years between 2007 and 2011, the authors compared the Pew Research Center's Project for Excellence in Journalism weekly content analysis detailing the most covered topics in four dozen American news outlets (the media network issue agenda) with monthly Gallup polls asking the 'most important problem' question (the public network issue agenda). The correlations between the media and the public agendas across the time period ranged from +0.65 to +0.87. An additional cross-lagged correlation analysis established that in the majority of cases the media network issue agenda influenced the public network issue agenda. Comparison of all five years combined of the media network issue agenda with the public network issue agenda yielded a correlation of +0.81.

Following the trend of earlier stages of agenda-setting research, initial explorations of network agenda setting concentrated in electoral campaigns in the United States. An innovative study[13] conducted during the 2012 election between Barack Obama and Mitt Romney examined the ways in which different issues were bundled on Twitter by the news media and how these bundles influenced how Twitter users discussed the election. For fifteen of the seventeen weeks of the campaign analysed, the network issue agenda of Obama supporters was positively correlated with newspapers' and broadcast channels' network issue agendas. At the same time, the network issue agenda of Romney supporters was significantly correlated with traditional media's network issue agendas in thirteen of the seventeen weeks analysed. These results were replicated when comparing the network agenda of both Obama and Romney supporters with the corresponding issue agendas of new media, such as MSNBC, Fox News, and the personal accounts of journalists working on these outlets. Other network-based studies of agenda setting have also been conducted in the context of recent US elections.[14]

Outside the United States, a study[15] applied the network agenda-setting model to data collected during Taiwan's 2012 presidential election. Networks of issues and candidate attributes in the media (newspapers and television) were compared with similarly measured networks of public opinion. As in the case of the Obama and Romney study, the overall correlation between the Taiwanese media and public network agendas was positive and significant, particularly at the attribute (instead of the issue) level.

Network agenda setting has also witnessed replications and extensions moving beyond political campaigns. Based on a similar method to that of the initial study on network agenda setting, news reports and responses to a public opinion survey conducted in Hong Kong about two different issues were compared using network analysis.[16] In both cases, the evidence shows strong attribute agenda setting effects at the third level. There also is research on network attribute agendas on the Iraq War comparing news coverage in the US, China, Taiwan, and Poland.[17] Another study focused on the network agendas of technology themes, products, and companies among so-called tech bloggers and the traditional news media.[18] An empirical work compares the network agendas of Greenpeace, news media, and Facebook's discussion of the actors and attributes involved in an environmental issue.[19]

A new gestalt perspective

Although third-level agenda setting and its network analysis statistical methodology are new aspects of agenda-setting theory, which have emerged in recent years, this is an extension of a gestalt perspective that has its roots in the earliest days of agenda setting. By a gestalt, we mean the collective mix of major public issues and news topics presented by the news media to the public. This gestalt perspective also describes what members of the public experience and absorb as they are exposed to the media agenda.

In the first days of agenda-setting research, Ray Funkhouser found a correlation of +0.78 in his comparison across the entire decade of the 1960s of the major issues in the news with the public's responses about the most important issues facing the United States across that decade.[20] More recently, Stromback and Kiousis[21] found that the total amount of attention to political news – attention to the gestalt presented by the media – predicted the salience of the issues most important to voters in deciding upon their vote, not their attention to specific news media.

Agenda-setting studies using network analysis have reinvigorated the theory's application to the current media environment. As argued in Chapter 1, for many years, agenda setting was thought to be dependent upon the fate of traditional news media. Many observers argued that, as the homogenous agendas of television, radio, and newspapers were replaced by the heterogeneous agendas of digital media, the possibility for agenda-setting effects diminished. However, network agenda-setting studies have incorporated data from Twitter, partisan websites, and other nontraditional media sources, finding strong evidence for the transfer of salience from one set of agendas to another.[22] Furthermore, the network approach has triggered a new round of cross-national research on agenda setting,[23] which has been a limitation for other communication theories.

Summing Up

Traditional first and second-level agenda-setting research examines the transfer of discrete message elements – issues or other objects and their attributes – from the media to the public. However, regarding the media agenda as a bundle of networked elements, a gestalt, and examining the connections among these elements offers a more comprehensive view of what the media present and what the public experiences.

Using network analysis has proved an important advancement in our understanding of media influence on public opinion. The cognitive and affective maps offered by news reports about candidates, issues, and their respective attributes are an important influence on media users' psychological maps of the 'world outside' – the bundle of objects and attributes conveyed by the media often become the bundle of objects and attributes that people have in their minds and conversations.

5 Why Agenda Setting Occurs

Sometime back in a high-school physics class you probably encountered the scientific principle 'Nature abhors a vacuum.' A similar proposition applies to human psychology. Innate within each of us is a need to understand our surrounding environment.[1] Whenever we find ourselves in a new situation, in a cognitive vacuum, so to speak, there is an uncomfortable feeling until we explore and mentally map that setting. Think back to your freshman year in college when you probably arrived on a new and unfamiliar campus to undertake a new intellectual voyage. Or your experience in moving to a new city – or even visiting a new city, especially one in a foreign country. In those situations, newcomers feel a need to orient themselves to the situation at hand. Colleges conduct extensive freshman orientation sessions. Publishers find it profitable to offer tourists guidebooks that contain maps, lists of hotels and restaurants, and a variety of other orienting information.

In the civic arena, there are also many situations where citizens feel a need for orientation. In primary elections to select a party's nominee for office, there are sometimes as many as a dozen candidates. Because it is a primary election, the orienting cue frequently used by voters, party affiliation, is moot. All the candidates belong to the same party. In this circumstance, many voters feel a strong need for orientation. Much the same situation exists in bond elections and other referenda elections, where again party labels are not pertinent, as well as in many elections for lower-level offices that present nonpartisan and, often, unfamiliar candidates. In all these circumstances, voters frequently turn to the news media for orientation, either to garner pertinent information about the situation at hand from the news coverage or directly to the editorial endorsements.[2]

Not every voter feels this need for orientation to the same degree, of course. Some citizens desire considerable background information before making their voting decision. Others desire no more than a simple orienting cue. Need for orientation is a psychological concept, which means that it describes individual differences in the desire for orienting cues and background information.

These patterns of behaviour frequently exhibited in election settings are one outcropping of psychologist Edward Tolman's general theory of cognitive mapping.[3] Earlier we encountered a similar idea in Lippmann's concept of the pseudo-environment, not the world as it is, but the picture of the world that is in our minds. What is common to both is the idea that we form maps – albeit many times sketchy and highly condensed maps – of the external environment. Emphasizing the purposive nature of this map-making, Robert Lane reviews our 'efforts to extract meaning from the political environment'.[4] Lane attributes the origins of these efforts variously to the innate nature of humans, the process of childhood socialization, and formal education. The psychological concept of need for orientation introduced by David Weaver in the 1972 Charlotte study of agenda setting, summarized in Chapter 1, describes these efforts at meaning and provides a psychological explanation for the transfer of salience from the media agenda to the public agenda.

Relevance and uncertainty

Conceptually, an individual's need for orientation is defined in terms of two lower-order concepts, relevance and uncertainty, whose roles occur sequentially. Relevance is the initial defining condition of need for orientation. Most of us feel no psychological discomfort and no need for orientation whatsoever in numerous situations, especially in the realm of public affairs, because we do not perceive these situations to be relevant. The internal politics of Armenia or New Zealand stir little interest among most citizens of Europe or North America. Much the same can be said of many issues of the day, even in our own country. There are many issues with little constituency among the public at large. In these situations, where relevance to the individual is low or even non-existent, the need for orientation is low.

Among individuals who for whatever reason perceive the relevance of a topic to be high – to keep matters simple, relevance is considered here as either low or high – the level of uncertainty about the topic must also be considered. As we see in Box 5.1, level of uncertainty is the second and subsequent defining condition of need for orientation. Frequently, individuals already have all the information that they desire about a topic. Their degree of uncertainty is low. This is the case for many public issues where public opinion is highly stable over long periods of time. In this circumstance, people do not usually ignore the news media, but they monitor the news primarily in order to detect any significant changes in the situation at hand.[5] Under these conditions of high relevance and low uncertainty, the need for orientation is moderate.

At other times, both relevance and uncertainty are high. This is often the case in party primary elections where there are many unfamiliar candidates and the easy orienting cue of party affiliation

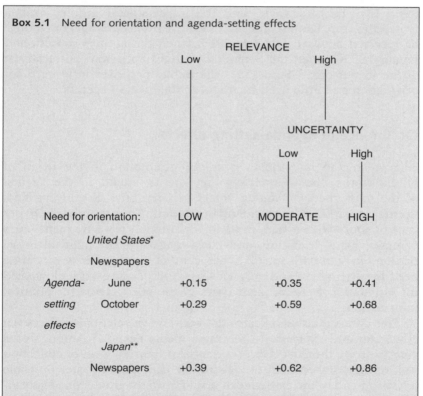

Box 5.1   Need for orientation and agenda-setting effects

| | | RELEVANCE | | |
| | | Low | | High |

| | | | UNCERTAINTY | |
| | | | Low | High |

Need for orientation:		LOW	MODERATE	HIGH
*United States**				
	Newspapers			
Agenda-	June	+0.15	+0.35	+0.41
setting	October	+0.29	+0.59	+0.68
effects				
*Japan***				
	Newspapers	+0.39	+0.62	+0.86

Source: David Weaver, 'Political issues and voter need for orientation', in *The Emergence of American Political Issues*, ed. Donald Shaw and Maxwell McCombs (St Paul, MN: West, 1977), pp. 107–19.
**Source*: Toshio Takeshita, 'Agenda-setting effects of the press in a Japanese local election', *Studies of Broadcasting*, 29 (1993), pp. 193–216.

is unavailable. This is also the case for what are essentially new issues on the public agenda, such as the extensive debate in recent times on health-care reform in the United States. The complexity and broad implications of this issue resulted in high relevance and high uncertainty for many Americans. In theoretical terms, those citizens had a high need for orientation.

In contrast, most Americans felt little need for orientation in regard to the sexual scandal involving president Bill Clinton and Monica Lewinsky in 1998. While most perceived the president's personal conduct as reprehensible, a majority also regarded this behaviour as irrelevant to his position as president. Poll after poll reported high job-performance ratings for Clinton as president, despite the continuing obsession of the news media with the scandal.[6] A similar trend may be observable with the impeachment inquiry against Donald Trump. Despite intensive negative news coverage, the ratings he received between October 2019, when the inquiry started, and January 2020, when the Senate acquitted him, remained steady at 40 to 45 per cent.[7] Sometimes the public perceives little need for orientation and little need to attend to the media's agenda.

Occurrence of agenda-setting effects

The greater an individual's need for orientation in the realm of public affairs, the more likely they are to attend to the agenda of the mass media.[8] Among voters in Charlotte, North Carolina, during the 1972 US presidential election, for example, 79.8 per cent of those with a high need for orientation were frequent users of newspapers, television, and news magazines for political information. In comparison, 62.5 per cent of those with a moderate need for orientation and only 47.4 per cent of those with a low need for orientation were frequent users of the mass media for political information.

This concept also explicates the well-known relationship between education and exposure to the mass media agenda.[9] Among Texas voters during the 2000 US presidential primaries, level of education was strongly linked both to viewing the candidate debates on cable television and to the existence of need for orientation defined specifically in terms of whether there was any personally relevant issue on the campaign agenda. Detailed analysis of these relationships revealed that need for orientation is an intervening variable that explains the link between education – a broad-brush, background predictor of an individual's cognitive orientation to public affairs – and viewing the candidate debates – a highly specific information-seeking behaviour. With increased education, particularly some college or more, there was more likely to be a need for orientation. In turn, the existence of this need was linked with debate watching.

During an election, voters frequently learn a great deal about the candidates and their issue positions from the news media and from political advertising. This learning includes significant adoption of the media agenda in direct relation to the voters' level of need for orientation. Below the conceptual diagram in Box 5.1 of need for orientation is a summary of the degree of agenda setting that occurred among voters in Charlotte during the 1972 US presidential election.[10] During the summer months as the campaign took shape and, later, during the autumn campaign, agenda-setting effects increased monotonically with the strength of the need for orientation. The metaphor of an election as an open civic classroom is bolstered by the increased degree of agenda setting that occurred from June to October. The students were doing their lessons.

This same pattern of agenda-setting effects was found in the Japanese mayoral election previously discussed in Chapter 1.[11] When these Japanese voters are stratified according to their level of need for orientation, Box 5.1 shows that the strength of the agenda-setting effect increases monotonically with the degree of need for orientation. Recall that the overall result among these voters was a modest, but positive, correlation of +0.39. This is a very low correlation in comparison to those found in most of the evidence.

However, Box 5.1 shows a correlation of +0.62 between the media agenda and voters with a moderate need for orientation and an astounding correlation of +0.86 for those voters with a high need for orientation. Further examination of the evidence from that election provides an explanation for the overall modest correlation of +0.39. A majority of the voters interviewed, some 57 per cent, had a low need for orientation. Only 21 per cent had a high need for orientation. In this situation, the concept of need for orientation provides a concise explanation for the low degree of correspondence overall between the media agenda and the public agenda. With a low need for orientation, the majority of voters had little motivation to attend to the media agenda or to adopt that agenda.

The concept of need for orientation also provides an explanation for the near-perfect match between the media agenda and the public agenda in the seminal Chapel Hill study.[12] The overall correlation obtained there was +0.97, a degree of correspondence that greatly encouraged the continued exploration of the agenda-setting phenomenon. Although the concept of need for orientation was not explicated as part of agenda-setting theory until a few years later, it is clear in retrospect that the original Chapel Hill evidence of agenda-setting effects was based exclusively on persons with a high need for orientation. Recall that the persons interviewed in Chapel Hill were selected randomly from the list of registered voters. In other words, the presidential election and its issue agenda were relevant to them. They were registered voters, but registered voters who had not yet made a commitment to a particular presidential candidate. The entire sample consisted of these undecided voters. In theoretical terms, all of these voters had high uncertainty. High relevance and high uncertainty define a high need for orientation, the theoretical condition under which the highest degree of correspondence is predicted between the media agenda and the public agenda. Chapel Hill's correlation of +0.97 is very high, but not astronomically high in comparison with the +0.86 found among those Japanese voters who also had a high need for orientation.

Additional evidence for the validity of the need for orientation concept is found in Box 5.2, which indicates that the importance voters attach to knowing the presidential candidates' positions on the issues increases with need for orientation.[13] In other words, this general concept of intellectual curiosity explains differences in the level of voter interest in a specific kind of information. The consistently higher levels of interest in the issue positions of Jimmy Carter, the relatively unknown challenger, compared to the issue positions of Gerald Ford, the incumbent president running for re-election, further validates the idea of need for orientation.

For a local environmental issue in the mid-western US, there was also a strong level of correspondence (+0.60) between the pictures in people's minds and local newspaper coverage on six facets of

Box 5.2 Need for orientation and average level of interest in political information

	Need for orientation		
	Low	Moderate	High
Ford's issue positions	4.8*	5.5	5.7
Carter's issue positions	5.0	5.6	6.3

* Maximum rating = 7

Source: David Weaver and Maxwell McCombs, 'Voters' need for orientation and choice of candidate: mass media and electoral decision making', paper presented at the American Association for Public Opinion Research, Roanoke, VA, 1978.

the development of a large, man-made lake.[14] And, in line with the patterns described above for object salience at the first level of agenda setting, the degree of correspondence between the newspaper's agenda of attributes and the pictures in people's heads also increased with their need for orientation. Among persons with a low need for orientation, the match between their attribute agenda and the newspaper's attribute agenda was only +0.26. Among those with a high need for orientation, the match was +0.77. Again, we see that increased need for orientation results in greater acquisition of the media agenda.

Relevance

Relevance is the core concept defining need for orientation. The relevance of a topic or issue springs from many sources, and these multiple origins of relevance have been elaborated in considerable detail in recent years. A creative investigation of eight different issues ranging from global warming to personal health used a set of thirteen bipolar semantic differential scales to measure the relevance of those public issues.[15] Analysis of these data revealed three underlying dimensions:

- Social relevance – measured by such scales as irrelevant/relevant and unimportant/important,
- Personal relevance – e.g. matters to me/doesn't matter to me, of no concern to me/of concern to me,
- Emotional relevance – e.g. boring/interesting, exciting/unexciting.

Spanish sociologist Fermín Bouza made a similar theoretical distinction regarding personal and social relevance:

> individuals maintain an important area of personal interests that is separated, to a certain degree, from what that individual considers to be public interests or everyone's interests. This clear distinction between an area of personal interests and another area of public interests marks the existence of an area that I will define as the impact area of political communications [...] because it is the area in which the individual feels a clear coincidence between the country and himself.[16]

These theoretical distinctions between social relevance, personal relevance, and emotional relevance neatly organize the findings from a pair of state-wide polls in Texas that explored why respondents named a particular issue in response to the widely used Gallup MIP question, 'What is the most important problem facing this country today?'[17] Analysis of a set of follow up questions developed to probe the resonance of the issue named in response to the MIP question identified a stable set of five sources of issue relevance that dovetail with these theoretical distinctions:

• Social relevance – Civic duty and peer influence
• Personal relevance – Self-interest and avocation
• Emotional relevance – Emotional arousal

Taking another approach to the personal relevance of issues, Sebastián Valenzuela found that Ronald Inglehart's materialist and postmaterialist values[18] are strongly related to agenda-setting effects.[19] Using a content analysis of major daily newspapers across Canada, survey data from the 2006 Canadian national election, and an original experiment, Valenzuela found that at both the aggregate and individual levels there were stronger agenda-setting effects among persons with materialist values than among those with post-materialist values. At the aggregate level, for example, the correlation between the media agenda and the public agenda was +0.55 for materialists and +0.35 for post-materialists. These findings are consistent with the media's more prominent coverage of materialist issues such as the economy and crime relative to post-materialist issues such as the environment and political reform.[20]

Emotions towards objects in the news matter, too. Despite the tradition in Western thought of downplaying emotion while highlighting reason, neuroscientists have long contended that affect and cognition are intertwined. In agenda setting, Joanne Miller found that certain emotions triggered by the news explained issue salience judgements.[21] Her experiments measured the extent to which participants felt angry, proud, hopeful, and happy as well as sad and afraid while reading news stories about crime. Only feelings of being sad or afraid mediated the agenda-setting effect. Neither a general measure of emotional arousal nor a general measure of valence created from combinations of all six emotional responses explained the link between exposure to crime news and naming crime as an important issue facing the nation. However, the creation of negative valence did result in a greater likelihood of naming crime.

This emerging gestalt elaborating the concept of relevance is an example of a major trend in agenda-setting research. Borrowing a term from physics, this renewed examination of the concept of relevance is a centripetal trend in which scholars have turned their attention inward to further explicate basic concepts of agenda-setting theory.

Another example of this trend is the set of scales developed by Jörg Matthes to measure need for orientation with survey questions.[22] Corresponding to the first level of agenda setting, there are scales to measure need for orientation towards the object itself. For example, 'It is important for me to observe this issue constantly.' Other scales measure the second level of agenda setting, both the substantive attributes of the object under consideration – 'I would like to be thoroughly informed about specific details' – and the affective attributes of the object reflected in the journalistic evaluations found in commentaries and editorials – 'I attach great importance to commentaries on this topic.' These three sets of measures can be summed to create a single need for orientation score for each questionnaire respondent.

In an investigation of the issue of unemployment in Germany, Matthes found that the strength of need for orientation measured by this composite measure predicted basic first-level agenda-setting effects. However, the strength of NFO measured by the composite scale did not predict media effects at the second level of agenda setting, specifically, the affective attribute of the unemployment issue.[23]

A controlled experiment comparing the strength of the traditional need for orientation measures and these new measures in predicting agenda-setting effects found that the traditional measure was the stronger predictor. However, comparison of the traditional measure with the first dimension of the new measure, the dimension directly concerned with first-level agenda setting, indicated that these two measures are very similar.[24]

Personal experience with public issues

The news media are not our only source of orientation to public affairs. Personal experience, which includes conversations with our family, friends, and co-workers, also informs us about many issues. The dominant source of influence, of course, will vary from person to person and from issue to issue. For an economic issue such as inflation, personal experience is almost certainly dominant. If there is significant inflation in the economy, personal experience with routine purchases will reveal its presence. We do not need the news media to alert us to this problem or to dispel any uncertainty about its significance. In contrast, for economic issues such as national trade deficits, the news media are likely to be our sole source of orientation. There are many other public issues, especially in the realm of foreign affairs, where personal experience is greatly limited, if not non-existent. In theoretical terms, some issues are obtrusive, that is, they obtrude into our daily lives and are directly experienced. Other issues are unobtrusive. We encounter them only in the news, not directly in our daily lives.[25]

Examination of the agenda-setting influence of the news media on the salience of three public issues in Canada found the pattern of results predicted by this distinction between obtrusive and unobtrusive issues.[26] In Box 5.3, there is very little correspondence (+0.28) between the pattern of news coverage for inflation and the salience of this issue among the Canadian public over a sixteen-month period of time. But for the abstract, unobtrusive issue of national unity, there is an extraordinary match (+0.96). We shall return shortly to the third issue, unemployment, which a priori would seem to be an obtrusive issue, but whose empirical outcome here (+0.67) more closely fits the prediction for unobtrusive issues. But first let us examine some additional evidence from the United States that sustains the validity of this distinction between obtrusive and unobtrusive issues.

This same pattern of results – a high degree of correspondence between public opinion and news coverage for unobtrusive issues

---

Box 5.3 Agenda-setting effects for obtrusive and unobtrusive issues (natural history perspective)

OBTRUSIVE ——————————————————— UNOBTRUSIVE

Canada*

| Inflation +0.28 | Unemployment +0.67 | National unity +0.96 |

United States**

Crime +0.19	Unemployment +0.60	Pollution +0.79
Cost of living +0.20		Drug abuse +0.80
		Energy +0.71

*Source: James Winter, Chaim Eyal and Ann Rogers, 'Issue-specific agenda setting: the whole as less than the sum of the parts', *Canadian Journal of Communication*, 8, 2 (1982), pp. 1–10.
**Source: Harold Zucker, 'The variable nature of news media influence', in *Communication Yearbook 2*, ed. Brent Ruben (New Brunswick, NJ: Transaction Books, 1978), pp. 225–40.

and little correspondence for obtrusive issues – was found across a decade of public opinion in the United States.[27] Box 5.3 displays high correlations for the unobtrusive issues of pollution, drug abuse and energy, but very low correlations for the obtrusive issues of crime and the cost of living. At the local level in the United States, the pattern of agenda setting in Louisville summarized in Chapter 1 also indicates a lack of media influence on obtrusive issues. Detailed comparisons between the issue rankings on the media agenda and public agenda in Louisville, whose overall correlation was +0.65, found that 'the major differences between the two agendas involve issues with which people would likely have personal experience: road maintenance, health care, the courts, drainage, and mass transit'.[28]

All this evidence about the differences between obtrusive and unobtrusive issues is based on the analysis of individual issues. In terms of the Acapulco typology, this evidence is based on the natural history perspective. There also is evidence pointing to the same conclusion that is based on the competition perspective, which considers the entire agenda of issues. Box 5.4 presents a series of comparisons in which the issues on the media and public agendas have been divided into two sets, an agenda of unobtrusive issues and an agenda of obtrusive issues.[29] The agenda of unobtrusive issues consists of seven items: government credibility, government spending, foreign affairs, the environment and energy, crime, race relations, and social problems. The four issues on the obtrusive issue

---

Box 5.4 Agenda-setting effects for obtrusive and unobtrusive issues (competition perspective)

	Agenda of obtrusive issues	Agenda of unobtrusive issues
New Hampshire		
Newspapers	+0.32	+0.67
Television news	+0.33	+0.74
Indiana		
Newspapers	+0.06	+0.60
Television news	+0.06	+0.59
Illinois		
Newspapers	+0.20	+0.95
Television news	+0.32	+0.95

Source: David Weaver, Doris Graber, Maxwell McCombs and Chaim Eyal, *Media Agenda Setting in a Presidential Election: Issues, Images, and Interest* (Westport, CT: Greenwood, 1981).

agenda are all economic concerns: unemployment, taxes, inflation, and the general state of the economy. In Box 5.4, all of the measures for unobtrusive issues show substantial agenda-setting effects.

The median correlation falls between +0.67 and +0.74. In contrast, there is very little correspondence between the media and public agendas of obtrusive issues. The median correlation falls between +0.20 and +0.32.

A general explanation for these striking differences in the public's response to media coverage of obtrusive and unobtrusive issues is provided by the concept of need for orientation. Because obtrusive issues are defined as issues obtruding into people's everyday lives, personal experience in many instances will sufficiently orient individuals to the situation at hand. The result is a low need for any additional orientation, a circumstance that predicts low correlations between the media agenda and the public agenda. On the other hand, personal experience is not a sufficient source of orientation for unobtrusive issues. For these, the theoretical assumption is that the media agenda is commonly the primary source of orientation, the source to which people turn to reduce their uncertainty.

Individual differences

When the concept of obtrusive and unobtrusive issues was added to the theory of agenda setting, this distinction was initially treated as a simple dichotomy. Issues were either obtrusive or unobtrusive. The examples in Box 5.4 are typical of this research. But Box 5.3 already anticipated a more subtle treatment of this concept in which obtrusive and unobtrusive are the polar anchors of a continuum.[30] Examination of the public's encounters with any issue will reveal individual differences in the degree of their personal experience.

The issue of unemployment, which we set aside earlier, illustrates the importance of treating this concept as a continuum rather than as a simple dichotomy. For persons who are unemployed or who know unemployed persons, this is an obtrusive issue. But for tenured university professors, affluent professionals and many others, unemployment is an abstract, unobtrusive issue. There is a vast range of personal experience regarding unemployment – and many other issues. In Box 5.3 this range of experience with unemployment is reflected by its location in the middle of the layout beneath the line that connects obtrusive and unobtrusive to illustrate a continuum. The values of the two correlations there, which are highly similar even though measured at different times in Canada and the United

States, suggest that for the majority of North Americans during those times, albeit certainly not for all, the issue of unemployment was essentially an unobtrusive one.[31]

A detailed look at individual differences regarding personal experience with issues is available from a panel study of American voters, who were asked to name 'the one most important problem that the national government in Washington should do something about'.[32] This analysis focused on three major issues. For the issue of unemployment, the distinction between obtrusive and unobtrusive was based on survey respondents' personal or household employment situation. For the issue of inflation, each respondent's household financial situation was the basis of this distinction. For the issue of crime, the distinction was based on perceptions about how safe it was to walk in their neighbourhood at night.

Among persons for whom these were obtrusive issues, the evidence supports the theoretical assumption that need for orientation is satisfied largely through personal encounters with these issues and that the media are not important sources of influence. High media users were no more likely to name any of these three issues than were low media users. Increased exposure to newspapers and television news did not increase the salience of these issues among this group.

However, among persons for whom these were unobtrusive issues, the evidence supports the tandem theoretical assumption that need for orientation is largely satisfied through use of the mass media and that the degree of media influence increases with greater exposure. Among voters for whom these issues are unobtrusive, their salience was higher among high media users than among low media users.

The role of the mass media vis-à-vis personal experience regarding the salience of public issues is not always so distinct. Evidence for the tandem influence of the frequency of media use and personal experience with public issues is found both in public opinion about crime in Syracuse, New York, and in Texans' level of agreement with a thirteen-issue media agenda.[33] In support of the basic hypothesis of agenda setting, the salience of local crime as an issue in Syracuse was greater among those with high exposure to news about local crime, and in Texas frequency of media use was the best predictor of agreement with the media agenda. However, personal experience was also a significant predictor of the salience of crime in Syracuse and of overall agreement with the media agenda in Texas. In both geographical settings – a middle-sized city in the northeastern US and a large southwestern state – media use and personal experience combined to produce strong agenda-setting effects. In Syracuse, for example, the salience of crime as a local issue was highest among those with high exposure to news about local crime on television and in the newspapers and some personal experience with crime. In Texas, the more that people used the news media and the more involved they were personally with public issues, the more the public agenda reflected the media agenda.

This positive, tandem relationship of media use and personal experience with agenda-setting effects would seem to contradict the evidence presented in Boxes 5.3 and 5.4. More fundamentally, however, this outcome contradicts the assumption of conflicting cues – media versus personal experience – for personal orientation that is implicit in all the early research on obtrusive and unobtrusive issues. In turn, negative evidence regarding this assumption prompts the explication of a more detailed theoretical map. Consider the possibility that personal experience with an issue does not always result in a psychologically satisfactory level of orientation. Parallel to individual differences in media use and personal involvement with issues are considerable individual differences in the amount of information that satisfies everyone's need for orientation. For some individuals, personal experience with an issue rather than satisfying the need for orientation may trigger a search in the mass media for further information and validation of the problem's social significance.[34] Sensitized to the issue, these individuals may become particularly apt students of the media agenda.

In conjunction with these individual differences in issue sensitization, recall Lane's observation at the beginning of this chapter about the influence of formal education upon 'efforts to extract meaning from the political environment'. In this regard, the educational background of the Texans whose surprising behaviour has been noted here was considerably higher than the national average. Explicit measurement in the future of the breadth and depth of need for orientation can clarify the roles of personal experience and media use in the agenda-setting process.

The Texas evidence[35] also introduces personal conversation, a channel of communication that has not been considered in any detail up to this point. Among those Texans, the frequency of talking about public issues was positively linked to the frequency of both media use and personal experience with public issues. Although talking about public issues was a companion of these other behaviours, it did not have an independent role, either positive or negative, in determining people's level of agreement with the media agenda. A similar result is reported from an investigation into whether people who rely more on interpersonal communication have the same agenda as people who rely more on the news media. No differences were found in the agendas of these two groups.[36]

This lack of a distinct role for talking about public issues represents a rough average of the accumulated evidence on the role of conversation in the agenda-setting process.[37] Sometimes, conversation reinforces the impact of media agendas.[38] A field experiment in Germany published an article about a new issue in a magazine and measured two days later changes in the public salience of that issue, as well as the interpersonal discussion triggered by the article.[39] The study found the article had a cascading effect, by first increasing conversation about the issue, which subsequently increased the salience of the issue, even among people not exposed initially to the article. At other times, conversation is a conflicting source of orientation that reduces the influence of the media.[40]

Incidental learning

Need for orientation, issue unobtrusiveness, and personal experience are important determinants of people's likelihood of adopting the media agenda. So is media attention – the active processing of media content when exposed to it – as we saw in Chapter 2. However, given the ubiquity of news, which the rise of social media platforms such as Facebook, Twitter, and Instagram has deepened, it is not clear whether attention is a necessary condition for agenda-setting effects any more.

In the past decade, research on this aspect has developed around the concept of incidental learning.[41] Incidental learning about a particular object, person, or situation is more likely when it is omnipresent.[42] The high degree of redundancy across agendas in the contemporary media environment increases the likelihood that the public will learn the media agenda, even at low levels of news exposure. Two experiments conducted in Germany demonstrated the role of incidental learning in the agenda-setting process.[43] In one of them, participants were instructed to visit a news website every day for two weeks. The coverage of the experimental issue was varied by frequency of coverage (daily vs. occasionally) and salience of presentation (lead story vs. short reports). The results show that for people who are not personally involved with the issue, incidental media cues (e.g. news format) were sufficient to produce agenda-setting effects. The incidental nature of learning the news agenda, in turn, helps issues move rather quickly from the media to the public agenda. The real-world experiment by Gary King and colleagues[44] described in Chapter 1 found that the public agenda reflected the news media agenda within six days. In sum, the transfer of salience between media and public agendas can occur both in active and incidental fashion. We come back to this conclusion in Chapter 6, when discussing the transfer of salience.

Agenda-melding

Agenda-melding (also spelled agendamelding) is a recent perspective incorporated into agenda-setting theory that further explicates the creation of the public agenda. Whereas most agenda-setting research has focused on the influence of the news media on the public agenda, agenda-melding incorporates these agenda-setting effects into a broader learning process that includes other sources. As Donald Shaw et al. noted:

> Agenda-melding is a process. It is inside our minds. It involves mixing messages from the larger world into the personal plays on the stage that is the mind. Traditional and social media play a role, as do our interactions with other people at all levels. Our values and experiences provide the magnets that attract and hold the pieces together.[45]

The result of this marriage of media agenda setting and other personal interactions is the construction of a personal reality that enables each of us to live comfortably in imagined civic communities.

A key element in the concept of agenda-melding is the distinction between mainstream, legacy media and various social media that represent a distinct point of view about the issues and topics of the day. A useful distinction is between vertical media and horizontal media.[46] The vertical media, such as newspapers and network television news, seek to reach across many different strata of society and build a broad-based audience and broad agenda. In contrast, horizontal media primarily seek out a homogenous audience built around a specific point of view or specific interest. On the internet some politically oriented social media seek a conservative audience while others seek a liberal audience. Put another way, vertical media disseminate agendas relevant to a large proportion of the public. Horizontal media disseminate agendas for a smaller proportion of the public that reflects a point of view, commonly liberal or conservative. Typically, these horizontal media utilize social platforms that allow a back-and-forth flow of information in which both sender and receiver can exert some degree of control over the framing of messages. The prominence of these strong feedback loops in horizontal media is a major characteristic of the expanded media landscape that has evolved in recent decades.

Agenda-melding's marriage of the distinct sources of personal agendas – vertical media and horizontal media reflecting opposing points of view – is a productive contribution towards understanding the agenda-setting process. Agenda-melding emphasizes that 'audiences do not passively absorb media agendas, but do so actively, if unconsciously. Audiences meld media agendas into personal pictures of civic community.'[47]

Traditional agenda-setting research, which established the field over the past half century with hundreds of empirical studies, examined the relationship between the media agenda and the public agenda. However, there is ample room for additional explanatory variables. Meta-analyses of the media-public agendas relationship found that the average of these correlations hovers around +0.50.[48] This means that it explains only 25 per cent of the variance in the dependent variable, leaving ample territory for other predictor and explanatory variables.

Agenda-melding research during the 2016 US presidential election found that the issue agenda of active Twitter users showed a high correspondence with both the vertical and horizontal media.[49] By election day, both Democrat and Republican tweets strongly correlated with the vertical media issue agenda (+0.96 for Democrats and +0.97 for Republicans). For horizontal media, Republicans showed a higher correspondence with Republican sources (+0.87) than Democrats did with Democrat sources (+0.75). All the correlations are strong, and the match of Democrats and Republicans with horizontal media is somewhat less than their match with vertical media.

Replication of these results in a reanalysis of data from the 2012 US presidential election using network analysis – reviewed in Chapter 4 – found similar patterns, except for a reverse in the use of compatible horizontal media. In that election Democrats showed a higher correspondence with Democrat sources than Republicans did with Republican sources.[50]

The salience of Democrat media to Democrats and the salience of Republican media to Republicans is obvious. But the shift in the extent to which Democrats and Republicans reflect the agenda of their party's horizontal media reflects what Richard Carter called a pertinence relationship,[51] the comparison of the value of two objects (in this case, partisan horizontal media). Given the candidates, Obama and Romney in 2012 and Hillary Clinton and Donald Trump in 2016, Democrats may have felt a more intensive need for information about Obama, then a relative newcomer on the political stage, whereas Republicans may have felt a more intensive need for information about the newcomer Trump in 2016.

These agenda-melding results are grounded in strong inter-correlations among the issue agendas of vertical media, conservative horizontal media and liberal horizontal media. In 2012, the median correlation among the three media agendas was +0.83, and in 2016 the median correlation was +0.65. These are contemporary examples of the homogeneity of media agendas noted in the original Chapel Hill study. To be clear, agenda-melding is not an additional level of agenda setting. Rather, it is a process that opens the way to an expanded explication of how individuals construct their personal agendas.

Summing up

Need for orientation is the cognitive version of the scientific principle 'Nature abhors a vacuum.'[52] In the realm of public affairs, the greater an individual's need for orientation, the more likely he or she is to attend to the agenda of the news media with their wealth of information on politics and government.[53] This concept also identifies the issues that are most likely to move from the media agenda to the public agenda, namely, issues that are relevant and unobtrusive. If an unobtrusive issue resonates with the public, need for orientation will be moderate to high. In contrast, for obtrusive issues, need for orientation may be satisfied largely by personal experience. However, on occasion personal experience will create a desire for more information and people will turn to the mass media for additional orientation.

Need for orientation provides a detailed psychological explanation for why agenda-setting effects occur and is the most prominent of the contingent conditions for agenda-setting effects, those factors that enhance or constrain the strength of these effects. Contingent conditions were introduced as the second aspect of agenda-setting theory during the early 1970s. The first aspect, of course, was the basic relationship between the media agenda and the public agenda inaugurated by the Chapel Hill study. These aspects of agenda-setting research are not marked by the closing of one line of inquiry and the opening of another. Rather they are continuing lines of inquiry that parallel each other in time. Both of these early phases of agenda-setting research continue to this day by adding new contingent conditions, such as issue obtrusiveness, personal experience, and incidental learning. They also take place in new settings, particularly the continuing proliferation of internet and social media channels, for which the concept of agenda-melding may prove particularly fruitful.

6 How Agenda Setting Works

The agenda-setting effects of media are widespread. Observations have found agenda-setting effects across the United States in a variety of small towns and large cities. These effects also have been found abroad in cities as diverse as Tokyo, Japan, and Pamplona, Spain, and in countries as different as Argentina, Canada, Chile, China, and Germany. Altogether, there are now more than 500 empirical studies of agenda setting,[1] many following the original Chapel Hill example and conducted during political campaigns, others monitoring public opinion in non-election periods. There is considerable diversity in the public issues that have been examined over the past fifty years, a diversity encompassing the economy, civil rights, drugs, the environment, crime, a wide variety of foreign policy questions, and dozens of other public issues. The topics studied now extend far beyond public issues to include public figures, a growing variety of other objects, the attributes of these objects, and the networks of all these objects and their attributes. Agenda setting is a robust and widespread effect of mediated communication, an effect that results from specific content in the media.

For many, one of the most surprising aspects of the theory is the tremendous variability of the geographical and cultural settings in which agenda-setting effects occur. The culture and politics of the United States are exceedingly different from the cultural and political setting of Spain, where numerous agenda-setting effects have been measured. There is even more of a cultural and political contrast when we shift from Western countries to the younger democracies of East Asia and South America, where agenda-setting effects also have been observed.

Some years ago, a seminar in Taiwan discussed this widespread international replication of media effects originally found in the United States and came to the conclusion that agenda-setting effects – the successful transfer of salience from the media agenda to the public agenda – occur wherever there is a reasonably open political system and a reasonably open media system. Arguably, there is no perfectly open political system in any country in the world today, no system where the principle of one person, one vote, fully applies to every adult in the population.[2] But the political systems of the United States, Spain, and Taiwan – to cite some countries previously mentioned – are reasonably open in that elections really matter and actually determine the course of political history. Moreover, most adults are eligible to participate in these elections. The media systems of these countries – or at least significant portions of them – are also open in that they are relatively independent sources of news and political expression and are free from the domination of the government. Where these conditions of openness exist, the public accepts considerable portions of the issue agenda put forward by the news media.[3]

Observations made during the 1994 Taipei mayoral election in Taiwan[4] underscore the validity of this axiom that explains the widespread occurrence of agenda setting. At the time of that election, there were three television stations serving Taipei, and all three in one way or another were controlled by the government and the long-dominant KMT political party. Not surprisingly, no agenda-setting effects were found for television news. To echo a signature expression of American political scientist V. O. Key, albeit in a different setting, 'The voters are not fools!'[5] In contrast, significant agenda-setting effects were found for the two dominant daily newspapers in Taipei. Although these newspapers, like most news outlets around the world, favour a particular political perspective, they are independent businesses free from any direct control by the Taiwan government or the KMT. This Taipei example is a useful comparison of the influence of open and closed media systems where all the other political and cultural factors are essentially held constant.[6]

An ongoing stream of public opinion evolves in these civic arenas around the world that are defined by open political and media systems. Over time, the salience of individual issues rises and falls as the attention of the communication media and the public shifts. The previous chapter presented several aspects of the psychology of this process, including the concept of need for orientation that explains individual differences in attention to the media agenda, the concept of obtrusive and unobtrusive issues that introduces the role of personal experiences external to the media that play a role in the formation of the public agenda, and the concept of incidental learning that explains why agenda-setting effects can occur even when people pay little attention to news content. Here we will outline additional aspects of the public opinion process as issues appear on the media agenda and then move to the public agenda. We shall consider the capacity of the public agenda and competition among issues for a place on this agenda, as well as the time-span that is involved in the evolution of the public agenda.

Carrying capacity of the public agenda

The intense competition among issues for a place on the media, public, and policymaking agendas is the most important aspect of the process of agenda setting. At any moment there are dozens of issues contending for public attention. But no society and its institutions can attend to more than a few issues at a time. The resource of attention in the news media, among the public, and in our various public institutions is a very scarce one.

One of the earliest insights about agenda setting was the limited size of the public agenda. For many years, a statement that the public agenda typically included no more than five to seven issues at any moment was accepted as an empirical generalization and regarded as another instance of what the psychologist George Miller called the 'magic number seven plus or minus two', a sweeping empirical generalization that describes the limits of a wide variety of sensory processes.[7]

The accumulation of evidence over subsequent years suggests an even smaller limit. Only a few problems demonstrate any sizeable constituency among the public when in the United States the Gallup Poll asks a national sample, 'What is the most important problem facing this country today?' Across the ten Gallup polls asking this most important problem (MIP) question from 1997 to 2000, only half found a public agenda on which as many as five issues had a constituency of 10 per cent or more – the level of concern among the public that has been identified as the threshold for significant public attention.[8] Five issues, of course, is the bottom of the range for Miller's axiom. Across all ten polls, the public agenda ranged from two to six issues. Another analysis of trends from 1954 to 1994 – also based on responses to Gallup's MIP question – found no change in the capacity of the US public agenda.[9] Updating this portrait, a recent analysis of Gallup data from 1975 through 2014 found that despite the proliferation of media channels, the rise of social media, and elite polarization occurring in the United States during this period, the capacity of the public agenda remained virtually flat – on average, three issues reached 10 percent of responses to the MIP question.[10] This trend is not particular to the United States, either. For instance, the Latinobarometer 2017 survey, which polled 18 Latin American countries on their most important problems, found that only four issues garnered 10 per cent or more responses.[11]

This tight constraint on the size of the public agenda is explained by the limits of the public's resources, limits that include both time and psychological capacity. Limits on the size of most media agendas are even more obvious – a limited amount of space in the newspaper and a limited amount of time for broadcast news. Even the supposedly limitless capacity of the internet has not changed this. Data from the 2012 News Coverage Index collected in the United States by the Project for Excellence in Journalism found that only four topics exceeded 10 per cent of the news hole (i.e. the amount of space in a publication that remains for journalism after advertising has been placed) among the twelve websites considered.[12]

All these constraints on the agendas of public issues within a society at any moment are summed up in the idea of the agenda-setting process as a zero-sum game in which the rise of an issue on an agenda is largely at the expense of another issue, a perspective that underscores the intense competition among issues for attention by the media and the public.[13]

Historically, one result of this limited agenda capacity and intense competition among issues is that a few perennial concerns have held centre stage in public opinion. For instance, in the United States, in the years immediately following the Second World War, foreign affairs and economics occupied centre stage, with foreign affairs nearly always in the leading role. Although other issues were able to garner a constituency from time to time, this pair of issues dominated the US public agenda.[14]

Diversity and volatility of the public agenda

Despite the limits on the capacity of the public agenda to carry more than a handful of issues at any given time, there have been fluctuations both in the diversity of issues and the relative size of the constituencies around these issues. Sometimes, the three top issues get roughly equal public attention. Other times, there are one or two dominant issues and a handful of minority issues. In the United

States, the diversity of the public agenda decreased from the 1950s to the 1980s. However, from the 1980s to the 2000s, the public agenda became more diverse over time,[15] especially after the economic recession of 2008–2009.[16]

What can explain why, despite the lack of change in the capacity of the public agenda during this time, the diversity of issues on it increased? Part of the answer to this puzzle lies in the rising levels of education. Between 1954 and 2014 – the years covered in the analyses of the capacity of the US public agenda – the average number of years of total schooling in the United States increased 56 per cent, from 8.5 to 13.3 years.[17]

In *The Reasoning Voter*, Samuel Popkin observes:

> Education affects politics not by 'deepening' but by broadening the electorate – by increasing the number of issues that citizens see as politically relevant, and by increasing the number of connections they make between their own lives and national and international events.[18]

His observation acknowledges the widely documented situation that most people, even highly educated persons, rarely possess detailed, in-depth knowledge of public issues. Persons with higher levels of education do follow the news and discuss these issues more frequently with their family, friends, and co-workers. The principal outcome of this activity, notes Popkin, is that educated persons 'will have limited information about a wider range of subjects, including national and international events, that are further from daily-life experience'.[19] This broadening effect of education on the public agenda is readily apparent in the growing diversity of issues found on the public agenda.

As previously noted, at the time of the Second World War and in the post-war years up to 1960, a single category, international affairs, largely dominated the public agenda. But in the next two decades, the 1960s and 1970s, a larger array of issues was prominent. International issues were still on the agenda, principally Vietnam and the Cold War, but there also were large constituencies for economic issues as well as for civil rights. In the 1980s and 1990s, the public agenda continued to broaden and diversify. Four major issues each claimed more than 10 per cent – jobs, personal economic issues, law and order, and international affairs. Another four minor issues concerned with other aspects of the economy and domestic issues each claimed a 5 to 10 per cent share.[20]

The relative stability in the capacity of the agenda, coupled with the increasing diversity of issues that make it to the public agenda, has resulted in more issue volatility – some issues now move on and off the public agenda faster than in previous decades. In other words, the explanation that reconciles these aspects of the agenda-setting process is that a collision between the expansive influence of education and the restrictive influence of limited agenda capacity has resulted in a more volatile public agenda. In the United States, one category, international affairs, dominated centre stage in the 1950s. But the cast of issues began to grow in the 1960s and 1970s, and this trend for major issues to share the stage with minor issues, at least for brief intervals, continued well into the 1980s and onwards. 'By the mid 1990s, an issue was about twice as likely to drop off the agenda in four to six months as it had been in 1975.'[21] As we see in Box 6.1, the long-reigning divas of public affairs continued to get starring roles on the public agenda, and the duration of their time on stage often exceeded two years or more. The trend for the last two decades is less clear, though, as there is some evidence that the probability of an issue falling off the agenda decreased from its peak in the 1990s. Still, it is evident that the major issues in the US public agenda – the economy and government affairs – now share the spotlight from time to time with an array of emergent issues, such as the environment, education, and health. While these other issues

Box 6.1   Duration of major issues on the public agenda

	Average duration per cycle (in months)*	Number of cycles, 1954–94*
Personal economic issues	47.4	7
Politics and government	40.8	8
Asia	27.8	4
General foreign policy issues	25.2	13
Government spending	21.8	5
Russia and Eastern Europe	19.3	4
Jobs	15.1	14
General economic issues	14.0	5
Law and order	10.3	12
Technology	8.7	3

* A cycle is the period of time beginning when 10% or more of the responses to the MIP question first name this issue and continuing until this issue is named in less than 10% of the responses.
Source: Maxwell McCombs and Jian-Hua Zhu, 'Capacity, diversity, and volatility of the public agenda: trends from 1954 to 1994', Public Opinion Quarterly, 59 (1995): 495–525. Details of the specific issues mentioned over time that fall in these ten categories are in Appendix A of the article.

do not appear nearly as often, nor is their duration on stage nearly as lengthy, they do appear despite the limited capacity of the public agenda. This supports the notion that rising educational levels have broadened the influence on public perspectives about the issues of the day.

Education and agenda setting

Further insight into the role of formal education in the agenda-setting process comes from a comparison of five demographic characteristics that appear time and again in public opinion polls: age, education, income, sex, and race. Using a mix of issues that received either very high or very low coverage in the local newspapers, their salience was examined among nearly a thousand Americans in three communities stretching diagonally across the United States, from Florida to the Pacific Northwest.[22] Only a single demographic characteristic was related to the pattern of salience for these issues. Citizens with more years of formal education more closely mirrored the media agenda. This primacy of the educational experience is striking throughout the realm of politics and public affairs.

Whether one is dealing with cognitive matters such as level of factual information about politics or conceptual sophistication in assessment; or such motivational matters as degree of attention paid to politics and emotional involvement in political affairs; or questions of actual behaviour, such as engagement in any of a variety of political activities from party work to vote turnout itself; education is everywhere the universal solvent.[23]

Education has the conjoint effect of increasing individuals' attention to the news media and sensitizing them to a wider range of issues appearing in the news. On the other hand, higher levels of education do not appear to increase individuals' defensive responses to the pattern of emphasis in the news. Well-educated persons do not show any greater tendency than less-educated persons to argue against or erect psychological barriers to acceptance of the media agenda.[24]

However, one must be careful not to overstate the role of education and individual differences in the agenda-setting process. To define further the role of education vis-à-vis the messages of the media in determining the public agenda, the salience of four issues among the American public between 1977 and 1986 – inflation, unemployment, international problems, and government spending – was compared to the pattern of coverage on national television during the same ten-year period.[25] Shifts in the salience for each of these four issues were examined separately for population subgroups defined by education and family income. The salience of all four issues was expected to be higher among the more educated. Family income was also used as a measure of issue sensitivity to these four issues because inflation and unemployment were assumed to be less relevant and international problems and government spending more relevant to higher income families.

There were massive shifts in the salience of these issues between 1977 and 1986. Each issue displays a pattern of peaks and valleys, rising and falling sharply both on the media agenda and among the income and education subgroups. In contrast, the differences among the demographic subgroups themselves are minimal.

Specifically in terms of the fit between the salience of each issue on the media agenda and its salience among the public, for three of the issues – inflation, unemployment and international problems – all the demographic subgroups followed a similar trajectory over time that paralleled the number of TV news stories. There are significant demographic differences, but, in statistical terms, individual differences defined by education and family income accounted for only 2 per cent of the variance in salience, while the wide swings from year to year attributable to variations in the news coverage accounted for 37 per cent. 'In other words, media agenda-setting effects are not manifested in creating different levels of salience among individuals, but are evident in driving the salience of all individuals up and down over time.'[26]

Finally, there is an important footnote on the lack of agenda-setting effects for the fourth issue, government spending. In the final three years of the decade that was examined, the salience of government spending rose sharply and remained at high levels among most sectors of the public, despite a low level of attention in television news. Part of the explanation for the high salience of this issue among the public may come from what we know about the limited capacity of the public agenda and about the recurring appearance of some issues. During those final three years, 1984 through 1986, the salience of two other aspects of the economy, unemployment and inflation, were low on both the media and the public agenda. Recall that unemployment was one of the reigning divas on the public agenda during the last half of the twentieth century and that inflation also made frequent appearances. Government spending is best described as one of the minor issues that make an occasional appearance on the stage of public opinion. Its move to centre stage during 1984–1986 may well have occurred because both unemployment and inflation were offstage during much of this period. This again calls attention to the powerful constraints on the size of the public agenda.

Explaining the transfer of salience

There are two countervailing trends in contemporary agenda-setting research, a centrifugal trend expanding agenda setting into new domains that range from the third level of agenda setting discussed in Chapter 4 to a variety of disparate settings to be discussed in Chapter 8, and a centripetal trend in which scholars are returning to further explicate key theoretical concepts. Focused on the core concept of the transfer of salience from the media agenda to the public agenda, Toshio Takeshita identified two distinct theoretical paths for this transfer process, a path of deliberative cognitive involvement and a more casual path of incidental involvement.[27]

The proposal of a dual process of agenda setting is reminiscent of the Elaboration Likelihood Model of persuasion, which posits the existence of a 'central' and a 'peripheral' route of information processing of persuasive messages.[28] Both routes can result in persuasion, but imply very different levels of cognitive effort and, hence, different consequences in terms of the duration of attitude change. In Chapter 5, we saw that agenda setting can occur through two different paths – an active one, through media attention, and a passive one, through incidental learning.[29] Subsequent research has further probed this dual-process approach within the agenda-setting tradition.

Two experiments in Germany investigated a dual path of agenda setting among participants who freely selected what to read on a news site over a period of time.[30] The time spent with news stories about the key issues of the experiment was determined from each individual's log file. Prior to visiting the website, each participant's level of involvement with the manipulated issues was measured, and the log files indicated that higher involved persons read more stories.

Results of the experiments also indicated that when there was less cognitive effort – reading few stories – the media cues (frequency of appearance on the website and lead story vs. short reports) exerted significant influence on subsequent judgements of issue importance. In contrast, with higher involvement and a greater level of cognitive effort – reading more stories – the media cues did not influence subsequent judgements of issue importance.

Strikingly, these experiments found that 'less involved persons, who initially did not assign much importance to an issue and did not pay much attention to the issue-related coverage, estimated the issue as important as the highly involved and attentive persons, if the media emphasis placed on the issue was strong enough'.[31]

Two experiments in the United States further explicated these dual information-processing paths, agenda-cueing and agenda-reasoning, that result in media agenda-setting effects. These experiments also introduced a contingent condition for the strength of these effects, gatekeeping trust. In contrast to more general measures of media trust or credibility, gatekeeping trust is the specific belief that news coverage is the result of systematic efforts by journalists to prioritize problems.[32]

High gatekeeping trust increased the impact of the media agenda in agenda-cueing situations. In other words, persons with high gatekeeping trust believe that in making a judgement about the most important problems of the day the pattern of news coverage is appropriate for use as a cognitive shortcut to avoid doing that task for oneself. However, in agenda-reasoning situations, persons with low gatekeeping trust, who do not believe that the pattern of issue coverage in the news is the result of the careful weighing of issue importance, rely upon the specific content of the news to arrive at judgements of issue importance.

Theoretically complementary in their explanation of agenda-setting effects, the German experiments examined online processing of media content while the US experiments examined memory-based processing of media content.

Further explicating these theoretical paths, a field study in Kosovo returned to an earlier definition of the need for orientation in which its components, relevance and uncertainty, were used to create a 2 × 2 typology.[33] Unlike the earlier conceptualization which merged the two high–low cells of the typology as a measure of moderate need for orientation, this new approach made a theoretical distinction between these two cells. High relevance and low uncertainty was defined as moderate NFO–active, a situation where people might be expected to turn to partisan news media to reinforce their existing predispositions. In contrast, low relevance and high uncertainty was defined as moderate NFO–passive, a situation where people will turn to more balanced news media in their effort to reduce uncertainty.[34]

As expected, citizens with moderate NFO–active used partisan TV, radio, and newspapers considerably more than citizens with moderate NFO–passive, a finding that can be interpreted as evidence of selective perception. However, these same citizens also used independent TV, radio, and newspapers more than did moderate NFO–passive citizens. In turn, citizens with moderate NFO–active also showed the strongest attribute agenda-setting effects regarding attributes of seven political institutions in Kosovo – corrupt/fair, dishonest/honest, inefficient/efficient, and selfish/caring. The strength of these effects was significantly stronger than those found among the low, high, and moderate-passive NFO groups.

With the proliferation of channels in the new communication environment, there has been considerable interest in selective exposure. In a detailed, empirically grounded explication of selective exposure, Natalie Stroud found that about a third of the US public engage in a pattern of partisan behaviour characterized by exposure to like-minded political sources without using any non-like-minded sources.[35] Additional citizens, of course, may tilt heavily towards likeminded sources.

In line with the Kosovo findings, there may be a number of distinct agenda-setting paths. For citizens who are not heavily invested in partisan politics, perhaps it is essentially the broad agenda-setting process that we have mapped in the decades since Chapel Hill. But for those with high partisan involvement, it is likely that very powerful niche agenda-setting processes are at work. Evidence of this possibility is available in a subsequent study by Lindita Camaj, in which she elaborated on her initial Kosovo findings, this time using content analysis and survey data from the 2012 US election.[36] She found that people with high NFO were more likely to seek information from television programming that offered balanced news reporting, while people with moderate NFO–active were more prone to seek information from partisan television programmes. Interestingly, individuals with moderate NFO–active were as likely as people with high NFO to consume news on network television, suggesting that partisans are more likely than non-partisans to use both partisan and independent or mainstream media.

This evidence of distinct theoretical paths that result in agenda-setting effects is strengthened by the counterbalanced study designs: in Germany, attention-based experiments in which participants determined the pattern of exposure; in the United States, both content-based experiments in which exposure to an agenda-cueing or agenda-reasoning stimulus was explicitly manipulated and cross-sectional analyses of media content and survey data; in Kosovo a field study grounded in content analysis and survey research. In each of these settings, dual paths led to significant agenda-setting effects.

Timeframe for effects

The mythic hypodermic needle theory of media effects viewed media influence as essentially immediate. In that view, media messages were injected into the audience much as medical injections are administered to patients and typically achieve rather quick effects. This perspective disappeared with the accumulation of empirical evidence in the 1940s and 1950s, a body of evidence summarized by the Law of Minimal Consequences.[37] In response, communication scholars such as Wilbur Schramm asserted that the truly significant effects of media were likely to be very long term, much as awesome formations of stalactites and stalagmites in caves are created drop by drop over eons of time. That is, media effects could eventually be strong and massive, but not when analysed in the short term.

Against that background, how long does it take for media attention to an issue to translate into significant salience for that issue on the public agenda? Does it really take the psychological equivalent of eons? Or could it be that the shift from attitude and opinion change to earlier points in the communication process, such as focus of attention and perceived importance, yields evidence of relatively short-term media effects?

Recall that the rise and fall of public concern about civil rights in the United States across a 23-year span of time reflected primarily the pattern of media attention to this issue in the preceding month.[38] Agenda-setting effects are far from instantaneous, but they are relatively short term. Experiments on agenda setting have shown that the time lag between news coverage and public salience can be measured in a few weeks, even days.[39] There is, of course, the question of how generalizable this picture is of the agenda-setting process. We know that the strength of agenda-setting effects can vary from issue to issue. However, two other investigations of the timeframe for agenda-setting effects also suggest that the span of time involved in the transfer of issue salience from the media agenda to the public agenda is generally in the range of four to eight weeks.

A longitudinal analysis of the public opinion trends for each of three major issues during the 1960s and 1970s – pollution, drug abuse, and energy – found a median correlation of +0.66 between the public agenda and the national television news agenda of the preceding month.[40] A three-wave panel study found a median correlation of +0.77 between the salience of the environment among the public and the agenda of three local newspapers during the preceding two months.[41] Our confidence that the public agenda typically reflects the media agenda of the preceding one to two months is enhanced by both the strength and the high degree of convergence among the correlations in all three investigations, which included both newspapers and television news and a variety of issues.

Under conditions of high personal involvement in the news, the timeframe for agenda-setting effects may be even shorter.[42] Use of the internet by individuals to discuss four public issues was monitored during the 1996 US presidential election. The frequency of discussion from September until a week after the November election for immigration, health care, taxes, and abortion was compared with the pattern of news coverage on these issues in the *New York Times*, Reuters, Associated Press, CNN, and *Time* magazine. Discussion of immigration responded immediately to news coverage. Discussions of health care and taxes had longer timeframes, but still the effects were evident within a week. Among the four issues examined, only the discussions of abortion were not linked to the pattern of news coverage, an outcome most likely linked to the highly controversial and emotional nature of this issue. For the three issues where the pattern of media coverage did influence the salience, the timeframe was much shorter than for the agenda-setting effects of traditional news media. This outcome is not surprising because the internet is an outcropping of the public agenda where persons with high interest in an issue can respond behaviourally.[43]

All this evidence about the timeframe for agenda-setting effects is based on analyses tracing the salience of individual issues on the public agenda across time, analyses that are designated in the Acapulco typology as the natural history perspective. Obviously, there are other perspectives to consider, notably the competition perspective that takes into account the full array of issues competing for positions on the agenda. While it is useful analytically to examine a single issue in order to understand the process underlying its natural history, the competition perspective provides a portrait of the real world where there is always a melange of issues in flux. From this perspective, what timeframe links the media and public agendas? A comprehensive investigation of the timeframe for agenda-setting effects examined an agenda of eleven public issues and a range of news media from local TV news and the local newspaper to national TV news and the weekly news magazines.[44]

Although there are variations across these news media in how many cumulative weeks of news coverage show the best fit with the public agenda, the variation is relatively small and falls in essentially the same range observed for individual issues. The range of time-spans producing the optimum match between the media and public agendas is one to eight weeks, with a median span of three weeks. In every case, the agenda-setting effects are sizeable. If our benchmark is the four to eight weeks typically found for the natural history of issues, the distribution found in this study based on a competition perspective falls towards the shorter end of that range.

An even shorter time-span was found in more recent analysis conducted in Germany using data collected between 2009 and 2014.[45] Using a sophisticated time-series analysis, the study found that the time lag between media coverage and the maximum public response ranged between one day and two weeks. 'Despite a lot of variation, agenda-setting effects typically peaked after 7 to 8 days; TV news came into effect faster, but also wore out more quickly than newspaper effects.'

Considering the complexity involved in the full array of issues on the media and public agendas, the time-span for the appearance of significant agenda-setting effects is rather short. Over the course of a relatively few weeks, the salience of topics featured in the news media is absorbed by significant numbers of the public.

Long ago, Paul Lazarsfeld described mass communication as an informal classroom where the students continuously come and go and, much like some students in more formal classrooms, do not always pay full attention even when they are present. But people do learn from the media. They learn a panoply of facts, many of which they incorporate into their images and attitudes about a variety of objects. They also learn about the most important issues of the moment, incorporating the agenda of the news media into their own agenda of the key issues facing society.

The news media are teachers whose principal strategy of communication is redundancy. With the proliferation of new communication channels in recent decades, the level of redundancy arguably is even higher than ever before. Over and over again, our media teachers repeat topics, at times with great emphasis, at other times just in passing. It is primarily the accumulation of these lessons over a period of one to eight weeks that is reflected in the responses of citizen students when we inquire about the most important issues facing the nation. Of course, in most cases the lessons did not begin abruptly eight weeks previously, but it is the pattern of coverage in the most recent weeks that has by far the greatest impact on the public.

There is also empirical evidence about the reverse side of the learning coin, the decay of information and the forgetting that takes place for any pattern of learning. Without delving into this aspect of learning in as much detail as we have spent on the acquisition of information, the timeframe for the decay of learning lacks the tight focus reflected in the acquisition of current public concerns.[46] The point of decay of agenda-setting effects, defined as the point in time where significant correlations between the media agenda and the public agenda disappear, ranges from eight to twenty-six weeks. In the study from Germany, some issues decayed even more quickly, in less than a week.[47]

These conclusions about the duration of issues on the public agenda, both the learning process involved in the rise of issues in public attention and the decay of learning as issues disappear from public attention, are essentially empirical generalizations. We know about these timeframes because the logs of various social scientists' exploratory voyages into this realm yield rather consistent data, especially in regard to the rise of issues on the public agenda. But empirical generalizations are less sound than empirical findings that are grounded in an explicit theoretical context.

In this regard, the current status of agenda-setting theory differs little from the larger literature on media effects. Examination of the indices of two comprehensive and widely used texts on communication theory reveals scant attention by scholars to the question of timeframes for various media effects.[48] This is simultaneously a theoretical deficit and an opportunity for advancement.

There are the beginnings of a theoretical framework for agenda-setting effects in an early discussion of time-related concepts.[49] These concepts include the time lag between the appearance of an issue on the media agenda and its appearance on the public agenda as well as the optimal effect span, the length of time yielding the peak association between the two agendas.[50] There is also a larger theoretical framework in the idea of the agenda-setting process as a zero-sum game.[51] However, considerable work remains to be done.

Diversity of salience measures

Methodologically, agenda-setting theory is well supported by increasingly diverse research designs and measures of object and attribute salience that are far beyond the seminal Chapel Hill study.

> Methodological skill [...] has increased rapidly over the years. Initially tied to procedures involving rank-order correlations, it has expanded to include the most sophisticated structural equations modelling, as well as cross-sectional data and multi-wave panels. Researchers also have used time series analysis of aggregated public opinion measures,

naturalistic experimental designs, and in-depth case studies to study agenda setting. Given the amount of activity surrounding agenda-setting research, we can conclude that it is one of the most vigorously pursued models in the field.[52]

There is also methodological strength in the wide variety of measures used to ascertain agenda-setting effects on the public agenda. Frequently, these effects are measured by responses to the question used by the Gallup Poll since the 1930s: 'What do you think is the most important problem facing this country today?'[53] This is a highly robust measure of issue salience.[54] A split-ballot design in a state-wide survey compared versions of the public agenda with a social frame of reference versus a personal frame of reference as well as versions using the traditional term 'problem' versus 'issue'. The results indicate the inter-changeability of MIP indicators that vary both in their frame of reference and choice of words.[55]

Although this MIP question – and similar open-ended questions assessing issue salience – continues to be widely used, there are numerous creative alternatives for measuring object and attribute salience on the public agenda. The experimental comparison of the printed and online versions of the *New York Times* supplemented the traditional MIP question with additional measures of salience, recognition, and recall of news stories that had appeared in the paper and ranking the importance of various sets of these news stories.[56] In another experiment, the salience of racism was measured by three five-point scales: the importance of the issue, the extent of discussion with friends, and the need for more government action.[57] Also recall the series of experiments discussed in Chapter 4 that used thirteen bipolar semantic differential scales to measure issue salience and to identify three underlying dimensions of salience.[58] Even online search activity from Google queries has been used as a proxy for measuring public salience.[59]

An analysis of public opinion about local crime in Syracuse, New York, used both a traditional rating scale and a behavioural measure to ascertain the salience of this issue:

Thinking about the issue of crime in the Syracuse area, on a scale from 1 to 10 where 1 is of no importance to you personally and 10 is most important to you personally, how would you rate the issue of crime? How concerned are you about being a victim of crime? Would you say you are not at all concerned, slightly concerned, or very concerned?[60]

The salience of the various attributes of an environmental issue, development of a man-made lake in the midwestern US, was ascertained in three different ways.[61] Two open-ended questions asked which aspects of this issue were of most interest and which had been discussed the most. The third measure of salience used paired comparisons, a scaling technique in which all possible pairs from a list of attributes are shown to survey respondents. For each pair, the respondent selects the one regarded as most important. These sets of judgements can then be used to create an interval scale of salience. As we see in Box 6.2, all three measures of attribute salience documented very similar attribute agenda-setting effects. The similarity of these replications attests to the robustness of these effects and their measurement.

Returning to an open-ended approach to measuring salience, analyses worldwide of attribute agenda setting for candidate images have used versions of the open-ended question originally devised for the 1976 presidential election study in the United States: 'Suppose you had some friends who had been away for a long time and were unfamiliar with the presidential candidates. What would you tell them about [candidate x]?'[62]

Finally, recent investigations of both object and attribute agendas have used non-response as an inverse measure of salience – arguably, the most fundamental of all measures of salience. For example, the smaller the number of persons who have no opinion about a public figure, the greater the salience of that person among the public.[63] Or, the greater the number of persons who have no opinion about a particular aspect of a public issue, the lower the salience of that attribute of the issue among the public.[64]

In the contemporary communication environment, there are a plethora of channels for public communication about public affairs. Methodologically, these social media provide a rich source of unobtrusive measures of the public agenda that parallels the long-standing advantage of content analysis as an unobtrusive

Box 6.2 A comparison of attribute agenda-setting effects based on three measures of attribute salience among the public for an environmental issue

Open-ended questions		Paired-comparison Scaling
'most interesting aspect'	'aspect discussed the most'	
+0.60	+0.61	+0.71

Source: David Cohen, 'A report on a non-election agenda setting study', paper presented to the Association for Education in Journalism, Ottawa, Canada, 1975.

methodology. We now have access to data on the media agenda and the public agenda that was produced without researchers in mind, a significant advantage over survey data. An innovative time-series analysis of the issue of same-sex marriage took advantage of this unobtrusive approach to compare the agenda-setting effects of local and national media in Chicago and Atlanta.[65] Computer automation also has considerable potential in this new environment. For example, an evaluation of the Lexicoder Sentiment Dictionary recommends its use for coding of the affective attribute agenda, a significant advance beyond the tedious – and often unreliable – coding of tone by traditional techniques.[66] With the increasing adoption of computational methods in communication research, agenda-setting studies using computer-assisted content analyses and social network analyses have become more frequent, especially for measuring the transfer of networked agendas from the news media to social media users.[67]

Summing up

Citizens are involved in a continuous learning process about public affairs. Their responses to a pollster's quiz about what are the most important issues typically reflect the media's lessons of the past few weeks. The agenda-setting effects that are frequently the outcome of this process are shaped to a considerable degree by characteristics of the media's messages and to a far lesser degree by the characteristics of the recipients of those messages. Public communication, including many of the new social media, is a process in which highly redundant messages are widely disseminated. Various characteristics of these messages influence how many persons pay attention and apprehend at least some portion of their content.

Ultimately, mediated communication is a transaction between a single member of the audience and the media message, a transaction in which individual differences might seem paramount. In a sense, communication effects are a large set of overlapping personal experiences. Although no two of these experiences are identical, it is fortunate for our goal of a parsimonious theory of communication effects that persons with vastly different personal characteristics frequently have highly similar experiences.

7 Shaping the Media Agenda

As more and more evidence accumulated about the agenda-setting influence of the news media on the public, scholars in the early 1980s began to ask, 'Who sets the media's agenda?' A new line of theoretical inquiry began to explore the various factors that shape the agenda presented by the news media. In this new line of inquiry, the media agenda becomes the dependent variable, the outcome that is to be explained.

Up to this point, the media agenda has been an independent variable, a key causal factor in the shaping of public opinion. Box 7.1 illustrates this broader, more comprehensive model of the agenda-setting process, which includes major antecedents of the media agenda. Thinking about the origins of the media agenda brings to

---

Box 7.1 An expanded view of agenda setting

OTHER AGENDAS	MEDIA AGENDA	PUBLIC AGENDA

Organizations
Interest groups
Public relations
Political campaigns

Object ======> | News norms | Object ========> Object

Transfer of salience

Attribute ======>| News norms | Attribute ========> Attribute

mind many other agendas, such as the agenda of issues and policy questions considered by legislative bodies and other public agencies that are routinely covered by the news media, the competing agendas in political campaigns, or the agenda of topics routinely advanced by public relations professionals. There are many organized agendas in modern societies.

A useful metaphor for understanding the relationships between all these other agendas and the agenda of the news media is 'peeling an onion'. The concentric layers of the onion represent the numerous influences at play in the shaping of the media agenda, which is the core of the onion. This metaphor also illustrates the sequential nature of this process in which the influence of an outer layer is, in turn, affected by layers more proximate to the core of the onion. A detailed elaboration of this onion contains many, many layers. Pamela Shoemaker and Stephen Reese's hierarchy of influence model, for example, identifies five distinct layers of influence on news media content, ranging from the prevailing culture to the psychology of the individual journalist.[1] A number of the intermediate layers in this onion describing the behaviour of news organizations and the professional norms of journalism constitute the sociology of news, an area of scholarship with which agenda-setting theory began to converge in the 1980s.[2]

In this chapter, a response to the question of who sets the media's agenda will be outlined in terms of the three fundamental layers illustrated in Box 7.2. At the surface of our theoretical onion are key external news sources, such as the president of the United States, routine public relations activities, and the efforts of political campaigns, both off- and online. Deep inside the onion are the interactions and influence of the various news media on each other, a phenomenon now commonly referred to as intermedia agenda setting. Social media like Facebook and Twitter, for instance, are now an important arena for intermedia interactions. To a considerable degree, these interactions validate and reinforce the social norms and practices of journalism. These norms and practices, which are the layer of the onion immediately surrounding the core, define the ground rules for the ultimate shaping of the media agenda.

That professional norms and practices are the most determinant factor on the news media agenda should be evident to anyone who has worked in journalism – news media themselves are the final arbiter of which events and issues will be reported and how they will be reported. For instance, the predilection for negative news[3] limits the range of events and issues covered by the media agenda, whereas investigative journalism can expand the media agenda by raising

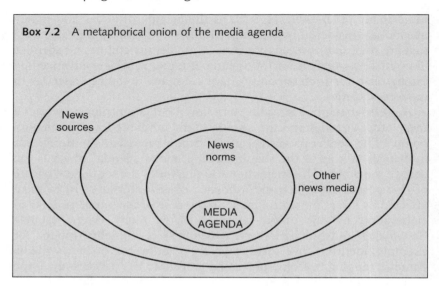

Box 7.2   A metaphorical onion of the media agenda

awareness about new issues, such as corruption. Nevertheless, those who hold the executive power – presidents and prime ministers – are typically considered the most important agenda setters of a country's news media.

The president and the national agenda

One way of describing and evaluating a national political leader, such as the president of the United States, is by his or her role in setting the national agenda. Increasingly, a major task for the president is to influence the focus of news coverage as a means of shaping supportive public opinion that, in turn, will leverage his influence on the actions of the Congress. There is considerable anecdotal evidence that the president is America's number one newsmaker. Virtually everything that a president does, from convening international conferences to stopping for a snack while on the campaign trail, is considered newsworthy.

Does being at the centre of media attention provide significant opportunities for the president to set the media's agenda? One rich opportunity for assessing the president's influence is the annual State of the Union address.[4] Required by the US Constitution, for more than a century this report was a written document submitted to the Congress. By the 1960s, the annual State of the Union address became a major media event, a public address in the Capitol by the president to a joint evening session of the House of Representatives and Senate that was broadcast live nationally by all the television networks.

The format of this address – essentially a shopping list of issues that the president wants the Congress to address – makes it ideal for assessing the president's agenda-setting influence. Here in a single message – a message that is weeks in the making with considerable input from numerous political and policy advisers – is a list of the president's priorities. Do these priorities reflected in the president's agenda have any significant influence on the subsequent media agenda, any influence on the pattern of news coverage extending beyond those days immediately surrounding the State of the Union address?

Surprisingly, the initial exploration of this question, which examined President Jimmy Carter's 1978 State of the Union address, found no significant impact on the subsequent month's coverage of his eight priority issues in the *New York Times* and the *Washington Post* or on the three national television networks.[5] However, there was evidence that the coverage of these eight issues in the *New York Times* and on the television networks during the month preceding the State of the Union address had influenced the president's agenda.

A replication based on the identical research design examined a very different American president, Richard Nixon.[6] In this instance, the agenda of fifteen issues in President Nixon's 1970 State of the Union address did influence the subsequent month's news coverage in the *New York Times* and the *Washington Post,* and on two of the three national television networks. There was no evidence of any media influence on the president. Enormous differences in presidential personalities are, of course, a major factor to be considered in these kinds of historical analyses. However, even with this factor in mind, there is also evidence of a shifting relationship between a president and the news media over the years of his administration. Analyses of President Franklin Roosevelt's first seven State of the Union addresses, which were delivered from 1934 to 1940, yielded highly mixed evidence about the relationship between the news media and the president.[7] Similar evidence of mixed effects is also found in analyses of President Reagan's 1982 and 1985 State of the Union addresses.[8]

Sometimes, the president can direct the attention of the news media towards certain issues and to set the agendas of the media and the public. At other times, the president follows the media and public opinion.[9] A similar conclusion is evident in studies conducted outside of the United States. In Canada, Stuart Soroka analysed data from 1985 and 1995 and found that for issues such as fiscal policy, the Throne Speech exerted a considerable effect on the news media agenda.[10] In Chile, Sebastián Valenzuela and Arturo Arriagada studied the influence of the president's annual message to Congress on both the public and news media agendas, using data collected between 2000 and 2005.[11] They found that across five issues, the president's speeches had a positive, statistically significant effect on subsequent television news coverage, even when controlling for the public agenda and the effects of real-world indicators.

These examinations of executive speeches provide considerably more than an answer to the question of who sets the media's agenda. They also illustrate one aspect of policy agenda setting, the process by which governments make decisions about what social issues will be the focus of their attention.[12] However, there has been considerably less empirical study of the role of the news media in the shaping of public policy than in the shaping of public opinion.[13] Perhaps the major reason for this situation is that the role of the news media is typically inconsistent for any particular issue over the lengthy periods of time usually required for the evolution of the public policy process. Media agendas are shaped far more by the news values of immediate events and situations than by the social value of deliberation.

Nevertheless, there is evidence that the media have exerted substantial influence on the policy agenda at both the national and the local level. Examples from studies conducted in the 1980s and 1990s include a seminal article on child abuse in the *Journal of the American Medical Association* that stimulated considerable media attention and subsequent actions by the Congress and many state legislatures;[14] a new year's community agenda on the editorial page of the *San Antonio Light* – supported by subsequent news reporting during the year – that resulted in vastly increased spending for children's programmes by the city government;[15] and two series of investigative reports by a Chicago television station that led to policy changes in the city's police and fire departments.[16]

More recently, a review[17] of works published between 2005 and 2015 found 32 studies that deal with the influence of the media agenda on the policy agenda, covering countries as diverse as Belgium, Chile, Denmark, the Netherlands, Spain, Switzerland, and the United States. Two-thirds were 'objective' studies; that is, they analyse the content of news coverage and policymakers' behaviour to examine the transfer of issue salience from one agenda to another. The remaining studies were 'subjective', based on the perceptions of political actors regarding media influence. This review concluded that there is, indeed, a media effect – a moderate one, in the case of objective studies, and a strong one, in the case of subjective studies. Which aspect of the policymaking process is most influenced by the media, though, was clear-cut: 'the media matters more for what politicians *say* than for what they *do*'.[18] That is, news coverage makes a large impact on symbolic agendas, such as presidential speeches, compared to substantive agendas, such as the fiscal budget.

Taking all this research together, it is evident that the relationship between news coverage and the evolution of public policy over time is circular, a pattern documented in careful detail for such diverse issues as AIDS,[19] global warming,[20] and drugs.[21] Because of both the intermittent and often circular role of the news media, examinations of media communication and public opinion have less frequently included the third member of the democratic triad, government policy.

Subsidizing the media agenda

Journalists can observe only a small fraction of each day's situations and events. Even with the routine exclusion of many kinds of events in many places, there are still not enough journalists to cover all aspects of even the major topics in the daily news. Much of what we know, for example, about the workings of government and business, from the international level down to the local level, originates with public information officers and other public relations practitioners who represent important news sources. These communication professionals 'subsidize'[22] the efforts of media organizations to cover the news by providing substantial amounts of organized information, frequently in the form of press and video news releases, news conferences, planned events, background briefings, and messages posted on Facebook, Twitter, and other social media.

A seminal examination of the *New York Times* and *Washington Post* across a twenty-year period found that nearly half of their news stories were substantially based on press releases and other direct information subsidies.[23] Some 17.5 per cent of the total number of news stories appearing in these newspapers was based, at least in part, on press releases. Press conferences and background briefings accounted for another 32 per cent. The *New York Times* and *Washington Post* are major newspapers with large staffs and immense resources. Their substantial reliance on public relations sources underscores the key role that information subsidies play in the daily construction of all media agendas.

Additional evidence of the key role of public relations in shaping the news agenda was found in an extensive 2006 investigation of five major British newspapers and four broadcast news outlets. Nineteen per cent of the newspaper stories and 17 per cent of the broadcast news stories 'were verifiably derived mainly or wholly from PR material or activity'.[24] Adding stories that were a mix of public relations and other information brought the totals to 30 per cent for newspapers and 31 per cent for broadcasters. News coverage of six state government agencies by Louisiana's major daily newspapers also was based substantially on information provided by those agencies' public information officers.[25] Slightly more than half of the information subsidies provided by these public information officers, primarily written news releases but occasionally personal conversations, appeared in subsequent news stories. The agenda of topics ranged from state finances and the general economy to ceremonial events and celebrations. Specifically, the correspondence during an eight-week period between the agenda originating with the public information officers and the agenda of the news stories using that information was +0.84. The correspondence between the agency-originated agenda and all stories on those state government agencies during that period was +0.57. Inquiries into the reasons for this high level of success underscored the central role of journalistic norms and traditions as the final layer of the onion that sets the ground rules for the shaping of the media agenda. Newsworthiness was the most important consideration 82 per cent of the time.

This substantial agenda-setting role for public relations is in many regards the inevitable outcome of journalists operating 'under economic, institutional and organizational constraints which require them to draft and process too many stories for publication'.[26] To signal a concern with the increasing reliance on PR, some observers distinguish journalism based on original reporting from 'churnalism',[27] content from organizations that do not necessarily serve the public interest.

The reporting of public health issues, such as AIDS or polio, also reflects information subsidies, though mainly through information provided by scientists and other expert news sources.[28] The sustained and rising coverage of AIDS during the 1980s was set in motion by the scientific agenda, but sustained by the appearance in the latter half of the decade of new frames for telling the AIDS story. Concomitant with the appearance of these new frames were shifts in the agenda-setting roles of the biomedical community and the news media. Just as with the interaction of presidents, the news media, and the public, there is a temporal dynamic to be considered in the natural history of nearly every issue.

An extensive and fundamental role for social scientists in the evaluation of major public works projects in twenty countries across the world and the subsequent use of the media to influence public opinion regarding these expenditures is detailed in Bent Flyvjberg, Todd Landman and Sanford Schram's *Real Social Science: Applied Phronesis*. Originating in Aristotle's ethics, phronesis refers to practical wisdom and political ability.[29] Over the past two decades, global warming has been another media issue where the information subsidies provided by scientists have proved key.[30] The political conflict around climate change has also meant that the agendas of NGOs, industry, even celebrities, are frequently aiming at influencing news media coverage.[31]

Without the subsidies routinely provided by public relations professionals in the public, non-profit, and private sectors, the media agenda would be considerably different in scope and content. After all, agenda setting is a significant part of what public relations is about.[32] Furthermore, public relations influence on the media agenda is sometimes considerably more than a simple information subsidy to augment the routine work of journalists. Examination of professional public relations interventions on behalf of foreign governments, many with highly negative international images, found two measures of success. Their total coverage in the *New York Times* declined as the media spotlight shone less frequently on these governments, and this reduced news coverage was more positive.[33]

Capturing the media agenda

Political campaigns are a special case of public relations activities. In presidential elections, candidates spend vast amounts of money on political advertising in an effort to set the voters' agenda. Major efforts are also exerted to influence the agenda of the news media because these messages are less obviously self-serving and therefore more credible to the public. At the national level, these campaign efforts enjoy considerable success in setting the media agenda during the early months of the election year. However, this influence diminishes as the campaign moves towards Election Day and garners more and more attention from journalists.[34] On the other hand, in state and local elections – settings where fewer journalistic resources are brought to bear – the candidates' influence on the media agenda is more consistent and tends to be stronger.

Although the ultimate goal of any political campaign is to win on election day, campaigns increasingly see their immediate purpose as capturing the media agenda.[35] Implicit in this campaign perspective is the idea of agenda setting because control of the media agenda implies significant influence on the public agenda. A portion of the communication agenda, of course, is under the immediate and direct control of a campaign. A great deal of money is spent on political advertising in the media, predominantly television in many countries, but increasingly on social media channels as well.[36] These messages convey exactly the agenda desired by the campaign.

A comparative analysis of the 1983 British general election and the 1984 US presidential election found considerable differences between the two countries in the political parties' influence on the news agenda.[37] In the 1983 British general election, the parties enjoyed considerable success in focusing the attention of the news media on their issues. Extensive comparisons between the Conservative, Labour, and Alliance parties' emphases on five key policy issues and the coverage of those issues on the BBC and ITV and in five newspapers, both broadsheets and tabloids, found a median correlation of +0.70. In these twenty-one comparisons – three political parties each compared with seven different news media – the range of the correlations was +0.30 to a perfect 1.0. Six actually reflected the median value of +0.70, and only five of the twenty-one correlations fell below +0.70. The parties were equally successful with newspapers and television.

The 1984 American presidential campaigns did not fare as well with the news media. Comparison of the Democrats' and Republicans' emphases on six key policy issues with the news coverage on the three national television networks found no correlation exceeding +0.31, and three of the six comparisons were zero or negative. Other evidence indicated that the parties had no better success with the newspapers.

This striking difference between the successes of political campaigns as media agenda setters is largely the result of cultural differences in American and British journalists' orientation towards elections. In other words, the final layer of our theoretical onion, the social norms and traditions of journalism, is substantially different in Britain and the United States. The pattern of American election news coverage results from a normative calculus that weighs its news value each day in strict competition with the newsworthiness of all other possible stories. In contrast, the sacerdotal normative orientation of British journalists considers election campaigns as being inherently significant and important activities, whose coverage cannot be determined solely by the application of news values. This difference in how elections are covered in the two countries can be described in explicit agenda-setting terms:

In Britain, most television news people are hesitant to define their campaign contributions in 'agenda-setting' terms. In their eyes, the phrase has 'an active' interventionist meaning, as if they are being accused of presenting issues they personally deemed significant, despite or even in contradistinction to those the parties wish to press for ... Most of the NBC journalists [in America] were less diffident about their roles. They were prepared to regard themselves as more active in the agenda-setting process than their BBC counterparts.[38]

A similar American view was reflected during the 2000 US presidential primary elections by the editor of the *New York Times* in regard to persistent press questioning of George W. Bush about the use of drugs in his youth, questions which he refused to entertain. 'There is here the question of who sets the agenda – the politicians or the press', remarked Executive Editor Joseph Lelyveld.[39] This is a central question that we explore here in considerable detail.

Although the evidence overall suggests a strong agenda-setting role for the US news media during most of the lengthy presidential election, politicians sometimes do have the edge at the outset. As we saw in Chapter 3's discussion of attributes and frames, there is evidence of candidate influence on the news coverage of the 1996 Republican contenders for their party's presidential nomination in the *New York Times*, *Washington Post*, and *Los Angeles Times* from 26 December (the day *The Times* began a series of in-depth candidate profiles) until 20 February (the date of the New Hampshire primary, the first primary in the lengthy US presidential election year).[40] Media depictions of the four major contenders for the Republican nomination – Lamar Alexander, Pat Buchanan, Robert Dole, and Steve Forbes – were compared with the press releases on these candidates' websites, and the consistency of the media attribute agenda with each candidate's presentation of himself is striking: Alexander, +0.74; Buchanan, +0.75; Forbes, +0.78; and Dole, +0.62. Dole's status as the front runner could well explain his slightly lower, but still robust, correlation.

However, a more narrowly focused analysis of television news coverage during the New Hampshire primary itself found only a moderate degree of correspondence (+0.40) with the topics of the candidates' speeches during the primary.[41] While nearly all of the candidates' speeches included public issues, less than a third of the TV news reports even mentioned issues. The long-standing predilection of American journalists for the horserace and their lesser interest in the issues were amply apparent.

Additional evidence for the horserace's number one position on the media agenda is found in an analysis of the autumn 1996 presidential campaign coverage on the four major television networks and in the *New York Times, Washington Post,* and *Los Angeles Times.*[42] For both print and TV, horserace coverage consumed about half the media agenda. Setting aside discussion of the campaign and focusing specifically on public issues, the analysis of this news coverage indicates that the candidates' issue agendas, at best, had only modest influence on any of the media agendas during the autumn campaign.

But, again, demonstrating candidate influence early in the election year, there is evidence from the 2000 presidential primaries that candidate issue agendas influenced network television news coverage.[43] Ten of the twelve comparisons between four candidate agendas and the three major networks yielded significant correlations, with the median value falling between +0.64 and +0.68. Further analysis using cross-lagged correlations to examine the patterns during the early months of the presidential race found about twice as many instances of candidate influence on the media agenda of issues than the reverse.

At the second level of agenda setting, although there is less overall evidence of influence, the strength of the significant correlations that were found compare favourably with the evidence for basic agenda setting. Only six of the twelve comparisons of the emphasis on various audience subgroups – the elderly, minorities, women, etc. – by the candidates and by television news were significant. Among those comparisons, all of which involved Republicans Bush and McCain and none Democrats Gore or Bradley, the median correlation fell between +0.77 and +0.85. For a set of campaign topics – polls, endorsements, debates, etc. – only three of the twelve comparisons were significant. All three involved Republican challenger McCain, who in the dominant media narrative played David to Bush's Goliath. For these three significant correlations, the median value was +0.69.

Referendums involve very different types of campaign organizations. In the 2006 Swiss referendum on a more restrictive political asylum law, 47 organizations were players.[44] Comparison of the pro and con agendas advanced by various organizations with the news coverage on TV and in the newspapers of seven key arguments regarding the proposed law found that the organizations supporting the new law, but not those opposed to it, were highly successful in gaining coverage for their arguments. The median correlation across a three-month period between the pro arguments and the news coverage was +0.78. In turn, there were strong agenda-setting effects of this coverage, but only among those members of the public with high reliance on the media. However, across the three months examined, these effects appeared only in the final weeks prior to the referendum. By that time, the correspondence between the media agenda and the agenda of high media users was +0.92.

Moving to the theoretical frontier of agenda setting, an analysis of information subsidies by the Obama and Romney campaigns – press releases, party platforms, blogs, and other social media used by the candidates – examined their first, second, and third-level agenda-setting effects on newspaper and TV coverage during the middle months of the 2012 US presidential election.[45] In line with previous research, strong correspondence between the campaign agendas and the media agenda, particularly the newspaper agenda, were found for the salience of issues and for the salience of stakeholder groups, ranging from the candidates and their staffs to activist groups and social institutions. Similar patterns also were found for issue attribute agendas and candidate attribute agendas.

Exploring new terrain, more modest correspondence was found at the third level of agenda setting between the campaign and media issue networks and issue attribute networks. However, high levels of correspondence for press releases, blogs, and party platforms with newspaper coverage (median of +0.66) and television coverage (median of +0.77) were found at the third level of agenda setting for stakeholder networks. For four social media used by the campaigns – Facebook, YouTube, Google+, and Twitter – the median correlation for the stakeholder networks with newspaper coverage was +0.51 and +0.88 for television.

An analysis of four national elections in Austria from 1970 to 2008 found that the issue priorities of the major political parties' press releases were reflected in the news coverage of the major newspapers.[46] Expanding the issue attribute agendas of the political parties and the newspapers to examine their contribution to political deliberation, four aspects of the quality of the information in the press releases and news stories were evaluated: reasons for issue positions, proposals for solutions, civility, and substantive criticism of issue positions. The newspapers exhibited these qualities of information far less than the political parties in their press releases. Further comparison of the roles of journalists as disseminators versus analysts revealed higher levels of quality in straight news than in analytical articles.

This analysis of the quality of information answers one aspect of a key normative question about the news media's role in presenting an agenda that has civic utility for citizens.[47] How useful are these agendas of topics and attributes as the basis of the decisions that citizens in a democracy are called upon to make about public affairs?

Three election agendas

Substantial evidence of the strong influence that journalistic norms can have on both the shaping of the media's issue agenda and the subsequent public agenda of issues comes from comprehensive national analyses of the 1992 and 2000 US presidential campaigns.[48] At first glance, the strong correlations in 1992 of the candidates' platforms with both the media agenda (+0.76) and the public agenda (+0.78) might appear to undercut the idea of an agenda-setting role for the media and, further, to suggest that the strong correlation between the media and the public (+0.94) is overstated. This is not the case. When all three elements are considered simultaneously, the strong correlation between the media and the public remains, while the correlation between the candidates' platforms and the public agenda is greatly diminished. This can be observed in several ways.

When the analysis of the relationship between the media agenda and the public agenda (+0.94) also takes into account the direct influence of the candidates' platforms on both the media and the public agenda, the outcome remains an extraordinary +0.85. Alternatively, when the media agenda is viewed as the key factor intervening between the candidates and the public, that is, as the principal bridge between the candidates and the public, the resulting partial correlation – as expected – is greatly diminished. The original relationship of +0.78 between the candidates' platforms and the public agenda is reduced to +0.33 when the intervening influence of the media is removed. Of course, the media agenda is by no means constructed from whole cloth – there is significant input from media sources, as evidenced by a correlation of +0.76 – but the light emanating from presidential campaigns is refracted through the prism of journalistic norms before reaching the public.

This substantial agenda-setting influence of the news media on the issue agenda – independent of the political campaigns to a considerable degree – was replicated during the autumn 2000 presidential campaign.[49] At the outset, the basic pattern of correlations was nearly identical: substantial correlations between the candidates' agenda of issues and both the media agenda (+0.79) and the public agenda (+0.76), as well as a strong correlation between the media and the public (+0.92).

Replicating the pattern found in 1992, when the analysis of this relationship between the media and the public takes into account the influence of the candidates on both, the correlation remains a robust +0.79. Alternatively, when the media agenda is viewed as the intervening element between the candidates and the public, the original relationship of +0.76 is reduced to +0.15. Repetition of these analyses separately for the agendas of the two major candidates, George W. Bush and Albert Gore, revealed the identical pattern. All of this is strong evidence for the agenda-setting role of the news media in focusing the public's attention on public issues.

Analysis of the 2000 presidential campaign also explored the attribute agenda-setting influence of the candidates and the news media in defining the public's perception of the social welfare issue, which ranked number one on the public agenda. Here the evidence clearly favours the primary role of the campaigns as agenda setters for this issue during the autumn 2000 campaign. The correlation of the campaign agenda for eight attributes of the social welfare issue with the news agenda is a hearty +0.76 and with the public an even stronger +0.86. Unlike the pattern found at the first level of agenda setting in both 1992 and 2000 for the overall set of issues, at the second level of agenda setting this latter relationship is only slightly dimmed (+0.78) when the media agenda is included in the analysis as an intervening factor. Furthermore, the relationship between the media and the public (+0.60) for this attribute agenda disappears when the candidate agenda is introduced into the analysis.

Media agendas in local elections

Analysis of the press releases issued by the competing candidates in nine state-wide elections in 2006 found a median correlation of +0.48 between the issue agendas of the candidates and the issue agendas of widely circulated newspapers in those states. At the second level, the median correlation of the issue attributes agendas of the candidates and the newspapers was +0.58.[50]

In the 2002 Florida gubernatorial election, comparison of the Republican and Democrat candidates' issue agendas in their news releases with the issue agendas of six major newspapers across the state showed a median correlation of +0.78.[51] In turn, the median correlation of the newspapers' issue agenda with the public agenda was +0.74. There also was substantial correspondence between the attribute agendas of the candidates' press releases and their images in the newspapers. For substantive attributes of the candidates, the median correlation was +0.79; for negative attributes, +0.81; and for positive attributes, +0.60.

During the 1990 Texas gubernatorial election, the combined issue agendas of the Democrat and Republican candidates' paid television advertising in Austin, the capital of Texas, was compared with the news coverage of those issues by the Austin newspaper and the three local television stations.[52] This campaign agenda exerted significant influence on both the local newspaper (+0.64) and the local television stations (+0.52), a pattern of influence that persisted even when other factors were taken into account.

However, the pattern of influence in the Texas gubernatorial election four years later – the election marking George W. Bush's political debut – was essentially the reverse. Comparison of the press releases from Bush and incumbent Governor Ann Richards with the coverage of the state's three major newspapers during the autumn 1994 election campaign revealed that the newspapers substantially influenced the candidates' issue agendas (+0.70), the overall focus of their press releases on issues, personal images and aspects of the political campaign itself (+1.0), and the overall positive or negative tone of their press releases (+0.80).[53]

At the second level of agenda setting, there is evidence from the 1995 local elections in the Spanish province of Navarra that political advertisements influenced the subsequent depiction of the candidates on TV news (+0.99), but only to a modest degree in the newspapers (+0.32).[54] The primary influence of the advertising was on descriptions of the candidates' qualifications. On television, the time devoted to qualifications increased more than eightfold from the early days of the campaign to the latter days. In the newspapers, mentions of this attribute doubled in the course of the campaign.

Attributes of local issues

At the local level of politics in the United States, the attribute agenda-setting effects of political advertising were observed in two elections in Victoria, Texas.[55] In a 1995 local sales tax referendum in Victoria, two patterns are apparent from a pair of public opinion surveys conducted among registered voters, the first survey conducted about a month prior to the referendum, the second about a week before the voting. There was a significant increase in learning among the voters during the campaign, and political advertising played an especially strong role in shaping the pictures in voters' minds of what the proposed sales tax would do for Victoria.

From survey one to survey two, the match between the voters' pictures and the local newspaper's presentation of the sales tax increased from +0.40 to +0.65. For the political ads, the match increased from +0.80 to +0.95. When the match of these Texas voters with one source (e.g. the newspaper) controlled for the other source (e.g. advertising), the correspondence between the newspaper and the public disappeared entirely. But for political ads the correlations resulting from these controls were +0.87 (compared to the original correlation of +0.80 in survey one) and +0.94 (compared to the original correlation of +0.95 in survey two). Political advertising was the primary source of learning about this local economic issue.

In the election for mayor of Victoria that year, the voters' images of the two candidates significantly matched the agenda of attributes in local newspaper coverage (+0.60 for each candidate), but matched even more each candidate's political advertising (+0.73 and +0.85). Further analysis led to the conclusion that political ads were, by far, the major agenda setter in this local election. When the influence of the candidates on both the media agenda and the public agenda is taken into account, the match between the newspaper and the public is reduced from +0.60 to +0.46 for one candidate, and there is essentially no correlation at all for the second candidate. However, when the relationship between the political advertising agenda and the public controlled for the media agenda, there is no evidence at all for a media role as the key bridge between the campaign and the public. The strong candidate agenda–public agenda correlations are unchanged.

Three elements of elections

These sets of evidence based on all three key elements of a political campaign – the candidates and political parties, the news media, and the public – provide the complex mix of documentation needed to examine the agenda-setting role of the news media in its full context. This rich mix addresses earlier criticisms that the evidence of agenda-setting effects by the media is fragmentary because so much of it has examined only two elements at a time, the media and the public in the opening phase of agenda-setting research and subsequently, beginning in the 1980s, news sources and the media. In particular, this evidence also addresses the basic question of who are the true agenda setters, the media or the political campaigns. If the campaigns dominate the formation of both the media agenda and the public agenda, then the media are only, at best, the proximate cause of the public agenda. In Britain, the national political parties have enjoyed considerable success in capturing the news agenda. Not so in the United States, where a different set of journalistic norms has resulted in media agendas only weakly corresponding to the agendas put forward by the national parties during the presidential campaign. Most importantly, where the US evidence encompasses all three elements, it is these media agendas, rather than the candidates' agendas, that have by far the greatest influence on the public agenda.

All in all, across the election year in the United States, the media are the agenda setters. However, at the outset of presidential election years in the United States and at the local level in both the United States and Spain, the situation is more mixed. In these circumstances, political campaigns frequently succeed in capturing the media agenda.

A broader portrait

Elections offer a particularly intensive setting for examining both the influence of news sources on the media and, in turn, the influence of the media on the public. In the larger realm of history, however, elections are only tiny blips impacting the continuous rise and fall of public opinion on the topics of the day. A detailed analysis of Canadian public opinion on three issues from 1985 to 1995 offers this broader view of the flow of issue salience from a variety of news sources to the news media and from there to the public.[56] The three issues selected for analysis – inflation, the environment, and the national debt and budget deficits – also provide another look at aspects of agenda-setting theory reviewed in earlier chapters, this time in the context of a full-scale model of the agenda-setting process.

First, in terms of media effects and the concept of obtrusive and unobtrusive issues previously discussed in Chapter 5, there is a clear pattern across this continuum of issues. In line with previous evidence on the obtrusive issue of inflation, there is no evidence of any agenda-setting influence by the media on public opinion. For the environment, the relationship between the media agenda and the public agenda is reciprocal – and the impact of the public on the media appears to be stronger.

Finally, for the unobtrusive and abstract issue of the Canadian national debt and budget deficits, there is evidence of significant media influence on the public agenda. This comprehensive examination also allows us to revisit the relationship between the media agenda and reality. None of the three analyses yields a significant relationship between the trend in the media agenda over these years and real-world measures of inflation, the environment and Canadian national finances. As common sense would seem to dictate, these real-world measures are linked to the trends in both the public agenda and the policy agenda for the issues of inflation and the environment. For the third issue, national finances, there is only a link with the policy agenda, which is defined in these analyses by such measures as the topics of the question period and committee reports in the Canadian parliament. Of course, elections are also an aspect of reality and a major source of news. But the occurrence of elections did not impact the media trend over time for any of these issues, and the occurrence of elections impacted the trend in public concern only for the environment.

Various manifestations of the policy agenda in the government are also potential sources of news for the media. Here the evidence is mixed. For inflation, there is evidence of a modest influence by the policy agenda on the news agenda. But for the environment and Canadian national finances there is a reciprocal relationship between the media and policy agendas – quite strong for the environment, rather modest for national finances.

A similarly mixed picture emerged from a year-long comparison of the activity of the city council in Bloomington, Indiana, and its coverage in the local daily newspaper.[57] Although there was considerable correspondence between the priorities of the council and the media agenda (+0.84), closer examination revealed major discrepancies in the rankings of seven of the nineteen categories. For four categories – arts and entertainment, nuclear freeze, utilities, and elections – the newspaper's emphasis was considerably greater. For awards, animal protection, and urban development, the newspaper's emphasis was considerably less. Even news coverage of formal government meetings, where almost stenographic coverage might be expected, demonstrates the interplay of news norms and news events. The reporter who covered the city council said that he liked 'subjects that involve controversy, debates, and several actors because these characteristics make for a better story'.[58] His perspective reflects the normative influence of the narrative imperative of journalism, to tell a good story. This perspective also accounts, at least in part, for the fact that only 59 per cent of the items described in the council minutes were reported in the local newspaper.

Finally, influencing all three of the agendas just considered – the policy agenda reflected by various government activities, the media agenda, and the public agenda – is frequently the goal of organized interest groups.[59] Often as well financed as election campaigns, issue campaigns by interest groups share a similar record of success. A nine-year analysis of the US debate about gun control found significant links between the attention of network television news and the flood of press releases from interest groups on both sides of the issue (+0.60) as well as congressional discussion (+0.32).[60] Analysis of how this issue was framed reveals that a 'culture of violence' theme was dominant in nearly half of the news stories, but in less than a quarter of the congressional statements on gun control and less than a sixth of the press releases. In short, largely independent of these news sources, the news media heeded the narrative imperative and opted for the dramatic 'culture of violence' frame. Although this may celebrate the independence of the media voice, it is simultaneously a failure to 'move the discussion beyond a simplified emotive framework to a more reasoned policy debate'.[61]

Intermedia agenda setting

The elite news media frequently exert a substantial influence on the agenda of other news media. In the United States this role of intermedia agenda setter is frequently played by the *New York Times*. Despite intensive coverage by local newspapers over many months, neither serious chemical contamination at Love Canal in western New York state nor the radon threat in nearby Pennsylvania and New Jersey gained national attention until these problems appeared on the *New York Times'* agenda.[62] Chapter 2 previously noted how *The Times'* discovery of the drug problem in late 1985 resulted in heavy coverage the following year in major newspapers across the United States and on national television news, a pattern that peaked with two national television specials in September of that year.[63] A South Korea study indicates that this intermedia influence of major news organization also exists in the online news environment.[64]

Sociologist Warren Breed conceptualized this diffusion of a news story from an elite news medium to a host of other media as a dendritic influence.[65] Analogous to a family tree, this arterial flow is from a progenitor to a multitude of descendants. Many times these journalistic offspring are absolute clones. In the mid twentieth century, when the *New York Times* and the now defunct *New York Herald Tribune* were in serious competition, the managing editors of both newspapers frequently ordered last-minute changes on their front pages in order to match their competitors' coverage.[66]

As Chapter 1's discussion of the new media landscape noted, journalists frequently observe – and subsequently copy – their peers' news coverage in order to validate their own news judgement about the day's events.[67] A classic example of this influence at work among individual journalists occurred during the 1972 US presidential campaign. The first major political event of a presidential election year in the United States is the Iowa caucuses, a series of local political party meetings across that state to select delegates to the state party convention. It is a highly ambiguous situation to report. Those who attend these dozens and dozens of local meetings are a self-selected group of voters who are interested enough to show up and participate. Furthermore, at this early point in the election year there is typically a large field of candidates vying for delegates. Journalists' task on the evening of these caucuses is to make sense of it all, to find the news amid all this activity.

> What happened was that Johnny Apple of the *New York Times* sat in a corner and everyone peered over his shoulder to find out what he was writing ... He would sit down and write a lead, and they would go write leads ... Finally, at midnight, the guy announced that Muskie had 32 per cent and McGovern had 26 per cent, and Apple sat down to write his final story. He called it something like 'a surprisingly strong showing for George McGovern'. Everyone peered over his shoulder again and picked it up. It was on the front page of every major newspaper the next day.[68]

A large-scale portrait of intermedia agenda setting among the elite US news media is found in the history of global warming from 1985 to 1992.[69] As the news coverage of this issue steadily accelerated towards its peak in 1989, major newspapers – the *New York Times, Washington Post,* and *Wall Street Journal* – significantly influenced the agenda of the three national television networks. For this complex scientific issue, a significant intermedia agenda-setting role also was played by science publications, those key specialized sources regularly scanned by science writers and editors.

The role of elite news media in initiating widespread coverage of new topics and the influence of key journalists in framing the news are dramatic examples of intermedia agenda setting. But prosaic versions of intermedia agenda setting take place every day as local news organizations construct their daily agenda from the huge file of news sent to them by the wire services. An examination of how twenty-four Iowa daily newspapers used the Associated Press wire report found major influence on the local news agenda.[70] Although each newspaper used only a small proportion of the available AP stories, their patterns of coverage reflected essentially the same proportion for each category of news as the total AP file.

A laboratory experiment, whose subjects were experienced newspaper and television wire editors, also found a high degree of correspondence (+0.62) across categories between the proportion of news stories in a large wire file and the small sample selected by the editors.[71] Additional evidence about the agenda-setting influence of the wire service was found in a control condition of the experiment where there were an equal number of stories in each news category. In this situation, there was no common pattern of selection at all, either in comparison with the perfectly balanced wire file and its lack of cues about salience or among the wire editors themselves, who might be expected to share similar news values.

Early investigations of gatekeeping, the decisions by journalists editing the wire at local news outlets about which items to delete and which to pass through the gate, emphasized the psychological characteristics of the gatekeepers themselves. In contrast, agenda-setting theory calls attention to the sociological setting of this task.[72]

A re-analysis[73] of the classic case study of Mr Gates[74] found substantial correspondence (+0.64) between the combined agenda of his wire services and Mr Gates' selections for his newspaper. Further examination of a replication that studied Mr Gates seventeen years later when he used only a single wire service[75] found a correlation of +0.80 between the wire agenda and his news selections.[76]

Moving to the level of local news, analysis of election coverage in Austin, Texas, during the 1990 gubernatorial campaign found that the issue agenda of the local daily newspaper influenced the issue agenda of local television news (+0.73).[77] Recall that this chapter earlier noted that the candidates' issue agenda influenced both the newspaper and the television coverage. But even when this influence is taken into account, there is still evidence of significant newspaper influence on the television coverage (+0.44).

In Spain, an examination of intermedia influence among newspapers and television during the 1995 local elections measured both first and second-level agenda-setting effects.[78] Intermedia agenda setting at the first level in Pamplona and in Austin was highly similar. Comparisons of the coverage on six local issues in two Pamplona newspapers yielded correlations of +0.66 and +0.70, respectively, with the subsequent television news agenda. At the second level, there was no evidence of attribute agenda-setting influence among the newspapers and local television news in the ways that they described the local political candidates. However, recall that the political advertising in the Pamplona newspapers did influence subsequent depictions of the candidates in the newspapers and on television.

Journalists validate their sense of news by observing the work of their colleagues. The outcome of these routine, continuous observations and the resulting intermedia influence is a highly redundant

news agenda. The original Chapel Hill study found a median correlation of +0.78 between the major issue agendas of the nine traditional
media analysed.[79] Forty years later, an analysis of campaign coverage
of the 2008 US elections collected by the Project for Excellence in
Journalism (PEJ) found similar strong correlations.[80] For example,
McCombs and Shaw (1972) found that the campaign issue agendas
of the *New York Times*, CBS News, and NBC News exhibited a rank-
order median correlation of +0.66. With the PEJ 2008 data, which
coded fifteen broad story topics, the median correlation for those
same media was +0.68.

Due to the ease with which different media organizations can now
check the issues covered by their competitors, the rise of digital media
has increased the redundancy in news media agendas. This process
of 'imitation in an age of information abundance'[81] has resulted in
fairly homogenous national media agendas. Going back to the 2008
PEJ data, the median correlation between the agendas of the news
websites CNN.com, Yahoo! News, MSNBC.com, Google News, and
AOL News increased from an average of +0.21 in the mornings (9
a.m.) to +0.51 in the evenings (4 p.m.) That is, convergence in terms
of which are the most important issues of the day increases as digital
journalists and editors catch up with their colleagues' work during
the day.[82]

This high degree of consistency in the media agenda is a worldwide
phenomenon. A similar comparison of the issue agendas for three
major daily newspapers and three television stations in Taipei during
the 1992 Taiwan legislative elections found a median correlation of
+0.75.[83] A study in Chile conducted between 2000 and 2005 found a
median correlation in the issue agendas of TV news and newspapers
of +0.83.[84] Another examination of 39 news outlets covering the
2013 election in Austria using time-series analysis found strong
evidence for agenda contagion between media.[85]

At the second level of agenda setting, recall that in Chapter 3
the framing of Japan's economic problem by a major newspaper,
Mainichi Shimbun, was examined for two sets of attributes – macro
problematic situation frames and attributes detailing micro-aspects of
the economic problem. A replication and extension of that research,
which compared these two sets of attributes in the economic
coverage of *Asahi* and *Yomiuri*, found that these two newspapers were
quite similar in regard to the salience of problematic situation frames
(+0.93) as well as for sub-issue attributes (+0.79).[86] A comparison
of the attributes of the economic issue in the United States found a
correlation of +0.80 between the newspaper and television agendas.[87]
This might be termed a quasi-comparison because the two newspaper

agendas and three television agendas had already been merged to create a newspaper agenda and a television agenda.

Merging the agendas of various news outlets to create a composite media agenda is commonplace in investigations of the agenda-setting role of the media because of the high degree of homogeneity among these various agendas. In the language of research methodology, these high inter-correlations among the agendas of the news media can be regarded as a measure of reliability, the extent of agreement among independent observers who are applying the same rules of observation. Applying the norms and traditions of journalism to the vast number of events and situations available each day for observation, journalists – aided, of course, by their intermedia observations – construct highly similar agendas. At the second level of agenda setting, the homogeneity of agendas extends beyond agreement on the attribute agendas for a particular object. There is also a high degree of similarity in the attribute agendas for related objects. A comparison of the attribute agendas in the major Taipei newspapers for three mayoral candidates found a median correlation of +0.93.[88] The norms of journalism exert a powerful pressure towards homogeneity in telling the news of the day, a homogeneity that in turn influences the way that news is passed along in a major social media channel, Twitter. An examination of 16.32 million tweets on 3,361 different trending topics by Hewlett Packard Labs between September and October 2010 found that these trending topics were 'largely news from traditional media sources, which are then amplified by repeated retweets on Twitter to generate trends'.[89]

Where intermedia agenda setting becomes more nuanced is in the digital realm. To a considerable degree, the agendas of the political blogs and legacy media show a high level of convergence, especially at the first level of agenda setting. Given the political diversity of these blogs, it is not surprising that their attribute agendas show less convergence. In terms of influence, the mainstream media continue to be the prime movers, but from time to time the political blogs and other social media do succeed in taking the lead. Regardless of who leads and who follows, the dominant pattern is a highly homogenous issue agenda and an attribute agenda with considerable convergence.[90]

Finally, moving on to other aspects of the new media landscape, an analysis during the 2008 US presidential election primaries found that the citizen activist issue agenda reflected in the 'Obama in 30 Seconds' online ad contest was more strongly related to the partisan news media coverage than to the issue priorities of the official Obama or MoveOn.org ads on YouTube.[91]

Summing up

Who sets the media's agenda? This question about which topics are brought to public attention is especially vital. Columnist Leonard Pitts observed that, 'in a world where media set the public agenda and drive the dialogue, those things media ignore may as well not exist'.[92] The outline of an answer in this chapter to who sets the media's agenda considers three key elements: major sources who provide the information for news stories, other news organizations, and journalism's norms and traditions.

At times, national leaders do succeed in setting the news agenda. Public information officers and other public relations professionals are also significant contributors. But these influence streams are filtered through the ground rules established by the norms of journalism, and they are very powerful filters. The evolution of the daily and weekly news agenda is further shaped and standardized by the interactions among news organizations. In this process of inter-media agenda setting, high status news organizations, such as the *New York Times*, set the agendas of other news organizations. At the city level, local newspapers and television stations influence the news agenda of their competitors. In recent years, a variety of social media has joined the communication chorus. On occasion, intermedia agenda setting takes a very different form – entertainment media can set the agenda of the news media.[93]

In addition to exploring the question of who sets the media's agenda, an inquiry that is of immediate interest to communication scholars and professionals, our awareness of these external agendas illustrates the expanding scope of agenda-setting theory. Although most of our knowledge about the agenda-setting process centres on the relationship between the media agenda and the public agenda, that is only one delimited application of the theory. Agenda-setting theory is about the transfer of salience from one agenda to another. The best developed portions of the theory focus on the link between the media agenda and the public agenda because of its theoretical roots in public opinion research and because most of the scholars whose work has built this theory were especially interested in media effects. Even with the shift in this chapter to the elements shaping the media agenda, the overall focus remains media-centric. But, as we shall see, there are many other agenda-setting relationships to consider.

Historically, research into the sources of influence shaping the media agenda opened a new phase of agenda-setting theory that marked a significant expansion beyond the media agenda–public agenda relationship. The initial phase, inaugurated by the Chapel Hill study, was centred on the influence of the media's issue agenda on the public's issue agenda. A second aspect of agenda-setting theory elaborated this influence of the news media, exploring a variety of contingent conditions that enhance or constrain agenda-setting effects among the public. A third aspect expanded the scope of agenda-setting influence by the media from effects on attention – agendas of objects – to effects on comprehension – attribute agendas. More recently, the theory is exploring network agenda setting, a third level of effects. This chapter introduced yet another aspect of the theory, the origins of the media agenda. Although there is a clear historical pattern in the initial appearance of all these aspects of agenda setting, they are not historical stages in the sense that, with the appearance of a new aspect, the book is closed on those that preceded it. All these theoretical aspects of agenda setting continue to be active sites of inquiry. And there remain many additional sites to explore!

8 Consequences of Agenda Setting

The evolutionary process typical of most social science, a process that contrasts sharply with the popular notion of dramatic scientific 'discoveries', was especially apparent for agenda-setting theory at the turn of the twenty-first century. The orderly and parsimonious canon of knowledge centred on the media agenda and the public agenda that is found in the previous chapters was poised at the brink of an expansive explosion of new relationships and new settings. However, rather than the dawn of dramatic discoveries about the role of media in the shaping of public opinion, these new perspectives were more a cumulative outcome of scholarship. As a result of scholarly perseverance, the idea of an agenda-setting role of media was converging with a host of other social science concepts and interests about communication and human behaviour. The intellectual history of agenda-setting theory from its origins in 1968 to the present reflects steady, albeit diffuse, progress in mapping this communication process. To the initial map of basic first-level agenda-setting effects sketched in Chapel Hill were added a rich lode of additional details about the public, the media, and their agendas that enhanced our understanding of media effects among the public. The previous chapters have presented these details about the core of agenda-setting theory. And in the newest versions of this theoretical map were details about the consequences of the agenda-setting process beyond the transfer of salience. This aspect of agenda-setting theory – namely, explicating consequences – had previously been sketched only in outline, as noted by Eugene Shaw in 1979:

> Attitudes and behaviour are usually governed by cognitions – what a person knows, thinks, believes. Hence, the agenda-setting function

of the news media implies a potentially massive influence whose full dimensions and consequences have yet to be investigated and appreciated.[1]

Chapter 3 ended with the observation that the combination of cognitive and affective elements in attribute agenda setting revives the consideration of communication effects on attitudes and opinions. The evidence in that chapter, as well as that of Chapter 4, on the salience of affective attributes in the public's descriptions of political candidates – salience acquired, at least in part, from the news media – reopens a psychological area of exploration that was largely abandoned in the mid twentieth century in the face of strong, empirically grounded assertions about the limited effects of media.

Media effects can sometimes result, as many of the early scholars believed, from the sheer volume of exposure. First-level agenda-setting effects demonstrate that phenomenon to some extent. But, as attribute agenda setting shows, closer attention to the specific content of media messages provides a more detailed understanding of the pictures in our heads and of the attitudes and opinions grounded in those pictures. Attribute agenda setting brings us back to the influence of mass communication on attitudes and opinions, the theoretical site where mass communication theory started in the 1940s and 1950s. This is a return to Carl Hovland's scientific rhetoric, the matching of message characteristics to attitude and opinion change.[2] However, unlike Hovland's pioneering work, there now exists a detailed theoretical map linking the media agenda and the public to guide our explorations.

To achieve dramatic effect, the opening scenes of some movies are in black and white or sepia tones. A sudden shift from these subdued tones to vibrant colours heightens their emotional impact. In much the same way, when the attribute agendas of the media and the public include affective tone as well as substantive attributes, these pictures of objects in the news can result in strong emotions and feelings, which is to say, opinions. In short, the concepts of public attribute agendas and personal opinions converge. However, this is not the only point of convergence between public agendas and personal opinions, so before we examine these relationships in detail we need to sketch some additional portions of our theoretical map for agenda setting.

From our previous maps illustrating the first and second levels of agenda setting, Box 8.1 reproduces object salience and attribute salience. The new elements in this map are two aspects of opinion, plus observable behaviour. The first new element in Box 8.1 is

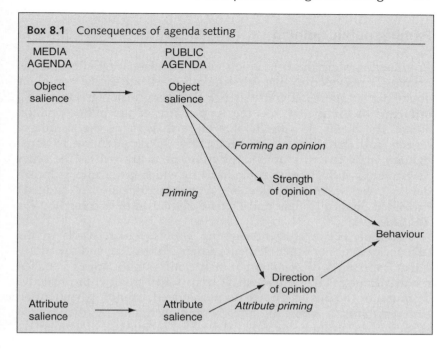

Box 8.1   Consequences of agenda setting

MEDIA AGENDA — Object salience → PUBLIC AGENDA Object salience

Forming an opinion → Strength of opinion

Priming

Behaviour

Direction of opinion

Attribute salience → Attribute salience   Attribute priming

the strength of opinion, beginning with the fundamental point of whether an opinion even exists. Strength of opinion also distinguishes between weakly and strongly held opinions regardless of whether those opinions are positive or negative. The second element added to Box 8.1 is very familiar, the direction of opinion, whether some object or attribute is regarded in a positive or negative light.

Linking object and attribute salience with these two aspects of opinions accounts for three major relationships. Considerable evidence exists for media priming, the link between object salience on the public agenda and the direction of opinion. Exploration of the second level of agenda setting introduced the idea of attribute priming, the link between attribute salience and the direction of opinion. The third relationship, forming an opinion, is the link between object salience and the strength of opinion. All three of these relationships, as well as their subsequent links with individuals' behaviour, are discussed in this chapter.

Priming public opinion

Prominent among the consequences of agenda-setting effects is the priming of perspectives that subsequently guide the public's opinions about public figures, a consequence that brings the agenda-setting influence of the media into the very centre of the public opinion arena. The media do considerably more than shape the agenda of objects and attributes in our heads. 'By calling attention to some matters while ignoring others, television news [as well as the other news media] influences the standards by which governments, presidents, policies, and candidates for public officials are judged', explained Shanto Iyengar and Donald Kinder in their seminal *News That Matters.*[3]

This link between agenda-setting effects, which result in the salience of issues or other elements among the public, and the subsequent expression of *opinions* about specific public figures is called media priming. The psychological basis for priming is the selective attention of the public. People do not, indeed, cannot, pay attention to everything, a situation already demonstrated by the limited capacity of the public agenda. Moreover, in making judgements – whether in casting a ballot on election day or simply in responding to a pollster's question – people use simple rules of thumb and intuitive shortcuts – what psychologists call heuristics.[4] Rather than engaging in comprehensive analyses based on their total store of information, most citizens routinely draw upon those bits of information that are particularly salient at the time judgement must be rendered.[5] In other words, citizens rely upon the agenda of salient objects and attributes in their minds, the agenda that is set to a considerable degree by the news media. This agenda determines the criteria – sometimes the single criterion – on which an opinion is based.

The series of agenda-setting experiments described in Chapter 1 also demonstrated the priming effects of television news on people's opinions about the president's overall performance in office.[6] To demonstrate that the shifting salience of specific issues influenced people's overall assessment of the president's performance, these experiments compared two groups: those who saw no news stories on a specific issue versus those who were exposed to television news coverage on the issue. Among subjects exposed to extensive news coverage on one or more of five different issues – defence, inflation, arms control, civil rights, and unemployment – their ratings on the issue or issues receiving heavy news coverage influenced their overall opinion about the president's performance more than among persons not exposed to this news coverage. This influence existed whether or not the news story implied a substantial degree of presidential responsibility for the issue. In subsequent experiments where the degree of presidential responsibility for an issue was explicitly manipulated, the impact of problem performance ratings on opinions about the president's overall performance was greater when the news stories emphasized presidential responsibility.

This is strong causal evidence based on controlled laboratory experiments that the influence of the news agenda on the salience of issues among the public primes the criteria that individuals use in judging the overall performance of a president.[7] A classic study was conducted during a major American political setting, the Iran–Contra scandal.[8] On 25 November 1986, the Attorney-General announced that funds obtained by the US government from the secret sale of weapons to Iran had been improperly diverted to the Contras, a group attempting to overthrow the Sandinista government in Nicaragua. This covert operation had been carried out by members of the National Security Council, and President Reagan subsequently revealed that the director of the council and a key staff member had been dismissed. As could be expected, all these revelations received major news coverage. By a fortuitous coincidence, the National Election Study's post-1986 presidential election survey was in the field at the time of these announcements, creating a natural before–after comparison of the elements of public opinion that influenced Americans' assessments of President Reagan.

> The importance of public opinion on the question of assistance to the Contras and US intervention in Central America [in assessments of the president's overall performance] increased substantially from the pre-revelation period to the postrevelation period [...] as did the importance of the public's view of the general choice between intervention and isolationism [...] Meanwhile, the public's view of the strength of the United States around the world was evidently unaffected by the revelation. This pattern of results corroborates the experimental findings noted earlier.[9]

Since these initial explorations, media priming effects have been identified for a wide variety of issues, including racial attitudes,[10] the economy,[11] corruption,[12] and foreign policy.[13] Importantly, these effects have been verified around the globe,[14] and over the short and long term.[15] Some of these studies also ask which members of the public are more susceptible to being influenced by the media. If priming occurs because people are politically unsophisticated, that would be a cause of concern – it would suggest that public opinion is easily malleable by the media and the elites that dominate news coverage. But if priming occurs among politically sophisticated individuals, it suggests that media influence results from a more deliberative process of filtering news content. There is some consensus that media priming is strongest among individuals with moderate levels of political sophistication, who are engaged enough to follow political news but have weaker attitudes and, thus, cannot easily reject media cues.[16]

In line with the discussion of civic osmosis in Chapter 1, priming effects result primarily from the cumulative information environment created by the media. Thus, media priming is a significant extension of agenda setting,[17] one of the routes through which the news media play a key role in the shaping of attitudes and opinions.[18] At times, these agenda-setting effects have very direct consequences for individuals' attitudes and opinions. This is particularly the case for attribute agenda setting, where the impact may be just as dramatic as the sudden shift in a movie from subdued tones to dynamic colour.

Attribute agendas and opinions

In mapping the news media's impact on opinions, it is crucial to distinguish the contribution of overall media attention to an issue, the first level of agenda setting, from the way that an issue is described in the media, the second level of agenda setting. The distinct consequences of object salience and attribute salience are illustrated by American public opinion regarding the 1990–1991 Gulf War.[19] Extensive television coverage resulted in the high salience of the war on the public agenda as the most important problem facing the country, a first-level agenda-setting effect. Analyses of public opinion about President Bush from 1988 to 1991 further indicated a shift in the basis of his popularity from economics to foreign policy, a media priming effect. And demonstrating the effects of attribute agenda setting on opinions, members of the public who reported higher levels of exposure to television news, which emphasized military options in its coverage of the war, favoured a military rather than a diplomatic solution in the Persian Gulf.

For topics of longer standing, such as nuclear power, pesticides, and smoking, increased news coverage not only brought increased public awareness, but this coverage also redefined these issues with subsequent shifts in public opinion.[20] Nuclear power and pesticides went from beneficial scientific applications to major threats to public safety. Smoking became increasingly defined as a threat to personal health. As the dominant attributes of these issues changed on the public agenda, public opinion became increasingly negative.

The various aspects of an issue presented by the media – the media's attribute agenda – shape both our perspective and our opinions. As Chapter 3 on attribute agenda setting noted, Cohen's classic summary must be revised to state that the media not only tell us what to think about, they also tell us how to think about it. And sometimes what to think about it.

For instance, the impact of the tone of news coverage on public opinion is a perennial scholarly concern. A typical finding is that shifting patterns of positive and negative tone in the media explain significant shifts in approval ratings of political leaders.[21] In agenda-setting terms, these results are evidence of attribute priming, which occurs when certain attributes of an object emphasized in the media become significant dimensions of the object's public evaluation.[22] Thus, positive (or negative) coverage of a candidate can translate into positive (or negative) poll ratings when the media are successful at priming positive (or negative) considerations of presidents or prime ministers among media users.[23]

In a more detailed analysis of attribute priming effects, Spanish citizens' ratings of six major political figures on a ten-point scale ranging from 'highly unfavourable' to 'highly favourable' were compared with their affective descriptions of these men in response to the widely used 'what would you tell a friend' question.[24] Responses to this open-ended question were coded into a descriptive matrix defined by six substantive categories and five affective categories, a finer shading of affect than found in any previous evidence. These responses to the open-ended question provide a richness of detail that explains the images behind the parsimony of the ratings. For the six Spanish political leaders, the range of correlations between the citizens' affective descriptions and their ratings for these men was +0.78 to +0.97, with a median of +0.86. Citizens who gave a leader a low rating on the ten-point scale produced descriptions with substantially negative content. Citizens who gave high ratings produced highly positive descriptions.

In the 2002 state and federal elections in Texas, there were significant attribute agenda-setting effects by the news media on citizens' attribute agendas for the candidates for governor and US senator and, subsequently, significant relationships between individuals' attribute agendas and their opinions of these four men. A greater number of the attributes predicted individuals' opinions towards the candidates for heavy readers than for light readers.[25]

These patterns were replicated in the 2006 Israeli elections. Attribute salience among the public changed in correspondence with attribute salience in the media during the campaign. In turn, voters evaluated the candidates in terms of the attributes that were most salient, especially among heavy newspaper readers.[26]

Effects of tone are not limited to attitudes and opinions about politics. A content analysis of fourteen years of news coverage of the economy in the UK was combined with two measures of economic evaluations and two indicators of real-world economic conditions.[27] The results of the statistical analyses showed that the media covered the economy negatively more often than positively. More importantly, the study found that there was an asymmetric public response to this pattern of coverage – consumer expectations about the future of the economy were affected by negative, but not positive, coverage. Thus, the media in the UK were more successful at priming pessimistic, rather than optimistic, evaluations of the economy.

Experimental manipulation of both issue salience (global warming) and attribute salience (belief in the likelihood for each of five attributes occurring as a consequence of global warming) found no impact of issue salience on participants' support for efforts to reduce global warming. However, in line with the concept of a compelling argument in which a particular attribute impacts the salience of an object among the public, one of the attributes, negative effects on the ecosystem, was significantly linked to participants' support for efforts to reduce global warming.[28]

The impressive change in attitudes towards same-sex marriage in the United States may be another example of attribute priming effects. In the late 1990s, more people opposed than supported same-sex marriage. By 2013, the trend had completely reversed, and in 2015, same-sex marriage was legalized across the country. A study[29] measured the salience of substantive and affective attributes – whether the issue was discussed in the context of religious beliefs, family values or legal rights, each in positive or negative tone – in the *New York Times* between 2003 and 2013, and correlated these with public opinion on the same-sex marriage issue. The results showed very high correlations, especially over the long term (one year).

This converging evidence about priming effects and about the effects of both substantive and affective attributes in media messages indicates that agenda setting can have consequences for the positive or negative direction of public opinion.

Forming opinions

To begin at the beginning, there is a fundamental link between the salience of objects in the news and the formation of opinions by the audience. With the increasing salience of public figures in the news, for example, more people form an opinion about these persons. Across the six US presidential elections between 1984 and 2004, there was considerable variation in the amount of news coverage. And there was a strong correspondence between this pattern and the proportion of citizens in each election who expressed an opinion about the candidates in the National Election Studies.[30] High salience for a candidate in the media was associated with a high number of people expressing an opinion. Conversely, low media coverage of the candidates corresponds to a greater number of people with no opinion about them. A similar pattern was found for the proportion of the public holding opinions about eleven political figures during the 1996 US presidential election.[31] Decreasing visibility of a political figure in the news was associated with decreasing numbers of people with an opinion about that political figure. Comparison of these eleven persons' frequency of coverage in the media with the proportion of the public expressing an opinion about each one found a correlation of +0.81.

Willingness to express an opinion to pollsters follows a similar path. Across the weeks of the 2004 US presidential election, the refusal rate in the Annenberg Election Study's national surveys was negatively associated with the frequency of election stories in the *New York Times* and three TV network news programmes. Higher levels of news coverage about the election resulted in lower refusal rates, that is, a greater willingness to participate in an opinion poll.[32]

Absent news coverage, opinions about unobtrusive issues or little-known public figures will tend to be neutral or nonexistent. Thus, agenda setting can influence, indirectly, both attitude formation and attitude strength. For instance, in the German state of Baden-Württemberg, the personal salience of two major issues, the reunification of East and West Germany and East German migrants, was strongly linked to both the strength and the direction of personal opinions.[33] For the strength of opinion on both issues, personal salience was a far stronger predictor than media exposure or demographic characteristics. For the direction of opinion, personal salience was a slightly stronger predictor than age for German reunification. For the direction of opinion about East German migrants, personal salience was equal in strength to the use of television and only a slightly weaker predictor than education.

Influencing behaviour

Influencing people's behaviours is the pinnacle of media effects. Whether the media can persuade people to act in one way or another – from voting for a political party to buying an advertised product – was the main focus of communication research when the field emerged eighty years ago. It still is, as a casual reader of any communication handbook can attest. Elihu Katz noted:

> Communications research, or media studies, is about effect. It might have been otherwise – consider the study of art, for example – but it is not. However, the field is subdivided [...] the underlying aim, not always acknowledged, is to account for the power of the media.[34]

There are many well-known examples of media influence on behaviour. One is the successful use of entertainment television programming to spread the idea among young adults of 'the designated driver', that member of a party group who abstains from drinking in order to drive his or her friends home safely afterwards.[35] Another is the positive effect of news coverage of influenza on parents' decision to vaccinate their children against it,[36] or visit a physician reporting influenza-like symptoms.[37]

Within agenda setting, initial explorations centred on studying the direct effects of mediated agendas on public behaviour. The classic example is an investigation on news about plane crashes and skyjackings conducted by Alexander Bloj for Maxwell McCombs' communication theory course at Syracuse University in 1973.[38] The analysis was explicitly grounded in agenda-setting theory and hypothesized that news about crashes in which ten or more persons died or news about skyjackers' control of an airborne plane increased the salience of the danger of flying. Two complementary sets of evidence about people's behaviour were collected in a middle-sized American city, the number of passengers purchasing tickets and purchasing flight insurance over a five-year period. Box 8.2 compares high salience weeks – those weeks when there were fatal crashes or skyjackings – with low salience weeks for each of the five years. As expected, ticket sales dipped in high salience weeks and, conversely, flight insurance sales increased. The differences in these complementary behaviours are striking. The media agenda does far more than influence the pictures in our heads. Many times the media influence our attitudes and opinions, and even our behaviour.

Box 8.2 Individual behaviour in response to news of plane crashes and skyjackings

	Average ticket sales		Average insurance sales	
	Low salience weeks	High salience weeks	Low salience weeks	High salience weeks
1969	4,493	4,030	52	56
1970	4,798	4,302	58	63
1971	5,014	4,601	60	64
1972	5,412	4,789	63	69
1973	5,667	5,021	68	74

Source: Study conducted by Alexander Bloj for McCombs' communication theory course, which was reported in Maxwell McCombs and Donald Shaw, 'A progress report on agenda-setting research', paper presented at the Association for Education in Journalism, San Diego, CA, 1974.

Subsequently, research examined whether issue salience can be a significant predictor of citizens' actual votes on election day.[39] Beyond influencing the salience of issues on the public agenda, the media's agenda can at times advantage a particular political party because of issue ownership, the perception among voters that one political party is more capable than another of handling certain issues. In the United States, Democrats own most social welfare issues while Republicans own most defence issues.[40] Media emphasis on one of these issues will not only influence its salience, which is the traditional agenda-setting effect. That salience can also translate into behaviour, votes for the party that owns the issue.[41]

Nevertheless, the communications field acknowledged a long time ago that media effects on behaviour do not follow a simple stimulus–response model. Accordingly, most contemporary research on agenda-setting effects in this area examines the mechanisms and indirect paths of media influence. A good example is a body of work using agenda setting to understand the political socialization of adolescents in the United States.[42] Based on a two-wave survey of adolescents and their parents from Arizona, Florida, and Colorado, the researchers found that when families talked about the gubernatorial election in 2002, adolescents' attention to news during the 2004 presidential election increased. Heightened news use led to more emphasis of the Iraq War and, most importantly, stronger feelings about how the Bush administration handled the issue of Iraq. Attitude strength, in turn, motivated teenagers to adopt a more global ideological identity and, ultimately, vote in the 2004 election.

Thus, basic agenda-setting effects on turnout resulted from multiple causal chains, through both specific and general political attitudes.[43]

In another study about the 2004 US election, Denis Wu and Renita Coleman[44] examined the relative strength of candidates' issue stances and personal attributes on citizens' voting intentions – a close antecedent of actual vote choice. They found that, first, both issue and attributes agendas were set to a considerable degree by the news media. These first and second-level agenda-setting effects, in turn, were predictive of voting intention, especially respondents' perception of candidates' traits.

The behavioural outcomes of attribute agenda setting have also been explored through multiple causal chains. By combining a content analysis of news coverage in Kosovo with a public opinion survey, Lindita Camaj[45] found that the aspects highlighted by the media when it described political institutions influenced people's confidence in institutions. Political trust, in turn, determined the likelihood of engaging in conventional political activities, such as voting or working for parties.

Investigations in the United States and Japan document a variety of complementary cognitive and behavioural outcomes that result from object salience on the media agenda. Box 8.3 details the results for three kinds of outcomes: discussion, reflection and a desire for more information, and attention and interest. In the United States, Granger analysis was used to assess the impact on each of these outcomes by the week-to-week salience of the 2000 US presidential campaign in national television news – measured by the amount of time devoted to election coverage.[46] Because a major determinant of any behaviour, such as discussing the election, is the level of that behaviour in previous weeks, the Granger analysis initially measured this impact for each of the three outcomes using national surveys across twenty nine weeks of the campaign. The analysis then added the salience of the election on the television agenda as an additional predictor for each outcome. As we see in Box 8.3, the media agenda significantly impacted all three outcomes.

In the Japanese experiment, the effects of object salience in the media are demonstrated in the amount of change found for three behaviours related to each subject's lowest priority issue among the four unobtrusive issues measured.[47] Half of the subjects read articles about their lowest priority issue that contained only bare facts, the typical objective and fragmentary style employed by journalists for spot news. The other half read interpretative articles about their lowest priority issue that forecast the impact of the issue on the reader. Although there is consistently greater change among subjects

Box 8.3 Impact on three behaviours of object salience on the media agenda

US 2000 presidential election[a]	Japanese experiment[b]	
[Granger analysis of impact]	[% of subjects who changed]	
	Exposed to Interpretative frame	Exposed to Fragmentary frame
'Discussed the campaign' $R^2 = +0.68^c$ Impact of media +7%	'Want to discuss the issue' 58.3%	50.2%
'Thought about the campaign' $R^2 = +0.65$ Impact of media +7%	'Want more information on the issue' 69.5%	60.6%
'Paid attention to the campaign' $R^2 = +0.54$ Impact of media +4%	'Greater interest in the issue' 53.5%	44.2%

[a] (US) Object is the presidential campaign.
[b] (Japan) Object is lowest priority issue.
[c] This Granger analysis uses the squared value of r, the correlation coefficient frequently cited in this book, as a measure of how much of the dependent variable (e.g., amount of recent discussion of the campaign) is explained by previous levels of the dependent variable plus exposure to the media. Because R^2 is based on r, the range of values is the same, namely 1 to 0 to −1.
Source: Robert L. Stevenson, Rainer Böhme and Nico Nickel, 'The TV agenda-setting influence on campaign 2000', *Egyptian Journal of Public Opinion Research*, 2, 1 (2001): 29–50, and Tsuneo Ogawa, 'Framing and agenda setting function', *Keio Communication Review*, 23 (2001): 71–80.

reading the interpretative news articles, both versions produced large amounts of change in all three outcomes. For example, Box 8.3 reports that more than half of the subjects (regardless of which version they saw) wanted more information about their lowest priority issue and wanted to discuss it more.

These complementary sets of behaviours from two very different cultures and based on very different techniques of investigation are compelling evidence for the consequences of media agenda setting.[48] These outcomes also have implications for need for orientation, the psychological concept discussed in Chapter 5. Arguably, there is impact here on both components of need for orientation, the perceived personal relevance of the topic and the adequacy of one's knowledge about the topic. Perceived personal relevance also accounts for the greater impact of the interpretative version in the Japanese experiment. In short, this evidence cantilevers from some core ideas in agenda-setting theory into new portions of our theoretical map.

A 1988 Indiana poll brought together all these aspects of agenda setting and its consequences.[49] Replicating a familiar pattern, the salience among the public of a major issue of that time – the US federal budget deficit – was significantly correlated with frequency of exposure to both newspapers and television news. Further, issue salience in conjunction with use of a single medium, television news, predicted the strength of people's opinions on this issue, while issue salience in combination with newspaper reading predicted actual behaviour, such as writing a letter or attending a meeting about the deficit. Here in a single setting is evidence of significant relationships between media exposure and issue salience and of subsequent effects on knowledge, opinions and observable behaviour.

Agenda setting role of business news

Evidence of a link between agenda-setting effects and public behaviour was found in investor reactions to stories in *Fortune*.[50] During a three-year period when the Standard and Poor 500 stock market index increased 2.3 per cent, the stocks of fifty-four companies featured in *Fortune* magazine increased 3.6 per cent. Companies receiving favourable coverage increased the most, 4.7 per cent, but any increase in the salience of these companies resulted in some increase, 1.9 per cent with negative coverage and 1.7 per cent with neutral coverage.

This investigation was an opening gambit in a growing new arena – the agenda-setting influence of business news on the public. One well-developed specialization in this arena is corporate reputations, particularly the agenda-setting influence of business coverage on the awareness and prominence of corporations and their CEOs among the public, on the influence of media descriptions of firms on the substantive attributes that people associate with these firms, and the impact of the tone of news coverage on the public's opinions of individual firms. Recent research in two dozen countries around the world, which included developed, emerging and frontier markets, also found these first-level and second-level agenda-setting effects.[51] In turn, there are significant economic consequences of these agenda-setting effects.[52]

Business journalism, ranging from venerable outlets such as the *Financial Times* and the *Wall Street Journal* to the proliferation of new cable channels, has a substantial range of agenda-setting effects with major consequences for opinions and behaviour. This nuanced multidimensional focus on business journalism is a microcosm of agenda-setting theory, including the emerging third level of agenda-setting effects.[53]

Another aspect of agenda-setting theory, the influence of news sources on the media agenda, also is key in this specialized arena. Chapter 7 discussed the influence of press releases in the context of public affairs. Press releases and corporate websites are key sources of business news,[54] everything from routine reports on corporate economic performance to major shifts in business strategies as well as efforts to influence stakeholder agendas in proxy fights and corporate take-overs.[55] The business news agenda has become a significant aspect of the agenda-setting role of mass communication.

Summing up

The agenda-setting effects of media have significant implications beyond the pictures created in people's heads. In the original, traditional domain of agenda setting, the salience of public issues, there is considerable evidence that the shifting salience of these issues is often the basis for public opinion about the overall performance in office of a public leader. In turn, the salience of a public figure in the news is also linked with whether an individual holds any opinion at all about that person. At the second level of agenda setting, the salience of affective attributes intertwined with the public's cognitive pictures of these leaders represents the convergence of attribute agenda setting with opinion formation and change. Beyond attitudes and opinions, the pictures of reality created by the media have implications for personal behaviours, ranging from flu vaccinations to voting on election day. The behavioural effects of agenda setting, however, are not direct, as in a simple model of stimulus-response. Instead, they occur indirectly, by first impacting cognitions, attitudes and opinions, which in turn may influence behaviours.

9 Communication and Society

Communication, especially through media channels, has three broad social roles: surveillance of the larger environment, achieving consensus among the segments of society, and transmission of the culture.[1] The process of agenda setting detailed in the previous chapters is a significant part of the surveillance role, contributing substantial portions of our pictures and thoughts about the greater environment. The agenda-setting process also has major implications for social consensus and transmission of culture, implications that take agenda-setting theory beyond its traditional setting in public affairs and political communication.

As the roving spotlights of the media move from object to object and across the attributes of those objects in their surveillance of the environment, the public acquires significant knowledge. Initially, through exposure to the media, people become aware of major elements in the environment beyond their immediate personal ken and ascribe particular importance to a select few. As a further consequence of the media's surveillance, the public forms its pictures about the important elements in that environment, the key objects and their most salient attributes. This aspect of learning is the core of the agenda-setting process.

Consideration of the media's role in achieving social consensus links these agenda-setting effects with the observation in Chapter 6 that 'media agenda-setting effects are not manifested in creating different levels of salience among individuals, but are evident in driving the salience of all individuals up and down over time'.[2] A reasonable inference from this outcome is that the differences often found between demographic groups in public opinion polls – differences between men and women, or younger and older adults, for example – decrease as a result of exposure to the news media. Specifically, the correspondence between the agendas of various demographic groups should increase with greater exposure to the news media.[3]

Seminal evidence from the North Carolina Poll supports this view of agenda setting and consensus.[4] Comparison of the issue agendas for men and for women who read a daily newspaper infrequently yielded a correlation of +0.55. However, for men and women who read a daily newspaper occasionally, the degree of correspondence was +0.80 for the agenda of the most important problems facing the nation. Among men and women who read regularly, the issue agendas were identical (+1.0). Similar patterns of increased consensus about the most important issues facing the nation as a result of greater exposure to the newspaper were found in comparisons between the young and the old and blacks and whites. Increased consensus among various demographic groups in conjunction with increased media exposure was also true for television news audiences.

Similar patterns of social consensus resulting from exposure to the news media have also been found in Taiwan and Spain.[5] These patterns of consensus among various demographic groups are summarized in Box 9.1. Of course, given the considerable cultural and political diversity underlying any comparison of Spain, Taiwan, and the United States, the lack of absolutely identical patterns in Box 9.1 is hardly surprising. Still, eleven of the nineteen comparisons in Box 9.1 show a pattern of increased consensus resulting from greater exposure to the mass media.

Similar patterns of increased consensus also have been found at the second level of agenda setting.[6] Surveys in fifteen European countries two months after the September 11, 2001 tragedy in New York examined two sets of attributes, eight substantive attributes of the European Union's response to 9/11, and five affective attributes of the Muslim and Arab community in Europe. For both sets of attributes there was increased consensus among younger and older adults and among those with high and lower levels of education with greater use of national television news in the vast majority of the fifteen countries. The same pattern also was found for the substantive attributes in the majority of countries among both demographic groups for newspaper reading, but not for the affective community attributes. For example, two-thirds of the countries showed increased consensus on the substantive attributes for newspaper reading among younger and older adults, but fewer than half the countries displayed this pattern for the community attributes.

Box 9.1 Patterns of social consensus with increasing use of the news media among demographic groups in Spain, Taiwan, and the USA

	Spain		Taiwan	USA	
Demographic Groups	Newspaper	TV news	TV news	Newspaper	TV news
Sex	YES*	NO	YES	YES	NO
Education	YES	YES	YES	NO	NO
Age	NO	NO		YES	YES
Income			YES	NO	NO
Race (black/white)				YES	YES

* YES means that, for demographic groups defined by this trait (e.g., men and women), the degree of correlation between the groups increases with greater use of newspapers or TV news. NO means that this pattern of increased correlation between the groups is absent.
Sources: Esteban López-Escobar, Juan Pablo Llamas and Maxwell McCombs, 'Una dimensión social do los efectos dó los medios de difusión: agenda-setting y consenso', *Comunicación y Sociedad* IX (1996): 91–125; Ching-Yi Chiang, 'Bridging and closing the gap of our society: social function of media agenda setting', unpublished master's thesis, University of Texas at Austin, 1995; Donald Shaw and Shannon Martin, 'The function of mass media agenda setting', *Journalism Quarterly*, 69 (1992): 902–20.

Comparisons between demographic groups are a useful starting point in exploring the extent to which the agenda-setting role of media contributes to social consensus. Everyone is familiar with these demographic comparisons that are so frequently found in the reporting on polling results. Further elaboration of the media's contribution to social consensus should include psychological characteristics that better tap individual differences and involvement in society. Demographics are, at best, broad-brush surrogates for people's life situation.

Transmission of culture

Aspects of communication's third social role, the transmission of culture, are also linked with the agenda-setting process. Media and public agendas of issues, political candidates and their attributes – all those elements that are the central focus of this book – rest on the foundations of the larger civic culture defined by a funda- mental agenda of normative beliefs about democracy and society. Intriguing new applications of the theory explore other agenda-setting institutions that are also part of this civic culture, such as schools and organized religion.

Exploration of the media's role in the transmission of yet other cultural agendas is moving agenda-setting theory across new intellectual frontiers and far beyond its traditional realm of public affairs. These new lines of cultural inquiry extend from the historical agenda defining a society's collective memory of the past to contemporary museum visits in Greece and global interest in professional basketball.

Beginning with the traditional focus of agenda setting on public issues, media issue agendas often simultaneously convey significant messages about the civic culture, the set of beliefs and activities that define the environment in which these issues arise and are acted upon. Taking the larger view, the agenda-setting influence of the media on these broad civic attitudes is far more important than any agenda-setting effects on specific issues and opinions. For example, the social health of any democracy is determined to a considerable degree by its civic culture regarding participation in elections.

In the United States, where politics does not occupy a prominent position on the personal agenda of most citizens, the most significant agenda-setting role of the media may be to stimulate political interest every four years and position the presidential election on citizens' agendas. An early look at this agenda-setting role during the 1976 US presidential election found that exposure to television news in the late spring stimulated political interest in the summer and autumn months leading up to the November election.[7] Unfortunately, this positive contribution to the civic culture is offset by an array of evidence that the predilection of US political journalists to emphasize the negative attributes of politics has significant negative consequences for the civic culture. This downside of media agenda setting is summarized by the titles of two widely cited books on political journalism and voters' responses: Joseph Cappella and Kathleen Hall Jamieson's *Spiral of Cynicism* and Thomas Patterson's *Out of Order*.[8] From the perspective of agenda-setting theory, these outcomes are hardly surprising. Repetition of negative civic themes year after year makes these negative perspectives about politics highly salient among the public.

New agenda-setting arenas

Another social institution with a major role in the definition of culture, as well as a major role in its transmission, is organized religion. Even within the relatively narrow civic realm of public affairs, religious agendas can exert major impact.[9] During the 1992 presidential election campaign, religious communication kept abortion on the public agenda even though news media attention was minimal. For a small number of subjects, all members of fundamentalist churches that encouraged their members to see a threat to their freedom, constitutional issues ranging from prayer in public schools to support for gun ownership were the most important issues even though those concerns were not part of media discourse about the presidential election.[10]

Quite apart from public affairs, religious agendas can have highly significant effects on the personal lives of adherents. The empirical evidence to date only hints at the agenda-setting influence of religious messages on people's patterns of behaviour past and present.[11] In medieval Germany and France individuals could bring an issue to the public agenda of Jewish communities through the ritual of delaying the prayer service in the synagogue. Moshe Hellinger and Tsuriel Rashi analyse this practice in terms of agenda-setting theory, discussing the parallels between the customs that gave rise to this practice and the process of communication described by agenda-setting theory.[12]

Sometimes overlapping the civic agenda, but occupying a broader cultural niche, is collective memory, which is the highly selective agenda of past events and situations that dominate the public's view of their historical identity.[13] These cultural myths, which are often highly salient in how a group, region, or nation recalls its past, frequently bear little resemblance to the factual historical situation. Understanding the nature and origins of our collective memories requires examining particularly the influence of media narratives on personal recollections about the past.

Deep personal recollections shape the collective memory in many nations of the Great Depression, the Second World War and other emotionally charged times. But as new generations join the age cohort who lived through those times, the narratives of the media begin to move towards centre stage.[14] In a very real sense, each generation writes its own history and develops its own collective memory of the past. For millions of Americans, their perspective on the assassination of President John F. Kennedy has been shaped largely by the agenda of filmmaker Oliver Stone. And in these people's picture of the Watergate scandal that drove President Richard Nixon from office, actor Robert Redford is *Washington Post* journalist Bob Woodward.

As we go farther back into the historical past, media narratives, which include popular books and school textbooks as well as films and the news media's commemoration of selected past events, hold even greater sway over the public agenda. This is true for both the first level of agenda setting – which past events are even salient – and the second level of agenda setting – the specific aspects and details of these events that are prominent in our memory. 'The media know how to tell stories, and they are more capable of creating legends than the traditional agents of memory', noted Israeli scholar Yoram Peri.[15]

There is a striking example of this ability of the media on the occasion of Israel's sixtieth anniversary as a nation.[16] Two sequential surveys asked representative national samples to name the two events they considered most important in Israel and the world over the past one hundred years. Content analyses of major newspapers and television channels measured the media's historical agenda. From time one, a week of routine news, to time two immediately after the sixtieth anniversary celebration, there was a fivefold increase in the number of events mentioned. And the correspondence between the media agenda and the public agenda at time one, +0.62, increased to +0.83 at time two. Most importantly, in line with the media coverage, mentions of international events and minor Israeli events declined, while mentions of major Israeli events increased more than six-fold.

Moving from images of the past to contemporary images, newspaper coverage influenced American and British opinions in 2004 about nine countries across the world, ranging from Germany, to Turkey, to North Korea.[17] The results were very similar for the United States and the United Kingdom. In both countries there was close correspondence between the tone of the news coverage and public opinion measured on a 100-point feeling thermometer, +0.72 in the United States and +0.73 in the United Kingdom. Separate analysis of the positive and negative coverage showed similar patterns in America, +0.87 for public opinion and positive coverage, +0.85 for negative coverage – but a stronger impact of negative coverage in Britain, +0.84 for negative coverage and +0.56 for positive coverage.[18]

Schools are another significant agenda setter for our collective memories. Content analyses of school textbooks identify those aspects of the past that a society wishes to emphasize or ignore. Here again the phenomenon of interest is the transfer of salience from one agenda to another, a role at least implicitly acknowledged from time to time as educators and the public debate how the past shall be remembered in school textbooks and the curriculum. Of course, collective memories are far from the only cultural and personal agendas influenced by schools. In Spain a creative application of agenda setting examined the agenda of professional values that is central in the education of future journalists in the university classroom.[19]

Other cultural agendas

'Our cultural sense of what is new and important – our cultural agenda – comes largely from what plays on television', observed Lawrence Wenner.[20] And today a significant portion of that televised agenda worldwide is professional sports. An example par excellence of the effects that this television agenda can produce is the ballooning popularity of professional basketball in the United States during recent decades. In *The Ultimate Assist,* John Fortunato details how the commercial partnership of the National Basketball Association and the US television networks used strategies grounded in both first and second-level agenda setting to build their audiences.[21] First-level effects, the increased salience of NBA games, was achieved, in part, by the careful positioning of the best teams and players on the national television schedule. Second-level effects, the enhancement of professional basketball's image, were achieved through the creative production of player and coach interviews, announcer commentary, illustrative graphics, instant replays, and other elements that framed the sport in exciting ways. And it worked, both on television and at the games themselves. In the 1969–1970 season, fourteen NBA teams played 574 games that drew 4.3 million fans to courtside. Thirty years later, in the 1999–2000 season, twenty-nine NBA teams played 1,198 games that drew 20.1 million fans to courtside. During this same thirty-year period, NBA revenue from television grew from less than $10 million to more than $2 billion dollars a season. Agenda setting, the theory, also can be agenda setting, the business plan.

News also can influence personal cultural agendas. Greek museums with higher visibility in the major Athenian newspapers have higher visitation than museums with lower visibility. Media visibility impacts visitation both in the current month and in the following month, with the impact in the subsequent month even stronger. Looking at the affective attribute agenda of the newspapers, museums that receive more favourable mentions had higher visitation, those that receive more negative mentions in the media have fewer visitors. Positive articles have a positive effect both in the current and the following month. However, negative articles are more likely to have a negative effect in the following month rather than in the current month.[22]

In a subsequent study, the same group of authors applied the concepts of first and second-level cultural agenda setting within the Greek market for art-house films. Using a film's weekly box office revenue as a measure of the public agenda, they found that the volume and tone of press coverage of the movies had a significant effect on ticket sales. Furthermore, the positive, neutral, or negative opinion of film critics had an additional, independent effect on public salience.[23]

Another aspect of the personal cultural agenda, perceptions regarding wine, also reflects agenda setting. The attribute agenda of press releases, brochures, and tasting notes that Oregon wineries sent to the wine writers of major magazines and newspapers were strongly reflected in these journalists' articles about Oregon wines (+0.67). In turn, a comparison of these media attribute agendas with the descriptions of Oregon wine found among consumers surveyed in five major US metropolitan areas also yielded a significant degree of correspondence (+0.44).[24]

There are two countervailing trends in contemporary agenda-setting research, the centripetal trend discussed in several preceding chapters in which scholars have further explicated key theoretical concepts, and the centrifugal trend detailed in this chapter about agenda setting's expansion into wide variety of new domains. Despite the conservative orthodoxy of many academics who oppose these departures from the original domain of agenda-setting theory, inquiries of this nature will certainly continue in the future. Back in the early 1980s, in response to the question 'Who sets the media's agenda?', there were also scholars who proclaimed that area beyond the realm of agenda-setting theory. But the theory continues to thrive in new settings and domains.

Concepts, domains, and settings

To understand fully the vast and continually expanding agenda-setting research literature, to have a grasp of what has been investigated and where new research may go in the future, it is useful to distinguish between the concepts, domains, and settings that are the focus of these investigations. The core concepts of agenda-setting theory are the object agenda, the attribute agenda, and the transfer of salience between agendas. The networked bundles of objects and attributes, as well as the key contingent condition for the transfer of salience, need for orientation, also should be included.

These theoretical concepts can be studied in many different domains and settings. Beginning with the Chapel Hill study and continuing to this day, the dominant domain of agenda-setting research is public affairs, particularly public issues. A very different set of domains with a significant literature dating from the past decade or so has been reviewed in this chapter. These civic and cultural domains range from educational and religious institutions to a society's collective memory of its past, contemporary museum visits and movie ticket sales in Greece, and global interest in professional basketball.

Within each of these domains, agenda setting can be studied in many contexts. That is to say, the operational definitions of the core concepts of agenda-setting theory can be particular aspects of many different domains. In the traditional domain of public affairs, the most studied setting is the news media–public dyad. But among the settings found in the traditional agenda-setting literature are the links among the various news media themselves, links between sources and the news media, and the influence of personal conversations on the public agenda. Other aspects of these domains include the kinds of agenda items studied (issues or candidates, for example). Finally, use of the concepts of agenda-setting theory to investigate these various domains has taken place in a wide variety of geographic settings worldwide at many points in time. The emerging new cultural domains of agenda setting introduce a vast array of new operational definitions for the sources of agendas and the items defining those agendas, all in settings far removed from public affairs.

Separating the core concepts of agenda-setting theory from their operational definitions, this rich variety of domains and settings found in the literature helps us to see the past more clearly and to envision new directions of research. This separation also clarifies the various – and sometimes confusing – definitions of agenda setting proffered by various scholars. Hewing to the original domain and setting of agenda-setting research, some narrowly define agenda setting as the transfer of issue salience from the media agenda to the public agenda. Evidence of this is the continued practice of citing the original Chapel Hill study of 1972. A broader definition that is frequently cited, but still essentially hews to the original domain and its settings, states that elements prominent on the media agenda frequently become prominent on the public agenda. Both definitions are correct, but neither encompasses the full range of agenda-setting theory and research that exists today.

Recognizing the distinction between concepts, domains and settings provides a useful context for defining agenda setting and for understanding the broad range of agenda-setting phenomena. In this variety of domains and settings, the core axiom of agenda-setting theory about the transfer of salience from one agenda to another provides parsimony in our theoretical vocabulary. Despite the juxtaposition from time to time in the literature of the terms agenda setting and agenda building, there is no fundamental difference between the two. It is a distinction without a difference. Agenda-setting theory fundamentally is about the transfer of salience among agendas, whatever the domain and setting. There are many agendas in the contemporary world and many different agenda setters. However, like Julius Caesar in ancient Rome, the news media frequently are first among equals in the shaping of contemporary agendas.

The important role played by the news media in setting the public and policy agendas is not set in stone – it may diminish, of course. Many contemporary observers hail Twitter, Facebook, Instagram, WhatsApp, and a plethora of other social media channels as the new chief agenda setters. As we discussed in Chapter 1, the empirical evidence about this possibility is, to date, mixed. This does not preclude the fact that for some groups, or in some contexts, social media already sets the agenda in a way the traditional, legacy media does not. In such a scenario, the concepts, domains, and settings of the theory of agenda setting are still valuable. That agenda setting has a very good chance of standing the test of time is recognized even by contemporary proponents of a new Law of Minimal Consequences:

> The increasing level of selective exposure thus presages a new era of minimal consequences, at least insofar as persuasive effects are concerned. But other forms of media influence, such as agenda setting or priming may continue to be important.[25]

Continuing evolution of agenda-setting theory

Our theoretical map of agenda setting began in Chapel Hill more than fifty years ago with an investigation of news media influence on the issues that voters regarded as most important. Over the following decades, this map has expanded into a multi-faceted theory with several distinct aspects. All of these continue to be productive areas of research as the idea of agenda setting has expanded to diverse domains in a broad range of international settings. And the future promises a continuing evolution beyond the contemporary theoretical map as research continues to explicate the process of agenda setting and explore the applications of this process to domains far beyond its original focus on public affairs. Turning back to theoretical basics concurrently with movement outwards to new domains presents an intriguing agenda for scholarly activity. To paraphrase Sherlock Holmes' call to adventure, 'Come, the game is afoot.'

Notes

Preface

1 Alan Cowell, 'New owner struggles at a London tabloid', *New York Times*, 26 February 2001, p. C15.

2 Max Frankel, *The Times of My Life and My Life with The Times* (New York: Random House, 1999), pp. 414–15.

3 Theodore White, *The Making of the President, 1972* (New York: Bantam, 1973), p. 327.

4 Maxwell McCombs and Donald Shaw, 'The agenda-setting function of mass media', *Public Opinion Quarterly*, 36 (1972): 176–87. The early history of this study offers a salutary note about new theoretical perspectives. A few months after the 1968 election, McCombs and Shaw submitted the paper later published in *Public Opinion Quarterly* to the annual convention of the Association for Education in Journalism. Their paper was summarily rejected, which explains the four-year gap between the election and the 1972 article.

5 Contrary to a published statement that the phrase 'agenda setting' was suggested by an anonymous reviewer of the original article published in the summer 1972 issue of *Public Opinion Quarterly*, Part I of the McCombs and Shaw report to the National Association of Broadcasters in June 1969 was titled 'The agenda-setting function of the mass media'. The title of the full report was 'Acquiring Political Information'. A revised version of this draft report was not submitted to *Public Opinion Quarterly* until several years later. The full statement about the phrase 'agenda setting' originating with an anonymous reviewer is in Robert L. Stevenson, Rainer Böhme, and Nico Nikel, 'The TV agenda-setting influence on campaign 2000', *Egyptian Journal of Public Opinion Research*, 2, 1 (2001), p. 29.

6 Maxwell McCombs and Jian-Hua Zhu, 'Capacity, diversity, and volatility of the public agenda: trends from 1954 to 1994', *Public Opinion Quarterly*, 59 (1995): 495–525; Jill A. Edy and Patrick C. Meirick, 'The fragmenting public agenda: capacity, diversity, and volatility in responses to the "most important problem" question', *Public Opinion Quarterly*, 82 (2018): 661–85.

7 My thanks to John Pavlik for this metaphoric comparison, made during a

conversation about the first edition of this book on 12 September 2003 in Bonn, Germany.

8 David Weaver, who came to the University of North Carolina to study for his PhD shortly after the original Chapel Hill study, quickly gained a major role in the development of agenda-setting theory. His contribution as a graduate student during the 1972 US presidential election is detailed in Chapter 6 and as a faculty member at Indiana University during the 1976 US presidential election in Chapter 1. Many other contributions from Indiana University in the subsequent years are noted in other chapters, along with continuing contributions from the University of North Carolina at Chapel Hill.

9 Michael Gurevitch and Jay Blumler, 'Political communication systems and democratic values', in *Democracy and the Mass Media*, ed. Judith Lichtenberg (Cambridge: Cambridge University Press, 1990), pp. 269–89.

10 Tom Bettag, 'What's news? Evolving definitions of news', *Harvard International Journal of Press/Politics*, 5, 3 (2000): 105.

11 Davis Merritt and Maxwell McCombs, *The Two W's of Journalism: The Why and What of Public Affairs Reporting* (Mahwah, NJ: Lawrence Erlbaum, 2003).

1 Influencing Public Opinion

1 Walter Lippmann, *Public Opinion* (New York: Macmillan, 1922), p. 29.

2 Robert Park, 'News as a form of knowledge', *American Journal of Sociology*, 45 (1940): 667–86.

3 Propaganda, however, can have agenda-setting effects. For instance, there is some evidence that 'fake news' websites – sites that deliberatively spread misperceptions and fabricated content – influenced the agenda of fact-based media during the 2016 US presidential election; see Chris J. Vargo, Lei Guo, and Michelle A. Amazeen, 'The agenda-setting power of fake news: a big data analysis of the online media landscape from 2014 to 2016', *New Media and Society*, 20 (2018): 2028–49.

4 Bernard Cohen, *The Press and Foreign Policy* (Princeton, NJ: Princeton University Press, 1963), p. 13.

5 Lippmann, *Public Opinion*, p. 3.

6 Ibid., p. 4.

7 Paul Lazarsfeld, Bernard Berelson, and Hazel Gaudet, *The People's Choice* (New York: Duell, Sloan, and Pearce, 1944).

8 Joseph Klapper, *The Effects of Mass Communication* (New York: Free Press, 1960), p. 8.

9 See, for instance, Robert E. Park, 'The city: suggestions for investigation of human behavior in the urban environment', in Robert E. Park and Ernest W. Burgess, eds., *The City* (Chicago, IL: University of Chicago Press, 1925), pp. 1–46; Paul F. Lazarsfeld and Robert K. Merton, 'Mass communication, popular taste and organized social action', in Guy E. Swanson, Theodore M.

Newcomb, and Eugene L. Hartley, eds., *Readings in Social Psychology* (rev. edn) (New York, NY: Henry Holt and Company, 1952), pp. 74–85.

10 Maxwell McCombs and Donald Shaw, 'The agenda setting function of mass media', *Public Opinion Quarterly*, 36 (1972): 176–87.

11 Yeojin Kim, Youngju Kim, and Shuhua Zhou, 'Theoretical and methodological trends of agenda-setting theory: a thematic analysis of the last four decades of research', *Agenda Setting Journal*, 1 (2017): 5–22.

12 Stanley Presser, 'Substance and method in *Public Opinion Quarterly*, 1937–2010', *Public Opinion Quarterly*, 75 (2011): 839–45. Details in Table 2 (p. 843). For additional background on citations to the Chapel Hill study, see W. Russell Neuman and Lauren Guggenheim, 'The evolution of media effects theory: a six-stage model of cumulative research', *Communication Theory*, 21 (2011): 169–96. For details, see p. 180.

13 W. Lance Bennett and Shanto Iyengar, 'A new era of minimal effects? The changing foundations of political communication', *Journal of Communication*, 58 (2008): 707–31. Quote from p. 708.

14 Yunjuan Luo, Hansel Burley, Alexander Moe, and Mingxiao Sui, 'A meta-analysis of news media's public agenda-setting effects, 1972–2015', *Journalism and Mass Communication Quarterly*, 96 (2019): 150–72.

15 Stephen A. Rains, Timothy R. Levine, and Rene Weber, 'Sixty years of quantitative communication research summarized: lessons from 149 meta-analyses', *Annals of the International Communication Association*, 42 (2018): 105–24.

16 Donald Shaw and Maxwell McCombs, eds., *The Emergence of American Political Issues* (St Paul, MN: West, 1977).

17 David H. Weaver, Doris A. Graber, Maxwell E. McCombs, and Chaim H. Eyal, *Media Agenda Setting in a Presidential Election: Issues, Images and Interest* (Westport, CT: Greenwood, 1981).

18 James Winter and Chaim Eyal, 'Agenda setting for the civil rights issue', *Public Opinion Quarterly*, 45 (1981): 376–83.

19 Stuart N. Soroka, 'Media, public opinion, and foreign policy', *Harvard International Journal of Press/Politics*, 8 (2003): 27–48.

20 Hans-Bernd Brosius and Hans Mathias Kepplinger, 'The agenda setting function of television news: static and dynamic views', *Communication Research*, 17 (1990): 183–211.

21 Adam Shehata, 'Unemployment on the agenda: a panel study of agenda setting effects during the 2006 Swedish national election campaign', *Journal of Communication*, 60 (2010): 182–203.

22 Kim Smith, 'Newspaper coverage and public concern about community issues', *Journalism Monographs*, 101 (1987).

23 Maria José Canel, Juan Pablo Llamas, and Federico Rey, 'El primer nivel del efecto agenda setting en la información local: los "problemas más importantes" de la ciudad de Pamplona' ['The first level agenda setting effect on local information: the "most important problems" of the city of Pamplona'], *Comunicación y Sociedad*, 9, 1 and 2 (1996): 17–38.

24 Toshio Takeshita, 'Agenda setting effects of the press in a Japanese local election', *Studies of Broadcasting*, 29 (1993): 193–216.

25   Federico Rey Lennon, *Los Diarios Nacionales y la Campaña Electoral: Argentina, 1997 Elecciones* [The national press and the electoral campaign: Argentina, the 1997 elections] (Buenos Aires: Freedom Forum and Universidad Austral, 1998).

26   Alicia Casermeiro de Pereson, Los medios en las elecciones: la agenda setting en la ciudad de Buenos Aires [The media in the elections: Agenda setting in the city of Buenos Aires] (Buenos Aires, Argentina, EDUCA, 2003).

27   Howard Eaton Jr, 'Agenda setting with bi-weekly data on content of three national media', *Journalism Quarterly*, 66 (1989): 942–8.

28   McCombs and Shaw, 'The agenda setting function of mass media.'

29   Shaw and McCombs, *The Emergence of American Political Issues.*

30   Weaver, Graber, McCombs and Eyal, *Media Agenda Setting in a Presidential Election.*

31   Winter and Eyal, 'Agenda setting for the civil rights issue.'

32   Eaton, 'Agenda setting with bi-weekly data on content of three national media.'

33   Brosius and Kepplinger, 'The agenda setting function of television news.'

34   Smith, 'Newspaper coverage and public concern about community issues.'

35   Shanto Iyengar and Donald R. Kinder, *News That Matters: Television and American Opinion* (Chicago: University of Chicago Press, 1987).

36   Scott L. Althaus and David Tewksbury, 'Agenda setting and the "new" news: patterns of issue importance among readers of the paper and online versions of the *New York Times*', *Communication Research*, 29 (2002): 180–207. Quote is on p. 199.

37   Michael Conway and J. R. Patterson, 'Today's top story? An agenda setting and recall experiment involving television and Internet news', *Southwestern Mass Communication Journal*, 24 (2008): 31–48.

38   Gary King, Benjamin Schneer, and Ariel White, 'How the news media activate public expression and influence national agendas', *Science*, 358 (2017): 776–80.

39   Matthew Gentzkow, 'Small media, big impact: Randomizing news stories reveals broad public impacts', *Science*, 358 (2017): 726–7. Quote is on p. 727.

40   Mike Gruszczynski and Michael W. Wagner, 'Information flow in the 21st century: the dynamics of agenda-uptake', *Mass Communication and Society*, 20 (2017): 378–402; Sharon Meraz, 'Using time series analysis to measure intermedia agenda-setting influence in traditional media and political blog networks', *Journalism and Mass Communication Quarterly*, 88 (2011): 176–94; Kevin Wallsten 'Agenda setting and the blogosphere: An analysis of the relationship between mainstream media and political blogs', *Review of Policy Research*, 24 (2007): 567–87.

41   For particular case studies, see Jacob Groshek and Megan Clough Groshek, 'Agenda-trending: reciprocity and the predictive capacity of social networking sites in intermedia agenda-setting across topics over time', *Media and Communication*, 1, 1, 2013: 15–27; Raymond A. Harder, Julie Sevenans, and Peter Van Aelst, 'Intermedia agenda setting in the social

media age: How traditional players dominate the news agenda in election times', *International Journal of Press/Politics*, 22, 3 (2017): 275–93; Ingrid Rogstad, 'Is Twitter just rehashing? Intermedia agenda setting between Twitter and mainstream media', *Journal of Information Technology and Politics*, 13, 2 (2016): 142–58; Ben Sayre, Leticia Bode, Dhavan Shah, Dave Wilcox, and Chirag Shah, 'Agenda setting in a digital age: tracking attention to California Proposition 8 in social media, online news and conventional news,", *Policy and Internet*, 2, 2 (2010): 7–32; Kathleen Searles and Glen Smith, 'Who's the boss? Setting the agenda in a fragmented media environment,", *International Journal of Communication*, 10 (2016): 2074–95; Sebastián Valenzuela, Soledad Puente, and Pablo M. Flores, 'Comparing disaster news on Twitter and television: An intermedia agenda setting perspective', *Journal of Broadcasting and Electronic Media*, 61 (2017): 615–37; Chris J. Vargo and Lei Guo, 'Networks, big data, and intermedia agenda setting: an analysis of traditional, partisan, and emerging online US news', *Journalism and Mass Communication Quarterly*, 94 (2017): 1031–55.

42 Hai Tran, 'Online agenda setting: a new frontier for theory development', in *Agenda Setting in a 2.0 World*, ed. Thomas J. Johnson (New York: Routledge, 2013), pp. 205–29.

43 Jason Martin, 'Agenda setting, elections and the impact of information technology', in *Agenda Setting in a 2.0 World*, ed. Thomas J. Johnson (New York: Routledge, 2013), pp. 28–52.

44 Conway and Patterson, 'Today's top story?'; Althaus and Tewksbury, 'Agenda setting and the "new" news.'

45 Yonghoi Song, 'Internet news media and issue development: a case study on the roles of independent online news services as agenda-builders for anti-US protests in South Korea', *New Media and Society*, 9 (2007): 71–92.

46 Jae Kook Lee, 'The effect of the Internet on homogeneity of the media agenda: a test of the fragmentation thesis', *Journalism and Mass Communication Quarterly*, 84 (2007): 745–60.

47 Ana S. Cardenal, Carol Galais, and Silvia Majó-Vázquez, 'Is Facebook eroding the public agenda? Evidence from survey and web-tracking data', *International Journal of Public Opinion Research*, 31, (2019): 589–608.

48 Pablo Barberá, Andreu Casas, Jonathan Nagler, Patrick J. Egan, Richard Bonneau, John T. Jost, and Joshua A. Tucker, 'Who leads? Who follows? Measuring issue attention and agenda setting by legislators and the mass public using social media data', *American Political Science Review*, 113 (2019): 883–901.

49 Ibid., p. 897.

50 G. R. Boynton and Glenn W. Richardson, Jr, 'Agenda setting in the twenty-first century', *New Media and Society*, 18 (2016): 1916–34.

51 Steven H. Chaffee and Miriam J. Metzger, 'The end of mass communication?', *Mass Communication and Society*, 4 (2001): 365–79; Bennett and Iyengar, 'A new era of minimal effects?'; Bruce A. Williams and Michael X. Delli Carpini, 'Monica and Bill all the time and everywhere: The collapse of gatekeeping and agenda setting in the new media environment', *American Behavioral Scientist*, 47 (2004): 1208–30.

52 Few argue that people's attention span has diminished as a consequence of a high-choice media environment. See, e.g. Philipp Lorenz-Spreen, Bjarke Mørch Mønsted, Philipp Hövel, and Sune Lehmann, 'Accelerating dynamics of collective attention', *Nature Communications*, 10, 1759 (2019). Active attention to media content, however, is not the only path through which people learn the media agenda, as there is evidence that the process can also operate incidentally, through cues. See Maxwell McCombs and Natalie J. Stroud, 'Psychology of agenda-setting effects: Mapping the paths of information processing', *Review of Communication Research*, 2 (2014): 68–93; Elizabeth Stoycheff, Raymond J. Pingree, Jason T. Peifer, and Mingxiao Sui, 'Agenda cueing effects of news and social media', *Media Psychology*, 21, 2 (2018): 182–201.

53 Yue Tan and David Weaver, 'Agenda diversity and agenda setting from 1956 to 2004: what are the trends over time?', *Journalism Studies*, 14, (2013): 773–89.

54 Monika Djerf-Pierre and Adam Shehata, 'Still an agenda setter: traditional news media and public opinion during the transition from low to high choice media environments', *Journal of Communication*, 67 (2017): 733–57.

55 Daniela Grassau, 'Has TV decreased impact on public opinion due to the transformations of the media environment in the 21st century?', paper presented to the International Association for Media and Communication Research, Madrid, 2019.

56 Renita Coleman and Maxwell McCombs, 'The young and agenda-less? Age-related differences in agenda setting on the youngest generation, baby boomers, and the civic generation', *Journalism and Mass Communication Quarterly*, 84 (2007): 495–508.

57 Jae Kook Lee and Renita Coleman, 'Testing generational, life cycle, and period effects of age on agenda setting', *Mass Communication and Society*, 17, 1 (2014): 3–25.

58 Yunjuan Luo, Hansel Burley, Alexander Moe, and Mingxiao Sui, 'A meta-analysis of news media's public agenda-setting effects, 1972–2015.'

59 Pablo Boczkowski, *News at Work: Imitation in an Age of Information Abundance* (Chicago: University of Chicago Press, 2010).

60 Maxwell McCombs, 'Civic osmosis: the social impact of media', *Communication and Society*, 25 (2012): 7–14.

61 James Webster and Thomas Ksiazek, 'The dynamics of audience fragmentation: public attention in an age of digital media', *Journal of Communication*, 62 (2012): 39–56. Quote is on p. 39.

62 Hyun, Ki Deuk, and Soo Jung Moon, 'Agenda setting in the partisan TV news context: attribute agenda setting and polarized evaluation of presidential candidates among viewers of NBC, CNN, and Fox News', *Journalism and Mass Communication Quarterly*, 93 (2016): 509–29.

63 Lazarsfeld, Berelson and Gaudet, *The People's Choice*, p. 122.

64 Maxwell McCombs, Esteban López-Escobar, and Juan Pablo Llamas, 'Setting the agenda of attributes in the 1996 Spanish general election', *Journal of Communication*, 50, 2 (2000): 77–92.

65 Coleman and McCombs, 'The young and agenda-less?.' Quote on p. 503.

66 Jesper Stromback and Spiro Kiousis, 'A new look at agenda setting effects – Comparing the predictive power of overall political news consumption and specific news media consumption across different media channels and media types', *Journal of Communication*, 60 (2010): 271–92. Quote is on p. 288 (emphasis in original).

67 Steven Chaffee and Donna Wilson, 'Media rich, media poor: two studies of diversity in agenda-holding', *Journalism Quarterly*, 54 (1977): 466–76. Also see Peter Jochen and Claes H. de Vreese, 'Agenda-rich, agenda-poor: a cross-national comparative investigation of nominal and thematic public agenda diversity', *International Journal of Public Opinion Research*, 15 (2003): 44–64.

68 See for example, Mark Boukes, 'Agenda-setting with satire: how political satire increased TTIP'S saliency on the public, media, and political agenda', *Political Communication*, 36 (2019): 426–51; Xiaoxia Cao, 'Hearing it from Jon Stewart: the impact of The Daily Show on public attentiveness to politics', *International Journal of Public Opinion Research*, 22 (2010): 26–46; J. Carroll Glynn, Michael Huge, James Reineke, Bruce Hardy and James Shanahan, 'When Oprah intervenes: political correlates of daytime talk show viewing', *Journal of Broadcasting and Electronic Media*, 51 (2007): 228–44.

69 William Gamson, *Talking Politics* (New York: Cambridge University Press, 1992).

70 William G. Mayer, *The Changing American Mind: How and Why American Public Opinion Changed between 1960 and 1988* (Ann Arbor: University of Michigan Press, 1992).

2 Reality and the News

1 Ray Funkhouser, 'The issues of the sixties', *Public Opinion Quarterly*, 37 (1973): 62–75.

2 Ibid., p. 72.

3 Hans Mathias Kepplinger and Herbert Roth, 'Creating a crisis: German mass media and oil supply in 1973–74', *Public Opinion Quarterly*, 43 (1979): 285–96.

4 Maxwell McCombs, Edna Einsiedel, and David Weaver, *Contemporary Public Opinion: Issues and the News* (Hillsdale, NJ: Lawrence Erlbaum, 1991), pp. 43–5. Also see Pamela Shoemaker, ed., *Communication Campaigns about Drugs* (Hillsdale, NJ: Lawrence Erlbaum, 1989), especially, Stephen Reese and Lucig Danielian, 'Intermedia influence and the drug issue: converging on cocaine', pp. 29–46; Danielian and Reese, 'A closer look at intermedia influences on agenda setting: the cocaine issue of 1986', pp. 47–66; and Pamela Shoemaker, Wayne Wanta, and Dawn Leggett, 'Drug coverage and public opinion, 1972–1986', pp. 67–80.

5 William Gonzenbach, *The Media, the President, and Public Opinion: A Longitudinal Analysis of the Drug Issue, 1984–1991* (Mahwah, NJ: Lawrence Erlbaum, 1996). This longitudinal study of the drug issue adds the policy

agenda to the traditional analysis of the media agenda–public agenda. Although the preponderance of evidence suggests that the major transmission of salience between the media and the public is from the media to the public, there is considerably more fluctuation, in the flow of influence between the policy agenda and the media agenda. James Dearing and Everett Rogers, *Agenda Setting* (Thousand Oaks, CA: Sage, 1996), among others, note that most of the research involving policy agendas has evolved in isolation from the media-centred theory of agenda setting discussed in this book.

6 Anthony Downs, 'Up and down with ecology: the "issue-attention cycle"', *The Public Interest*, 28 (1972): 38–50.

7 Salma Ghanem, 'Media coverage of crime and public opinion: an exploration of the second level of agenda setting', unpublished doctoral dissertation, University of Texas at Austin, 1996. Ghanem's study of the discrepancy in Texas between the pattern of news coverage and the reality reflected in crime statistics is a detailed microcosm of the national situation. See Richard Morin, 'Crime time: the fear, the facts: how the sensationalism got ahead of the stats', *Outlook, Washington Post* (30 January 1994), p. C1, and Dennis Lowry, Tam Ching, Josephine Nio, and Dennis Leitner, 'Setting the public fear agenda: a longitudinal analysis of network TV crime reporting, public perceptions of crime, and FBI crime statistics', *Journal of Communication*, 53, (2003): 61–73.

8 Margaret T. Gordon and Linda Heath, 'The news business, crime and fear', in *Reactions to Crime*, ed. Dan Lewis (Beverly Hills, CA: Sage, 1981). Excerpt reprinted in *Agenda Setting: Readings on Media, Public Opinion, and Policymaking*, eds. David Protess and Maxwell McCombs (Hillsdale, NJ: Lawrence Erlbaum, 1991), pp. 71–4. Another example of the disparity between news coverage and reality, in this case, local television news and the occurrence of crime in nineteen different US communities, is presented by James T. Hamilton, *Channeling Violence: The Economic Market for Violent Television Programming* (Princeton, NJ: Princeton University Press, 1998).

9 George Gerbner, Larry Gross, Michael Morgan, Nancy Signorielli, and James Shanahan, 'Growing up with television: cultivation processes', in *Media Effects: Advances in Theory and Research*, 2nd edn, eds. Jennings Bryant and Dolf Zillmann (Mahwah, NJ: Lawrence Erlbaum, 1994), pp. 43–68. Also see R. Andrew Holbrook and Timothy Hill, 'Agenda setting and priming in prime time television: crime dramas as political cues', *Political Communication*, 22 (2005): 277–95.

10 Kimberly Gross and Sean Aday, 'The scary world in your living room and neighborhood: using local broadcast news, neighborhood crime rates, and personal experience to test agenda setting and cultivation', *Journal of Communication*, 53 (2003): 411–26.

11 Magdalena Browne and Sebastián Valenzuela, 'Temor a la delincuencia en Chile: [Fear of crime in Chile], in *(In)seguridad, medios y miedos* [(In) security, media and fears], eds. Brenda Focás and Omar Rincón (Buenos Aires: Ediciones Imago Mundi, 2018), pp. 63–84.

12 'The statistical shark', *New York Times*, 6 September 2001, p. A26.

13 Christine Ader, 'A longitudinal study of agenda setting for the issue of environmental pollution', *Journalism and Mass Communication Quarterly*, 72 (1995): 300–11.

14 Stuart N. Soroka, *Agenda-Setting Dynamics in Canada* (Vancouver: UBC Press, 2002).

15 Downs, 'Up and down with ecology: the "issue-attention cycle".'

16 An excellent early example of research examining individual issue agendas is Jack McLeod, Lee B. Becker, and J. E. Byrnes, 'Another look at the agenda setting function of the press', *Communication Research*, 1 (1974): 131–66.

17 See the numerous citations to attention-based studies in Wayne Wanta, *The Public and the National Agenda* (Mahwah, NJ: Lawrence Erlbaum, 1997).

18 Jesper Stromback and Spiro Kiousis, 'A new look at agenda setting effects – Comparing the predictive power of overall political news consumption and specific news media consumption across different media channels and media types', *Journal of Communication*, 60 (2010): 271–92. Quote is on p. 288.

19 Magdalena Browne and Sebastián Valenzuela, 'Temor a la delincuencia en Chile' [Fear of crime in Chile].

20 Richard L. Merritt, *Symbols of American Community, 1735–1775* (New Haven, CT: Yale University Press, 1966).

21 David Paul Nord, 'The politics of agenda setting in late 19th century cities', *Journalism Quarterly*, 58 (1981): 563–74, 612.

22 Ibid., p. 570.

23 Jean Lange Folkerts, 'William Allen White's anti-populist rhetoric as an agenda setting technique', *Journalism Quarterly*, 60 (1983): 28–34.

24 Funkhouser, 'The issues of the sixties.'

25 James Winter and Chaim Eyal, 'Agenda setting for the civil rights issue', *Public Opinion Quarterly*, 45 (1981): 376–83.

26 Edward Caudill, 'An agenda setting perspective on historical public opinion', in *Communication and Democracy: Exploring the Intellectual Frontiers in Agenda setting Theory*, eds. Maxwell McCombs, Donald Shaw, and David Weaver (Mahwah, NJ: Lawrence Erlbaum, 1997), p. 179.

27 Ibid., p. 181.

28 Chris J. Vargo, Lei Guo, and Michelle Amazeen, 'The agenda-setting power of fake news: A big data analysis of the online media landscape from 2014 to 2016', *New Media and Society*, 20 (2018): 2028–49.

29 William Safire, 'Like father, unlike son', *New York Times*, 2 September 2002, p. A17.

3 The Pictures in our Heads

1 Walter Lippmann, *Public Opinion* (New York: Macmillan, 1922).

2 Maxwell McCombs and Donald Shaw, 'The agenda-setting function of mass media', *Public Opinion Quarterly*, 36 (1972): 176–87.

3 Maxwell McCombs, 'Explorers and surveyors: expanding strategies for agenda setting research', *Journalism Quarterly*, 69 (1992): 815.

 4 Stuart N. Soroka, *Agenda-Setting Dynamics in Canada* (Vancouver: UBC Press, 2002). For a similar study conducted in Israel, see Dan Caspi, 'The agenda-setting function of the Israeli press', *Knowledge: Creation, Diffusion, Utilization*, 3 (1982): 401–14.
 5 William J. McGuire, 'Theoretical foundations of campaigns', in *Public Communication Campaigns*, 2nd edn., eds. Richard E. Rice and Charles K. Atkin (Newbury Park, CA: Sage, 1989): 43–65.
 6 *New York Times*, 1 November 2002, p. A28.
 7 Bernard Cohen, *The Press and Foreign Policy* (Princeton, NJ: Princeton University Press, 1963), p. 13.
 8 David Swanson and Paolo Mancini, eds., *Politics, Media, and Modern Democracy: An International Study of Innovations in Electoral Campaigning and their Consequences* (Westport, CT: Praeger, 1996).
 9 Maxwell McCombs, 'The future agenda for agenda setting research', *Journal of Mass Communication Studies* [Japan], 45 (1994): 171–81; Maxwell McCombs and Dixie Evatt, 'Los temas y los aspectos: explorando una nueva dimensión de la agenda setting' ['Objects and attributes: exploring a new dimension of agenda setting'], *Comunicación y Sociedad*, 8, 1 (1995): 7–32.
10 Lee Becker and Maxwell McCombs, 'The role of the press in determining voter reactions to presidential primaries', *Human Communication Research*, 4 (1978): 301–7.
11 David H. Weaver, Doris A. Graber, Maxwell E. McCombs, and Chaim H. Eyal, *Media Agenda Setting in a Presidential Election: Issues, Images and Interest* (Westport, CT: Greenwood, 1981).
12 Maxwell McCombs, Esteban López-Escobar, and Juan Pablo Llamas, 'Setting the agenda of attributes in the 1996 Spanish general election', *Journal of Communication*, 50, 2 (2000): 77–92.
13 Rosa Berganza and Marta Martin, 'Selective exposure to highly politicized media'; and José Javier Sánchez-Aranda, María José Canel, and Juan Pablo Llamas, 'Framing effects of television political advertising and the selective perception process', papers presented at the World Association for Public Opinion Research regional conference, Pamplona, Spain, 1997.
14 Pu-Tsung King, 'The press, candidate images, and voter perceptions', in *Communication and Democracy*, eds. Maxwell McCombs, Donald Shaw, and David Weaver (Mahwah, NJ: Lawrence Erlbaum, 1997), pp. 29–40.
15 Esteban López-Escobar, Juan Pablo Llamas, and Maxwell McCombs, 'Una dimensión social de los efectos de los medios de difusión: agenda-setting y consenso' ['A social dimension of media effects: agenda-setting and consensus'] *Comunicación y Sociedad*, IX (1996): 91–125. Also see Maxwell McCombs, Juan Pablo Llamas, Esteban López-Escobar, and Federico Rey, 'Candidate images in Spanish elections: second-level agenda setting effects', *Journalism and Mass Communication Quarterly*, 74 (1997): 703–17.
16 Soo Jung Moon, 'Attention, attitude, and behavior: second-level agenda-setting effects as a mediator of media use and political participation', *Communication Research*, 40 (2013): 698–719.
17 Spiro Kiousis, Philemon Bantimaroudis and Hyun Ban, 'Candidate image

attributes: experiments on the substantive dimension of second-level agenda setting', *Communication Research*, 26, 4 (1999): 414–28.

18 Renita Coleman and Stephen Banning, 'Network TV news' affective framing of the presidential candidates: evidence for a second-level agenda-setting effect through visual framing', *Journalism and Mass Communication Quarterly*, 83 (2006): 313–28.

19 Ibid., p. 321. Extending this analysis of affective agenda-setting effects from visuals, Coleman and Wu introduced a theoretical distinction between affect as emotion and affect as positive and negative cognitive evaluations. No significant correlations were found between their measures of nonverbal behaviour by Bush and Gore in the TV news shots with either the public's cognitive evaluations of the candidates' traits or the public's positive emotional responses to the candidates. Significant relationships were found for negative emotional responses. See Renita Coleman and H. Denis Wu, 'Proposing emotion as a dimension of affective agenda setting: separating affect into two components and comparing their second-level effects', *Journalism and Mass Communication Quarterly*, 87 (2010): 315–27.

20 Hyun, Ki Deuk and Soo Jung Moon, 'Agenda setting in the partisan TV news context: attribute agenda setting and polarized evaluation of presidential candidates among viewers of NBC, CNN, and Fox News', *Journalism and Mass Communication Quarterly*, 93 (2016): 509–29.

21 Toshio Takeshita and Shunji Mikami, 'How did mass media influence the voters' choice in the 1993 general election in Japan?: a study of agenda setting', *Keio Communication Review*, 17 (1995): 27–41.

22 Marc Benton and P. Jean Frazier, 'The agenda-setting function of the mass media', *Communication Research*, 3 (1976): 261–74.

23 Mikami, Shunji, Toshio Takeshita, Makoto Nakada, and Miki Kawabata, 'The media coverage and public awareness of environmental issues in Japan', *International Communication Gazette*, 54 (1995), 209–26.

24 Michael Salwen, 'Effects of accumulation of coverage on issue salience in agenda setting', *Journalism Quarterly*, 65 (1988): 100–6,130.

25 Maxwell McCombs and John Smith, 'Perceptual selection and communication', *Journalism Quarterly*, 46 (1969): 352–5.

26 Salma Ghanem, 'Filling in the tapestry: the second level of agenda-setting', in *Communication and Democracy*, eds. Maxwell McCombs, Donald Shaw and David Weaver (Mahwah, NJ: Lawrence Erlbaum, 1997), pp. 3–14.

27 Salma Ghanem, 'Media coverage of crime and public opinion: an exploration of the second level of agenda setting', unpublished doctoral dissertation, University of Texas at Austin, 1996.

28 Amy Jasperson, Dhavan Shah, Mark Watts, Ronald Faber, and David Fan, 'Framing and the public agenda: media effects on the importance of the federal budget deficit', *Political Communication*, 15 (1998): 205–24. Also see David Fan, Kathy Keltner and Robert Wyatt, 'A matter of guilt or innocence: how news reports affect support for the death penalty in the United States', *International Journal of Public Opinion Research*, 14 (2002): 439–52.

29 Klaus Schoenbach and Holli Semetko, 'Agenda setting, agenda reinforcing

or agenda deflating? A study of the 1990 German national election', *Journalism Quarterly*, 68 (1992): 837–46.

30 Thomas Birkland, *After Disaster: Agenda Setting, Public Policy, and Focusing Events* (Washington, DC: Georgetown University Press, 1997).

31 Jan Váně and František Kalvas, 'Focusing events and their effect on agenda setting', paper presented to the World Association for Public Opinion Research, Hong Kong, 2012.

32 Spiro Kiousis, 'Compelling arguments and attitude strength – exploring the impact of second-level agenda setting on public opinion of presidential candidate images', *Harvard International Journal of Press/Politics*, 10 (2005): 3–27.

33 W. Russell Neuman, Marion Just, and Ann Crigler, *Common Knowledge: News and the Construction of Political Meaning* (Chicago: University of Chicago Press, 1992).

34 Original analysis by McCombs based on data reported in Neuman, Just and Crigler, *Common Knowledge*.

35 Paul F. Lazarsfeld and Robert Merton, 'Mass communication, popular taste and organized social action', in *The Communication of Ideas*, ed. Lyman Bryson (New York: Institute for Religious and Social Studies, 1948): 95–118.

36 Walter Lippmann, *'Public Opinion'*; Dan Nimmo and Robert L. Savage, *Candidates and their Images* (Pacific Palisades, CA: Goodyear, 1976).

37 Pamela Shoemaker and Tim Vos, *Gatekeeping Theory* (New York: Routledge, 2009).

38 George Gerbner, Larry Gross, Michael Morgan, Nancy Signorielli, and James Shanahan, 'Growing up with television', in *Media Effects*, 2nd edn, eds. Jennings Bryant and Dolf Zillmann (Mahwah, NJ: Lawrence Erlbaum, 1994), pp. 43–68.

39 Also see Margaret T. Gordon and Linda Heath, 'The news business, crime and fear', in *Reactions to Crime*, ed. Dan Lewis (Beverly Hills, CA: Sage, 1981).

40 Elisabeth Noelle-Neumann, *The Spiral of Silence: Our Social Skin*, 2nd edn (Chicago: University of Chicago Press, 1993).

41 Maxwell McCombs and David Weaver, 'Toward a merger of gratifications and agenda-setting research', in *Media Gratifications Research*, eds. K. E. Rosengren, L. Wenner and P. Palmgreen (Beverly Hills, CA: Sage, 1985), pp. 95–108.

42 Mark Miller, Julie Andsager, and Bonnie Riechert, 'Framing the candidates in presidential primaries: issues and images in press releases and news coverage', *Journalism and Mass Communication Quarterly*, 75 (1998): 312–24. The correlations reported here were calculated by McCombs' seminar on agenda setting theory at the University of Texas at Austin in spring semester 2000.

43 Toshio Takeshita, 'Expanding attribute agenda setting into framing: an application of the problematic situation scheme', paper presented to the International Communication Association, Seoul, Korea, 2002.

44 Alex Edelstein, Youichi Ito, and Hans Mathias Kepplinger, *Communication*

and Culture: A Comparative Approach (NewYork: Longman, 1989). Although Edelstein, Ito and Kepplinger did not explicitly relate the concept of the problematic situation with framing, the usefulness of that link was pointed out subsequently by Salma Ghanem. See 'Filling in the tapestry: the second level of agenda setting', in *Communication and Democracy*, eds. Maxwell McCombs, Donald Shaw, and David Weaver (Mahwah, NJ: Lawrence Erlbaum, 1997), p. 13.

45 Michael Cacciatore, Dietram Scheufele, and Shanto Iyengar, 'The end of framing as we know it ... and the future of media effects', *Mass Communication and Society*, 19 (2016): 7–23. Quote is on p. 20 (italics added).

46 Daniel Kahneman and Amos Tversky, 'Choices, values and frames', *American Psychologist*, 39 (1984): 341–50.

47 McGuire, 'Theoretical foundations of campaigns.' There continues to be some debate about whether the primary effects of the mass media are reinforcement of prevailing perspectives or the creation of new perspectives. The distinction between the first and second levels of agenda setting has implications for this debate, more so when considered in tandem with Carter's observation about media effects in terms of salience and pertinence as two aspects of psychological relevance:

> If all one is looking for is evidence of the salience aspect of value, then reinforcement of value is probably all one is going to find. On the other hand, if one looks at how the individual structures his cognitive environment in terms of the values he assigns elements, this must be accomplished through information processing of pertinence aspects of value. Thus, the apparent paradox conceivably can be dissolved by this distinction. (Richard Carter, 'Communication and affective relations', *Journalism Quarterly*, 57 (1,866): 108).

48 Frank R. Baumgartner and Bryan D. Jones, *Agendas and Instability in American Politics*, 2nd edn (Chicago: University of Chicago Press, 2009).

4 Networks of Issues and Attributes

1 Y. J. Son and David Weaver, 'Another look at what moves public opinion: media agenda setting and polls in the 2000 US election', *International Journal of Public Opinion Research*, 18 (2006): 174–97.

2 Lei Guo, 'Toward the third level of agenda setting theory: A network agenda setting model', in Thomas J. Johnson, ed., *Agenda Setting in a 2.0 World* (New York: Routledge, 2013), pp. 112–33.

3 John R. Anderson, *The Architecture of Cognition* (Cambridge, MA: Harvard University Press: 1983).

4 Stephen Kaplan, 'Cognitive maps in perception and thought', in *Image and Environment: Cognitive Mapping and Spacial Behavior*, eds. Roger M. Downs and David Stea (Chicago: Aldine, 1973), pp. 63–78.

5 Allan M. Collins and Elizabeth F. Loftus, 'A spreading activation theory of semantic processing', *Psychological Review*, 82 (1975): 402–8.

6 Daniel S. Levine, 'Neural population modeling and psychology: A review', *Mathematical Biosciences*, 66 (1983): 1–86.

7 Peter H. Lindsay and Donald A. Norman, *Human Information Processing: An Introduction to Pychology* (New York: Academic Press, 1977); Vincent Price and David Tewksbury, 'News values and public opinion: a theoretical account of media priming and framing' in *Progress in Communication Sciences: Advances in Persuasion*, eds. G. A. Barnett and F. J. Boster (Greenwich, CT: Ablex, 1997), pp. 173–212; David E. Rumelhart and Donald A. Norman, 'Accretion, tuning and restructuring: Three modes of learning', in *Semantic Factors in Cognition*, eds. John Wealdon Cotton and Roberta L. Klatzky (Hillsdale, NJ: Lawrence Erlbaum, 1978).

8 Lei Guo and Maxwell McCombs, 'Network agenda setting: a third level of media effects', paper presented to the International Communication Association, Boston, 2011.

9 Kihan Kim and Maxwell McCombs, 'News story descriptions and the public's opinions of political candidates', *Journalism and Mass Communication Quarterly*, 84 (2007): 299–314.

10 Lei Guo and Maxwell McCombs, 'Toward the third-level agenda setting theory: a network agenda setting model', paper presented to the Association for Education in Journalism and Mass Communication, St Louis, 2011.

11 Lei Guo and Maxwell McCombs, 'Network agenda setting: A third level of media effects.'

12 Hong Vu, Lei Guo, and Maxwell McCombs, 'Exploring "the world outside and the pictures in our heads": a network agenda setting study', *Journalism and Mass Communication Quarterly*, 91 (2014): 669–86.

13 Chris Vargo, Lei Guo, Maxwell McCombs, and Donald L. Shaw, 'Network issue agendas on Twitter during the 2012 US presidential election', *Journal of Communication*, 64 (2014): 296–316.

14 Spiro Kiousis, Ji Young Kim, Matt Ragas, Gillian Wheat, Sarab Kochhar, Emma Svensson, and Maradith Miles, 'Exploring new frontiers of agenda building during the 2012 US presidential election pre-convention period', *Journalism Studies*, 16 (2015): 363–82;

15 H. Denis Wu and Lei Guo, 'Beyond salience transmission: linking agenda networks between media and voters', *Communication Research* (2017): Advance online publication.

16 Yang Cheng, 'The third-level agenda-setting study: an examination of media, implicit, and explicit public agendas in China', *Asian Journal of Communication*, 26 (2016): 319–32.

17 Lei Guo, Yi-Ning Katherine Chen, Radoslaw Aksamit, Damian Guzek, Qian Wang, Hong Vu, and Maxwell McCombs, 'How the world pictured the Iraq War: a transnational network analysis', *Journalism Studies*, 16 (2015): 343–62.

18 Nirit Weiss-Blatt, 'Role of tech bloggers in the flow of information', in *The Power of Information Networks*, eds. Lei Guo and Maxwell McCombs (New York: Routledge, 2016), pp. 88–103.

19 Michael Etter and Anne Vestergaard, 'Third level of agenda building and agenda setting during a corporate crisis', in *The Power of Information*

Networks, eds. Lei Guo and Maxwell McCombs (New York: Routledge, 2016), pp.175–89.

20 Funkhouser, 'The issues of the sixties.'
21 Stromback and Kiousis, 'A new look at agenda setting effects.'
22 Chris J. Vargo and Lei Guo, 'Networks, big data, and intermedia agenda setting: an analysis of traditional, partisan, and emerging online US news', *Journalism and Mass Communication Quarterly*, 94 (2017): 1031–55.
23 For book-length treatment of additional studies, see Lei Guo and Maxwell McCombs, eds. *The Power of Information Networks: New Directions for Agenda Setting* (New York, Routledge: 2016).

5 Why Agenda Setting Occurs

1 Pamela Shoemaker, 'Hardwired for news: using biological and cultural evolution to explain the surveillance function', *Journal of Communication*, 46, 3 (1996): 32–47.
2 David Weaver, 'Political issues and voter need for orientation', in *The Emergence of American Political Issues*, eds. Donald Shaw and Maxwell McCombs (St Paul, MN: West, 1977), pp. 107–19; David Weaver, 'Audience need for orientation and media effects', *Communication Research*, 7 (1980): 361–76. Bruce Westley and Lee Barrow, 'An investigation of news seeking behavior', *Journalism Quarterly*, 36 (1959): 431–8; Maxwell McCombs, 'Editorial endorsements: a study of influence', *Journalism Quarterly*, 44 (1967): 545–8; J. E. Mueller, 'Choosing among 133 candidates', *Public Opinion Quarterly*, 34 (1970): 395–402.
3 Edward C. Tolman, *Purposive Behavior in Animals and Men* (New York: Appleton-Century-Crofts, 1932). Also see Tolman, 'Cognitive maps in rats and men', *Psychological Review*, 55 (1948): 189–208; and W. J. McGuire, 'Psychological motives and communication gratification', in *The Uses of Mass Communication: Current Perspectives on Gratifications Research*, eds. J. G. Blumler and Elihu Katz (Beverly Hills, CA: Sage, 1974), pp. 167–96.
4 Robert E. Lane, *Political Life: Why and How People Get Involved in Politics* (New York: Free Press, 1959), p. 12.
5 Davis Merritt and Maxwell McCombs, *The Two W's of Journalism* (Mahwah, NJ: Lawrence Erlbaum, 2003), chapter 6. Also see Michael Schudson, *The Good Citizen: A History of American Civic Life* (New York: Free Press, 1998), pp. 310–11.
6 Going beyond the concept of need for orientation to provide an in-depth explanation for this failure at agenda setting, Julie Yioutas and Ivana Segvic drew upon two other aspects of agenda-setting theory that are the subjects of Chapter 3, the concept of compelling arguments and the convergence of attribute agenda setting and framing. See Julie Yioutas and Ivana Segvic, 'Revisiting the Clinton/Lewinsky scandal: the convergence of agenda setting and framing', *Journalism and Mass Communication Quarterly*, 80 (2003): 567–82.
7 Jeffrey M. Jones, 'As Senate Trial Begins, 44% Approve of Trump', Gallup.

com, https://news.gallup.com/poll/283364/senate-trial-begins-approve-trump.aspx.

8 Weaver, 'Political issues and voter need for orientation', p. 112.
9 Paula Poindexter, Maxwell McCombs, Laura Smith, and others, 'Need for orientation in the new media landscape', unpublished paper, University of Texas at Austin, 2002.
10 Weaver, 'Political issues and voter need for orientation', pp. 113, 115.
11 Toshio Takeshita, 'Agenda-setting effects of the press in a Japanese local election', *Studies of Broadcasting*, 29 (1993): 193–216.
12 Maxwell McCombs and Donald Shaw, 'The agenda-setting function of mass media', *Public Opinion Quarterly*, 36 (1972): 176–87.
13 David Weaver and Maxwell McCombs, 'Voters' need for orientation and choice of candidate: mass media and electoral decision making', paper presented to the American Association for Public Opinion Research, Roanoke, VA, 1978.
14 David Cohen, 'A report on a non-election agenda setting study', paper presented to the Association for Education in Journalism, Ottawa, Canada, 1975.
15 Dixie Evatt and Salma Ghanem, 'Building a scale to measure salience', paper presented to the World Association for Public Opinion Research, Rome, Italy, 2001.
16 Fermín Bouza, 'The impact area of political communication: citizenship faced with public discourse', *International Review of Sociology*, 14 (2004): 245–59 (quote is on p. 250, emphasis added).
17 Maxwell McCombs, 'Personal involvement with issues on the public agenda', *International Journal of Public Opinion Research*, 11 (1999): 152–68.
18 Ronald Inglehart, *Culture Shift in Advanced Industrial Society* (Princeton, NJ: Princeton University Press, 1990).
19 Sebastián Valenzuela, 'Materialism, post-materialism and agenda-setting effects: the values-issues consistency hypothesis', *International Journal of Public Opinion Research,* 23 (2011): 437–63.
20 For further discussion about the role of values in explicating agenda setting, see Sebastián Valenzuela and Gennadiy Chernov, 'Explicating the values-issue consistency hypothesis through need for orientation', *Canadian Journal of Communication*, 41, 1 (2016); Sebastián Valenzuela, 'Value resonance and the origins of issue salience', in *Agenda Setting in a 2.0 World*, ed. Thomas J. Johnson (New York: Routledge, 2013), pp. 53–64.
21 Joanne Miller, 'Examining the mediators of agenda setting: A new experimental paradigm reveals the role of emotions', *Political Psychology*, 28 (2007): 689–717.
22 Jörg Matthes, 'The need for orientation towards news media: revising and validating a classic concept', *International Journal of Public Opinion Research*, 18 (2006): 422–44.
23 Jörg Matthes, 'Need for orientation as a predictor of agenda-setting effects: causal evidence from a two-wave panel study', *International Journal of Public Opinion Research*, 20 (2008): 440–53.
24 Gennadiy Chernov, Sebastián Valenzuela and Maxwell McCombs, 'An

experimental comparison of two perspectives on the concept of need for orientation in agenda-setting theory', *Journalism and Mass Communication Quarterly*, 88 (2011): 142–55.

25 Harold Zucker, 'The variable nature of news media influence', in *Communication Yearbook 2*, ed. Brent Ruben (New Brunswick, NJ: Transaction Books, 1978), pp. 225–40.

26 James Winter, Chaim Eyal and Ann Rogers, 'Issue-specific agenda setting: the whole as less than the sum of the parts', *Canadian Journal of Communication*, 8, 2 (1982): 1–10.

27 Zucker, 'The variable nature of news influence.'

28 Kim Smith, 'Newspaper coverage and public concern about community issues: a time-series analysis', *Journalism Monographs*, 101 (1987): 13.

29 David H. Weaver, Doris A. Graber, Maxwell E. McCombs, and Chaim H. Eyal, *Media Agenda Setting in a Presidential Election: Issues, Images and Interest* (Westport, CT: Greenwood, 1981).

30 Warwick Blood, 'Unobtrusive issues in the agenda setting role of the press', unpublished doctoral dissertation, Syracuse University, 1981.

31 For additional evidence on the unobtrusive nature of unemployment, especially as a national issue, see Donald Shaw and John Slater, 'Press puts unemployment on agenda: Richmond community opinion, 1981–1984', *Journalism Quarterly*, 65 (1988): 407–11.

32 Warwick Blood, 'Competing models of agenda-setting: issue obtrusiveness vs. media exposure', paper presented to the Association for Education in Journalism, Boston, 1980. This is a secondary analysis of data originally reported in Thomas Patterson, *The Mass Media Election: How Americans Choose Their President* (New York: Praeger, 1980).

33 Edna F. Einsiedel, Kandice L. Salomone, and Frederick Schneider, 'Crime: effects of media exposure and personal experience on issue salience', *Journalism Quarterly*, 61 (1984): 131–6; Dominic Lasorsa and Wayne Wanta, 'Effects of personal, interpersonal and media experiences on issue saliences', *Journalism Quarterly*, 67 (1990): 804–13.

34 Elisabeth Noelle-Neumann, 'The spiral of silence: a response', in *Political Communication Yearbook 1984*, eds. Keith Sanders, Lynda Lee Kaid, and Dan Nimmo (Carbondale: Southern Illinois University Press, 1985), pp. 66–94. Also see Lutz Erbring, Edie Goldenberg and Arthur Miller, 'Front-page news and real-world cues', *American Journal of Political Science*, 24 (1980): 16–49.

35 Lasorsa and Wanta, 'Effects of personal, interpersonal and media experiences on issue saliences.'

36 Jin Yang and Gerald Stone, 'The powerful role of interpersonal communication on agenda setting', *Mass Communication and Society*, 6 (2003): 57–74.

37 James P. Winter, 'Contingent conditions in the agenda-setting process', in *Mass Communication Review Yearbook*, eds. G. C. Wilhoit and Harold de Bock (Beverly Hills, CA: Sage, 1981), pp. 235–43; and G. Gumpert and R. Cathcart, eds., *Inter/Media: Interpersonal Communication in a Media World* (New York: Oxford University Press, 1986).

38 There is an example of the reinforcement role for conversation in Wayne

Wanta, *The Public and the National Agenda* (Mahwah, NJ: Lawrence Erlbaum, 1997), p. 59, where the role of conversation in the agenda setting process is significantly stronger than the role of media exposure. For a different perspective in which the news media are the prime movers, see the discussion of the French sociologist Gabriel Tarde's model of opinion formation in Susan Herbst, 'The cultivation of conversation', in *The Poll with a Human Face: The National Issues Convention Experiment in Political Communication*, eds. Maxwell McCombs and Amy Reynolds (Mahwah, NJ: Lawrence Erlbaum, 1999), esp. pp. 201–4; and Joohan Kim, Robert Wyatt and Elihu Katz, 'News, talk, opinion, participation: the part played by conversation in deliberative democracy', *Political Communication*, 16 (1999): 361–85.

39 Hong Nga Nguyen Vu and Volker Gehrau, 'Agenda diffusion: an integrated model of agenda setting and interpersonal communication', *Journalism and Mass Communication Quarterly*, 87 (2010): 100–16.

40 Tony Atwater, Michael Salwen and Ronald Anderson, 'Interpersonal discussion as a potential barrier to agenda setting', *Newspaper Research Journal*, 6, 4 (1985): 37–43.

41 Jessica T. Feezell, 'Agenda setting through social media: the importance of incidental news exposure and social filtering in the digital era', *Political Research Quarterly*, 71 (2018): 482–94.

42 Peter A. Frensch, 'One concept, multiple meanings: on how to define the concept of implicit learning', in *Handbook of Implicit Learning*, eds. Michael A. Stadler and Peter A. Frensch (Thousand Oaks, CA: Sage, 1998), pp. 47–104.

43 Kristin Bulkow, Juliane Urban, and Wolfgang Schweiger, 'The duality of agenda-setting: The role of information processing', *International Journal of Public Opinion Research*, 25 (2012): 43–63.

44 Gary King, Benjamin Schneer, and Ariel White, 'How the news media activate public expression and influence national agendas', *Science*, 358 (2017): 776–80.

45 Donald L. Shaw, Milad Minooie, Deb Aikat, and Chris J. Vargo, *Agendamelding: News, Social Media, Audiences and Civic Community* (New York: Peter Lang, 2019).

46 Donald L. Shaw, Bradley J. Hamm, and Thomas C. Terry, 'Vertical vs. horizontal media: Using agenda setting and audience agenda-melding to create public information strategies in the emerging Papyrus Society', *Military Review*, 86, 6 (2006): 13–25.

47 Shaw, Minooie, Aikat, and Vargo, p. 194.

48 Yunjuan Luo, Hansel Burley, Alexander Moe, and Mingxiao Sui, 'A meta-analysis of news media's public agenda-setting effects, 1972–2015', *Journalism and Mass Communication Quarterly*, 96 (2019): 150–172; Wayne Wanta and Salma Ghanem, 'Effects of agenda setting', in *Mass Media Effects Research: Advances through Meta-Analysis*, eds. Raymond W. Preiss, Barbara Mae Gayle, Nancy Burrell, Mike Allen, and Jennings Bryant (Mahwah, NJ: Lawrence Erlbaum, 2006), pp. 37–51.

49 Shaw, Minooie, Aikat, and Vargo, Chapter 4.

50 Ibid., Chapter 5.
51 Richard F. Carter, 'Communication and affective relations', *Journalism Quarterly*, 42 (1965): 203–12. For further discussion of the link between Carter's concepts of salience and pertinence and agenda setting, see Maxwell McCombs, 'Myth and reality in scientific discovery: The case of agenda setting theory', in *Communication: A Different Kind of Horse Race*, eds. Brenda Dervin and Steven Chaffee (Cresskill, NJ: Hampton Press, 2003), pp. 25–37.
52 For discussion of the link between need for orientation and another communication theory, the spiral of silence, see Maxwell McCombs and David Weaver, 'Toward a merger of gratifications and agenda-setting research', in *Media Gratifications Research: Current Perspectives*, eds. Karl Erik Rosengren, Lawrence Wenner, and Philip Palmgreen (Beverly Hills, CA: Sage, 1985), pp. 95–108.
53 Also see Jay Blumler, 'The role of theory in uses and gratifications research', *Communication Research*, 6 (1979): 9–36.

6 How Agenda Setting Works

1 Yeojin Kim, Youngju Kim, and Shuhua Zhou, 'Theoretical and methodological trends of agenda-setting theory: a thematic analysis of the last four decades of research', *Agenda Setting Journal*, 1 (2017): 5–22.
2 Larry M. Bartels, *Unequal Democracy: The Political Economy of the New Gilded Age*, 2nd edn (New York, NY: Russell Sage Foundation, 2016); Kay Lehman Schlozman, Sidney Verba, and Henry E. Brady, *The Unheavenly Chorus: Unequal Political Voice and the Broken Promise of American Democracy* (Princeton, NJ: Princeton University Press, 2013).
3 A significant corollary of this system perspective is that news coverage alone is not sufficient to create agenda-setting effects. Focusing on the issue of European integration, television news coverage of the June 1999 European election campaign was compared with postelection surveys carried out in all European Union countries. More EU coverage did not automatically increase the perceived importance of European integration. The more EU stories people watched in countries in which political elites disagreed about European integration, the more important they considered European integration. If elite opinion about European integration was consensual, this effect did not occur. See Jochen Peter, 'Country characteristics as contingent conditions of agenda setting: the moderating influence of polarized elite opinion', *Communication Research*, 30 (2003): 683–712.
4 Pu-Tsung King, 'The press, candidate images, and voter perceptions', in *Communication and Democracy*, eds. Maxwell McCombs, Donald Shaw, and David Weaver (Mahwah, NJ: Lawrence Erlbaum, 1997), pp. 29–40.
5 V. O. Key, *The Responsible Electorate: Rationality in Presidential Voting 1936–1960* (Cambridge, MA: Belknap Press of Harvard University Press, 1966). Original quote is on p. 7.
6 Additional evidence about the axiom of media openness is provided by

studies that fail to find robust agenda-setting effects for state-controlled media in mainland China, such as: Guoliang Zhang, Guosong Shao, and Nicholas David Bowman, 'What is most important for my country is not most important for me: agenda-setting effects in China', *Communication Research*, 39 (2012): 662–78.

7 George A. Miller, 'The magic number seven, plus or minus two: some limits on our capacity for processing information', *Psychological Review*, 63 (1956): 81–97.

8 W. Russell Neuman, 'The threshold of public attention', *Public Opinion Quarterly*, 54 (1990): 159–76.

9 Maxwell McCombs and Jian-Hua Zhu, 'Capacity, diversity and volatility of the public agenda: trends from 1954–1994', *Public Opinion Quarterly*, 59 (1995): 495–525.

10 Jill A. Edy and Patrick C. Meirick, 'The fragmenting public agenda: capacity, diversity, and volatility in responses to the "most important problem" question', *Public Opinion Quarterly*, 82, (2018): 661–85.

11 Sebastián Valenzuela, 'Agenda setting and journalism', in *Oxford Research Encyclopedia of Communication,* ed. Jon F. Nussbaum (New York, NY: Oxford University Press, 2019).

12 Ibid.

13 Jian-Hua Zhu, 'Issue competition and attention distraction: a zero-sum theory of agenda setting', *Journalism Quarterly*, 68 (1992): 825–36.

14 Tom Smith, 'America's most important problems – a trend analysis, 1946–1976', *Public Opinion Quarterly*, 44 (1980): 164–80.

15 McCombs and Zhu, 'Capacity, diversity and volatility of the public agenda'; Edy and Meirick, 'The fragmenting public agenda: capacity, diversity, and volatility in responses to the "most important problem" question.'

16 Mike Gruszczynski, 'Evidence of partisan agenda fragmentation in the American public, 1959–2015', *Public Opinion Quarterly*, 83 (2020): 749–81.

17 Jong-Wha Lee and Hanol Lee, 'Human capital in the long run', *Journal of Development Economics*, 122 (2016): 147–69; Robert J. Barro and Jong-Wha Lee, 'A new data set of educational attainment in the world, 1950–2010', *Journal of Development Economics*, 104 (2013): 184–98.

18 Samuel Popkin, *The Reasoning Voter* (Chicago: University of Chicago Press, 1991), p. 36 (emphasis in original).

19 Ibid., p. 43.

20 McCombs and Zhu, 'Capacity, diversity and volatility of the public agenda'; Edy and Meirick, "The fragmenting public agenda: capacity, diversity, and volatility in responses to the "most important problem" question.'

21 Edy and Meirick, 'The fragmenting public agenda', p. 674.

22 Wayne Wanta, *The Public and the National Agenda: How People Learn about Important* Issues (Mahwah, NJ: Lawrence Erlbaum, 1997), pp. 22–4.

23 Philip E. Converse, quoted by Jian-Hua Zhu, with William Boroson, 'Susceptibility to agenda setting: a cross-sectional and longitudinal analysis of individual differences', in *Communication and Democracy*, eds. Maxwell McCombs, Donald Shaw, and David Weaver (Mahwah, NJ: Lawrence Erlbaum, 1997), p. 71. Further explicating Converse's citation of 'conceptual

sophistication' is a study finding that the attribute agenda-setting effects of the media on candidate images are moderated by political sophistication, such that high sophistication citizens are less influenced despite high exposure. Moderately sophisticated voters, who have enough interest to be exposed to political messages in the media, show the greatest influence. See Sungtae Ha, 'Attribute priming effects and presidential candidate evaluation: the conditionality of political sophistication', *Mass Communication and Society*, 14 (2011): 315–42.

24 Michael MacKuen, 'Social communication and the mass policy agenda', in *More Than News: Media Power in Public Affairs*, eds. Michael MacKuen and Steven Coombs (Beverly Hills, CA: Sage, 1981), pp. 19–144.

25 Zhu with Boroson, 'Susceptibility to agenda setting.'

26 Ibid., p. 82 (emphasis in original).

27 Toshio Takeshita, 'Current critical problems in agenda-setting research', *International Journal of Public Opinion Research*, 18 (2006): 275–6.

28 Richard E. Petty and John T. Cacioppo, *Communication and Persuasion: Central and Peripheral Routes to Attitude Change* (New York, NY: Springer, 1986).

29 While the proposal of a dual path of agenda setting is becoming common, the labels of these paths still receive different names: 'casual' and 'deliberative', 'passive' and 'active', 'cueing' and 'reasoning', and so forth. See Na Yeon Lee, 'How agenda setting works: a dual path model and motivated reasoning', *Journalism* (2019); Raymond Pingree and Elizabeth Stoycheff, 'Differentiating cueing from reasoning in agenda setting effects', *Journal of Communication*, 63 (2013): 852–72.

30 Kristin Bulkow, Juliane Urban, and Wolfgang Schweiger, 'The duality of agenda-setting: the role of information processing', *International Journal of Public Opinion Research*, 25 (2013): 43–63.

31 Ibid., p. 17.

32 Raymond Pingree, Andrea Quenette, John Tchernev, and Ted Dickinson, 'Effects of media criticism on gatekeeping trust and implications for agenda setting', *Journal of Communication*, 63 (2013): 351–72; Pingree and Stoycheff, 'Differentiating cueing from reasoning in agenda setting effects.'

33 David Weaver, 'Audience need for orientation and media effects', *Communication Research*, 7 (1980): 361–76.

34 Lindita Camaj, 'Need for orientation, selective exposure, and attribute agenda-setting effects', *Mass Communication and Society*, 17 (2014): 689–712.

35 Natalie Stroud, *Niche News: The Politics of News Choice* (New York: Oxford University Press, 2011).

36 Lindita Camaj, 'Motivational theories of agenda-setting effects: an information selection and processing model of attribute agenda-setting', *International Journal of Public Opinion Research*, 31 (2019): 441–62.

37 Joseph Klapper, *The Effects of Mass Communication* (New York: Free Press, 1960), p. 8.

38 James Winter and Chaim Eyal, 'Agenda setting for the civil rights issue', *Public Opinion Quarterly*, 45 (1981): 376–83.

39 Shanto Iyengar and Donald R. Kinder, *News That Matters: Television and American Opinion* (Chicago, IL: University of Chicago Press, 1987); Pingree and Stoycheff, 'Differentiating cueing from reasoning in agenda setting effects.'

40 Harold Zucker, 'The variable nature of news media influence', in *Communication Yearbook 2*, ed. Brent Ruben (New Brunswick, NJ: Transaction Books, 1978), pp. 225–40.

41 Michael Salwen, 'Effects of accumulation of coverage on issue salience in agenda setting', *Journalism Quarterly*, 65 (1988): 100–6, 130.

42 Marilyn Roberts, Wayne Wanta, and Tzong-Houng (Dustin) Dzwo, 'Agenda setting and issue salience online', *Communication Research*, 29 (2002): 452–65.

43 For other studies using digital data as proxy of the public agenda, see Gary King, Benjamin Schneer and Ariel White, 'How the news media activate public expression and influence national agendas', *Science*, 358 (2017): 776–80; Michael Scharkow and Jens Vogelgesang, 'Measuring the public agenda using search engine queries', *International Journal of Public Opinion Research*, 23 (2011): 104–13; Brian Weeks and Brian Southwell, 'The symbiosis of news coverage and aggregate online search behavior: Obama, rumors, and presidential politics', *Mass Communication and Society*, 13 (2010): 341–60.

44 Wayne Wanta and Y. Hu, 'Time-lag differences in the agenda setting process: an examination of five news media', *International Journal of Public Opinion Research*, 6 (1994): 225–40.

45 Stefan Geiß, 'The media's conditional agenda setting power: how baselines and spikes of issue salience affect likelihood and strength of agenda setting', *Communication Research* (2019). Quote is from p. 22.

46 Similar variability in the decay of agenda-setting effects was found by James H. Watt, Mary Mazza and Leslie Synder, 'Agenda-setting effects of television news coverage and the memory decay curve', *Communication Research*, 20 (1993): 408–35.

47 Geiß, 'The media's conditional agenda setting power.'

48 Don W. Stacks, Michael B. Salwen, and Kristen C. Eichhorn, eds., *An Integrated Approach To Communication Theory And Research*, 3rd edn (New York, NY: Routledge, 2019); Mary Beth Oliver, Arthur A. Raney, and Jennings Bryant, eds., *Media Effects: Advances in Theory and Research*, 4th edn (New York, NY: Routledge, 2020).

49 Chaim Eyal, James Winter, and William DeGeorge, 'The concept of time frame in agenda setting', in *Mass Communication Review Yearbook*, vol. 2, eds. G. Cleveland Wilhoit and Harold de Bock (Beverly Hills, CA: Sage, 1981), pp. 212–18.

50 A full chapter discussing the issue of timeframe for agenda setting is available in Stuart N. Soroka, *Agenda-Setting Dynamics in Canada* (Vancouver: UBC Press, 2002).

51 Zhu, 'Issue competition and attention distraction.'

52 Gerald Kosicki, 'Problems and opportunities in agenda setting research', *Journal of Communication*, 43 (1993): 117.

53 Maxwell McCombs and Jian-Hua Zhu, 'Capacity, diversity, and volatility of the public agenda', *Public Opinion Quarterly*, 59 (1995): 495–525. See also Smith, 'America's most important problem – a trend analysis, 1946– 1976', *Public Opinion Quarterly*, 44 (1980): 164–80. Some agenda setting studies paraphrase the Gallup MIP question rather than use the original wording.

54 Will Jennings and Christopher Wlezien, 'Distinguishing between most important problems and issues?', *Public Opinion Quarterly*, 75 (2011): 545–55.

55 Young Min, Salma Ghanem and Dixie Evatt, 'Using a split-ballot survey to explore the robustness of the "MIP" question in agenda setting research: a methodological study', *International Journal of Public Opinion Research*, 19 (2007): 221–36.

56 Scott L. Althaus and David Tewksbury, 'Agenda setting and the "new" news: patterns of issue importance among readers of the paper and online versions of the *New York Times*', *Communication Research*, 29 (2002): 180–207.

57 Tai-Li Wang, 'Agenda setting online: an experiment testing the effects of hyperlinks in online newspapers', *Southwestern Mass Communication Journal*, 15, 2 (2000): 59–70.

58 Dixie Evatt and Salma Ghanem, 'Building a scale to measure salience', paper presented to the World Association for Public Opinion Research, Rome, Italy, 2001.

59 Brian Weeks and Brian Southwell, 'The symbiosis of news coverage and aggregate online search behavior: Obama, rumors, and presidential politics', *Mass Communication and Society*, 13 (2010): 341–60.

60 Edna F. Einsiedel, Kandice L. Salomone and Frederick Schneider, 'Crime: effects of media exposure and personal experience on issue salience', *Journalism Quarterly*, 61 (1984): 131–6.

61 David Cohen, 'A report on a non-election agenda setting study', paper presented to the Association for Education in Journalism, Ottawa, Canada, 1975.

62 David H. Weaver, Doris A. Graber, Maxwell E. McCombs and Chaim H. Eyal, *Media Agenda Setting in a Presidential Election: Issues, Images and Interest* (Westport, CT: Greenwood, 1981).

63 Spiro Kiousis and Maxwell McCombs, 'Agenda-setting effects and attitude strength: political figures during the 1996 presidential election', *Communication Research*, 31 (2004): 36–57.

64 Sei-Hill Kim, Dietram Scheufele, and James Shanahan, 'Think about it this way: Attribute agenda-setting function of the press and the public's evaluation of a local issue', *Journalism and Mass Communication Quarterly*, 79 (2002): 7–25.

65 Joe Bob Hester and Rhonda Gibson, 'The agenda setting function of national versus local media: a time-series analysis for the issue of same sex marriage', *Mass Communication and Society*, 10 (2007): 299–317.

66 Lori Young and Stuart Soroka, 'Affective news: the automated coding of sentiment in political texts', *Political Communication*, 29 (2012): 205–231.

67 Chris J. Vargo and Lei Guo, 'Networks, big data, and intermedia agenda setting: an analysis of traditional, partisan, and emerging online US news',

Journalism and Mass Communication Quarterly, 94 (2017): 1031–55; Chris J. Vargo and Lei Guo, 'Exploring the network agenda setting model with big social data', in Lei Guo and Maxwell McCombs, eds. *The Power of Information Networks: New Directions for Agenda Setting* (New York, Routledge: 2016), pp. 55–65.

7 Shaping the Media Agenda

1 Pamela Shoemaker and Stephen D. Reese, *Mediating the Message in the 21st Century: A Media Sociology Perspective* (New York, NY: Routledge, 2014). For an application of the hierarchy of influence model to the current news media environment: Stephen D. Reese and Pamela J. Shoemaker, 'A media sociology for the networked public sphere: the hierarchy of influences model', *Mass Communication and Society*, 19 (2016): 389–410.

2 Frequently cited classics from this vast literature include Warren Breed, 'Social control in the newsroom', *Social Forces*, 33 (May 1955): 326–35; Gaye Tuchman, 'Telling stories', *Journal of Communication*, 26, 4 (1976): 93–7; and Herbert Gans, *Deciding What's News: A Study of CBS Evening News, NBC Nightly News, Newsweek and Time* (New York: Pantheon, 1979).

3 Stuart Soroka and Stephen McAdams, 'News, politics, and negativity', *Political Communication*, 32, 1 (2015): 1–22.

4 Functional equivalents of the State of the Union address in other countries are, for instance, the Queen's Speech (UK), the Throne Speech (Canada), and the annual Messages to Congress (Brazil and Chile). Some of these speeches are readily coded and available for using in agenda-setting studies in the website of the Comparative Agendas Project, https://www.comparativeagendas.net/.

5 Sheldon Gilberg, Chaim Eyal, Maxwell McCombs, and David Nicholas, 'The State of the Union address and the press agenda', *Journalism Quarterly*, 57 (1980): 584–8.

6 Maxwell McCombs, Sheldon Gilberg and Chaim Eyal, 'The State of the Union address and the press agenda: a replication', paper presented to the International Communication Association, Boston, 1982.

7 Thomas J. Johnson and Wayne Wanta, with John T. Byrd and Cindy Lee, 'Exploring FDR's relationship with the press: a historical agenda-setting study', *Political Communication*, 12 (1995): 157–72.

8 Wayne Wanta, Mary Ann Stephenson, Judy VanSlyke Turk, and Maxwell McCombs, 'How president's State of Union talk influenced news media agendas', *Journalism Quarterly*, 66 (1989): 537–41. For evidence of influence on the national agenda from presidential news conferences and speeches, see Spiro Kiousis and Jesper Stromback, 'The White House and public relations: examining the linkages between presidential communications and public opinion', *Public Relations Review*, 36 (2010): 7–14.

9 William Gonzenbach, *The Media, the President and Public Opinion* (Mahwah, NJ: Lawrence Erlbaum, 1996); Wayne Wanta and Joe Foote, 'The president–news media relationship: a time-series analysis of agenda setting', *Journal*

of Broadcasting and Electronic Media, 38 (1994): 437–48. Wayne Wanta, *The Public and the National Agenda* (Mahwah, NJ: Lawrence Erlbaum, 1997), chapter 7, extends these analyses of the State of the Union address to the impact on the public agenda. An ingenious comparison of four groups of issues – those emphasized by the president but not by the news media; those emphasized only by the media; those emphasized by both; and those emphasized by neither – found that news media exposure, not exposure to the actual State of the Union address on television, was the key predictor for the salience of all the issues except those emphasized only by the president. In the case of issues emphasized by both, media exposure alone was the significant predictor, suggesting that the redundancy of the media agenda outweighs the authority of the president.

10 Stuart N. Soroka, *Agenda-Setting Dynamics in Canada* (Vancouver: UBC Press, 2002).

11 Sebastián Valenzuela and Arturo Arriagada, 'Politics without citizens? Public opinion, television news, the president, and real-world factors in Chile, 2000–2005. *Harvard International Journal of Press/Politics*, 16 (2011): 357–81.

12 R. W. Cobb and C. D. Elder, *Participation in American Politics: The Dynamics of Agenda-Building* (Baltimore: Johns Hopkins University Press, 1972).

13 Peter van Aelst and Stefaan Walgrave, 'Political agenda setting by the mass media: ten years of research, 2005–2015', in *Handbook of Public Policy Agenda Setting*, ed. Nikolaos Zahariadis (Cheltenham, UK: Edward Elgar, 2016), pp. 157–78.

14 Barbara Nelson, *Making an Issue of Child Abuse: Political Agenda Setting for Social Problems* (Chicago: University of Chicago Press, 1984).

15 Marcus Brewer and Maxwell McCombs, 'Setting the community agenda', *Journalism and Mass Communication Quarterly*, 73 (1996): 7–16.

16 David Protess, Fay Cook, Jack Doppelt, James Ettema, Margaret Gordon, Donna Leff, and Peter Miller, *The Journalism of Outrage: Investigative Reporting and Agenda Building in America* (New York: Guilford, 1991). Also see David Protess and Maxwell McCombs, eds., *Agenda Setting: Readings on Media, Public Opinion, and Policymaking* (Hillsdale, NJ: Lawrence Erlbaum, 1991), esp. part IV.

17 Peter van Aelst and Stefaan Walgrave, 'Political agenda setting by the mass media.'

18 Ibid., p. 174 (emphasis in original).

19 Everett Rogers, James Dearing, and Soonbum Chang, 'AIDS in the 1980s: the agenda-setting process for a public issue', *Journalism Monographs*, 126 (1991).

20 Craig Trumbo, 'Longitudinal modelling of public issues: an application of the agenda-setting process to the issue of global warming', *Journalism Monographs*, 152 (1995).

21 Gonzenbach, *The Media, the President and Public Opinion.*

22 Oscar J. Gandy, *Beyond Agenda Setting: Information Subsidies and Public Policy* (Norwood, NJ: Ablex, 1982); Jarol B. Manheim, *Strategic Public Diplomacy and American Foreign Policy: The Evolution of Influence* (New York:

Oxford University Press, 1994), chapter 8; Judy VanSlyke Turk, 'Information subsidies and media content: a study of public relations influence on the news', *Journalism Monographs*, 100 (1986).

23 Leon Sigal, *Reporters and Officials: The Organization and Politics of Newsmaking* (Lexington, MA: D. C. Heath, 1973), p. 121.

24 Justin Lewis, Andrew Williams, and Bob Franklin, 'A compromised Fourth Estate? UK news journalism, public relations and news sources', *Journalism Studies*, 9 (2008): 1–20. Quote is on p. 7 (italics in original). For an even more negative assessment of British journalism's reliance on public relations materials, see Nick Davies, *Flat Earth News: An Award-winning Reporter Exposes Falsehood, Distortion and Propaganda in the Global Media* (London: Chatto and Windus, 2008).

25 Judy VanSlyke Turk, 'Public relations influence on the news', *Newspaper Research Journal*, 7 (1986): 15–27; Judy VanSlyke Turk, 'Information subsidies and influence', *Public Relations Review*, 11 (1985): 10–25.

26 Ibid., quote is on p. 18.

27 Daniel Jackson and Kevin Moloney, 'Inside churnalism: PR, journalism and power relationships in flux', *Journalism Studies*, 17 (2015): 1–18.

28 Rogers, Dearing, and Chang, 'AIDS in the 1980s'; Liz Watts, 'Coverage of polio and AIDS: agenda setting in reporting cure research on polio and AIDS in newspapers, news magazines and network television', *Ohio Journalism Monograph Series* [School of Journalism, Ohio University], 4 (1993).

29 Bent Flyvbjerg, Todd Landman, and Sanford Schram, eds., *Real Social Science: Applied Phronesis* (Cambridge: Cambridge University Press, 2012), chapter 7.

30 Helen Ingram, H. Brinton Milward, and Wendy Laird, 'Scientists and agenda setting: advocacy and global warming', in *Risk and Society: The Interaction of Science, Technology and Public Policy*, ed. Marvin Waterstone (Dordrecht, the Netherlands: Springer, 1992); Spencer R. Weart, *The Discovery of Global Warming* (Cambridge, MA: Harvard University Press, 2008).

31 Alison Anderson, 'Sources, media, and modes of climate change communication: the role of celebrities', *Wiley Interdisciplinary Reviews: Climate Change*, 2, (2011): 535–46.

32 John V. Pavlik, *Public Relations: What Research Tells Us* (Newbury Park, CA: Sage, 1987), chapter 4.

33 Jarol B. Manheim and R. B. Albritton, 'Changing national images: international public relations and media agenda setting', *American Political Science Review*, 73 (1984): 641–7. Also see Spiro Kiousis and Xu Wu, 'International agenda-building and agenda setting: exploring the influence of public relations counsel on US news media and public perceptions of foreign nations', *International Communication Gazette*, 70 (2008): 58–75.

34 John C. Tedesco, 'Intercandidate agenda setting in the 2004 Democratic presidential primary', *American Behavioral Scientist*, 49 (2005): 92–113.

35 *Political Public Relations: Principles and Applications*, eds. Jesper Stromback and Spiro Kiousis (New York: Routledge, 2011); Kathleen Hall Jamieson

and Karlyn Kohrs Campbell, *The Interplay of Influence: News, Advertising, Politics and the Mass Media* (Belmont, CA: Wadsworth, 1992).

36 Nicholas O'Shaughnessy, *The Phenomenon of Political Marketing* (London: Macmillan, 1990).

37 Holli Semetko, Jay Blumler, Michael Gurevitch, and David Weaver, with Steve Barkin and G. C. Wilhoit, *The Formation of Campaign Agendas: A Comparative Analysis of Party and Media Roles in Recent American and British Elections* (Hillsdale, NJ: Lawrence Erlbaum, 1991).

38 Semetko, Blumler, Gurevitch, and Weaver, *The Formation of Campaign Agendas*, p. 49. The quoted material is from Michael Gurevitch and Jay Blumler, 'The construction of election news at the BBC: an observation study', in *Individuals in Mass Media Organizations: Creativity and Constraint*, eds. James Ettema and Charles Whitney (Beverly Hills, CA: Sage, 1982): 179–204. Also see Heinz Brandenburg, 'Who follows whom? The impact of parties on media agenda formation in the 1997 British general elections campaign', *Harvard International Journal of Press/Politics*, 7, 3 (2002): 34–54.

39 Joseph Lelyveld, *New York Times*, 22 August 1999, p. 18.

40 Mark Miller, Julie Andsager, and Bonnie Riechert, 'Framing the candidates in presidential primaries', *Journalism and Mass Communication Quarterly*, 75 (1998): 312–24. The correlations reported here and in Chapter 3 were calculated by McCombs' seminar on agenda setting theory at the University of Texas at Austin in spring semester 2000.

41 Robert Lichter and Ted Smith, 'Why elections are bad news: media and candidate discourse in the 1996 presidential primaries', *Harvard International Journal of Press/Politics*, 1, 4 (1996): 15–35.

42 Thomas P. Boyle, 'Intermedia agenda setting in the 1996 presidential primaries', *Journalism and Mass Communication Quarterly*, 78 (2001): 26–44.

43 John Tedesco, 'Issue and strategy agenda setting in the 2000 presidential primaries', unpublished paper, Virginia Technological University, 2001.

44 Werner Wirth, Jörg Matthes, Christian Schemer, Martin Wettstein, Thomas Friemel, Regula Hänggli, and Gabriele Siegert, 'Agenda building and setting in a referendum campaign: investigating the flow of arguments among campaigners, the media, and the public', *Journalism and Mass Communication Quarterly*, 87 (2010): 328–45.

45 Spiro Kiousis, Ji Young Kim, Matt Ragas, Gillian Wheat, Sarab Kochhar, Emma Svensson, and Maradith Miles, 'Exploring new frontiers of agenda building during the 2012 US presidential election pre-convention period: examining linkages across three levels', paper presented to the International Communication Association convention, London, 2013.

46 Roland Burkart and Uta Russmann, 'Quality of understanding in political campaign communication: an analysis of political parties' press releases and media coverage in Austria (1970–2008)', working paper, University of Vienna, 2013.

47 Michael Gurevitch and Jay Blumler, 'Political communication systems and democratic values', in *Democracy and the Mass Media*, ed. Judith Lichtenberg (Cambridge: Cambridge University Press, 1990), pp. 269–89.

Also see Davis Merritt and Maxwell McCombs, *The Two W's of Journalism* (Mahwah, NJ: Lawrence Erlbaum, 2003), chapter 6.

48 Russell Dalton, Paul Allen Beck, Robert Huckfeldt, and William Koetzle, 'A test of media-centered agenda setting: newspaper content and public interests in a presidential election', *Political Communication*, 15 (1998): 463–81. The original, zero-order correlations between the various agendas are reported in this article. For this chapter, McCombs calculated the partial correlations that introduce the various controls.

49 Sungtae Ha, 'The intermediary role of news media in the presidential campaign: a mediator, moderator, or political agent?', unpublished paper, University of Texas at Austin, 2001. For a replication of this pattern in a US Senate election, see Jason Martin, 'Agenda setting, elections, and the impact of information technology', in *Agenda Setting in a 2.0 World*, ed. T. Johnson (New York: Routledge, 2013).

50 Spiro Kiousis, Soo-Yeon Kim, Michael McDevitt, and Ally Ostrowski, 'Competing for attention: information subsidy influence in agenda building during election campaigns', *Journalism and Mass Communication Quarterly*, 86 (2009): 545–62.

51 Spiro Kiousis, Michael Mitrook, Xu Wu, and Trent Seltzer, 'First- and second-level agenda-building and agenda-setting effects: exploring the linkages among candidate news releases, media coverage, and public opinion during the 2002 Florida gubernatorial election', *Journal of Public Relations Research*, 18 (2006): 265–85.

52 Marilyn Roberts and Maxwell McCombs, 'Agenda setting and political advertising: origins of the news agenda', *Political Communication*, 11 (1994): 249–62.

53 Dixie Evatt and Tamara Bell, 'Upstream influences: the early press releases, agenda setting and politics of a future president', *Southwestern Mass Communication Journal*, 16, 2 (2001): 70–81. Also see S. W. Dunn, 'Candidate and media agenda setting in the 2005 Virginia gubernatorial Election', *Journal of Communication*, 59 (2009): 635–52.

54 Esteban López-Escobar, Juan Pablo Llamas, Maxwell McCombs, and Federico Rey Lennon, 'Two levels of agenda setting among advertising and news in the 1995 Spanish elections', *Political Communication*, 15 (1998): 225–38.

55 Kenneth Bryan, 'Political communication and agenda setting in local races', unpublished doctoral dissertation, University of Texas at Austin, 1997.

56 Stuart Soroka, 'Issue attributes and agenda setting by media, the public, and policymakers in Canada', *International Journal of Public Opinion Research*, 14 (2002): 264–85. For a broader, more detailed analysis of eight major Canadian issues, see Stuart Soroka, *Agenda-Setting Dynamics in Canada* (Vancouver: UBC Press, 2002).

57 David Weaver and Swanzy Nimley Elliot, 'Who sets the agenda for the media? A study of local agenda-building', *Journalism Quarterly*, 62 (1985): 87–94.

58 Ibid., p. 93.

59 Also see Kyle Huckins, 'Interest-group influence on the media agenda:

a case study', *Journalism and Mass Communication Quarterly*, 76 (1999): 76–86.

60 Karen Callaghan and Frauke Schnell, 'Assessing the democratic debate: how the news media frame elite policy discourse', *Political Communication*, 18 (2001): 183–212.

61 Ibid., p. 197.

62 Penelope Ploughman, 'The creation of newsworthy events: an analysis of newspaper coverage of the man-made disaster at Love Canal', unpublished doctoral dissertation, State University of New York at Buffalo, 1984; Allen Mazur, 'Putting radon on the public risk agenda', *Science, Technology, and Human Values*, 12, 3–4 (1987): 86–93.

63 Stephen Reese and Lucig Danielian, 'Intermedia influence and the drug issue', in *Communication Campaigns about Drugs*, ed. P. Shoemaker (Hillsdale, NJ: Lawrence Erlbaum, 1989), pp. 29–46.

64 Jeongsub Lim, 'A cross-lagged analysis of agenda setting among online news media', *Journalism and Mass Communication Quarterly*, 83 (2006): 298–312.

65 Warren Breed, 'Newspaper opinion leaders and the process of standardization', *Journalism Quarterly*, 32 (1955): 277–84, 328.

66 Richard Kluger, *The Paper: The Life and Death of the New York Herald Tribune* (New York: Alfred A. Knopf, 1986).

67 See, for example, the account of a story that was bumped from page 1A of *USA Today* until it appeared as the lead story on the 'CBS Evening News', in Peter Pritchard, 'The McPapering of America: an insider's candid account', *Washington Journalism Revue* (1987): 32–7. Another example, a case study of how a specific news story about deviant behaviour by a Catholic priest triggered a flood of negative stories about clergy over a four-year period, is presented by Michael J. Breen, 'A cook, a cardinal, his priests, and the press: deviance as a trigger for intermedia agenda setting', *Journalism and Mass Communication Quarterly*, 74 (1997): 348–56.

68 Timothy Crouse, *The Boys on the Bus* (New York: Ballantine, 1973), pp. 84–5.

69 Trumbo, 'Longitudinal modelling of public issues.'

70 David Gold and Jerry Simmons, 'News selection patterns among Iowa dailies', *Public Opinion Quarterly*, 29 (1965): 425–30.

71 D. Charles Whitney and Lee Becker, '"Keeping the gates" for gatekeepers: the effects of wire news', *Journalism Quarterly*, 59 (1982): 60–5.

72 Lee Becker, Maxwell McCombs, and Jack McLeod, 'The development of political cognitions', in *Political Communication: Issues and Strategies for Research*, ed. Steven Chaffee (Beverly Hills, CA: Sage, 1975), p. 39.

73 Donald Shaw's calculations of the intermedia agenda-setting correlations from the classic gatekeeping studies are reported in Maxwell McCombs and Donald Shaw, 'Structuring the unseen environment', *Journal of Communication*, 26, spring (1976): 18–22.

74 David Manning White, 'The "gate keeper": a case study in the selection of news', *Journalism Quarterly*, 27 (1950): 383–90.

75 Paul Snider, 'Mr Gates revisited: a 1966 version of the 1949 case study', *Journalism Quarterly*, 44 (1967): 419–27.

76 Shaw's calculations reported in McCombs and Shaw, 'Structuring the unseen environment.'

77 Roberts and McCombs, 'Agenda setting and political advertising.'

78 López-Escobar, Llamas, McCombs, and Lennon, 'Two levels of agenda setting among advertising and news in the 1995 Spanish elections.'

79 Maxwell McCombs and Donald Shaw, 'The agenda-setting function of mass media', *Public Opinion Quarterly*, 36 (1972): 183.

80 Sebastián Valenzuela, 'Agenda setting and journalism', in *Oxford Research Encyclopedia of Communication*, ed. Jon F. Nussbaum (New York, NY: Oxford University Press, 2019).

81 Pablo Boczkowski, *News at Work: Imitation in an Age of Information Abundance.* (Chicago: University of Chicago Press, 2010).

82 Valenzuela, 'Agenda setting and journalism.'

83 Pu-Tsung King, 'Issue agendas in the 1992 Taiwan legislative election', unpublished doctoral dissertation, University of Texas at Austin, 1994.

84 Sebastián Valenzuela and Arturo Arriagada, 'Competencia por la uniformidad en noticieros y diarios chilenos 2000–2005' [The competition for similarity in Chilean news broadcasts and newspapers 2000–2005], *Cuadernos.info*, 24 (2009): 41–52.

85 Ramona Vonbun, Katharina Kleinen-von Königslöw, and Klaus Schoenbach, 'Intermedia agenda-setting in a multimedia news environment', *Journalism*, 17 (2016): 1054–73.

86 Toshio Takeshita, 'Agenda setting and framing: two dimensions of attribute agenda-setting', *Mita Journal of Sociology* [Japan], 12 (2007): 4–18. This research is a replication and extension of Takeshita, 'Expanding attribute agenda setting into framing', paper presented to the International Communication Association, Seoul, Korea, which was discussed in Chapter 3.

87 Marc Benton and P. Jean Frazier, 'The agenda-setting function of the mass media at three levels of information-holding', *Communication Research*, 3 (1976): 261–74.

88 Pu-Tsung King, 'The press, candidate images, and voter perceptions', in *Communication and Democracy*, eds. M. McCombs, D. Shaw, and D. Weaver (Mahwah, NJ: Lawrence Erlbaum, 1997), pp. 29–40.

89 Sitaram Asur, Bernardo A. Huberman, Gabor Szabo, and Chunyan Wang, 'Trends in social media: persistence and decay', Social Computing Lab Hewlett Packard, Palo Alto, CA (2011). Quote on p. 8. http://mashable.com/2011/02/14/twitter-trending-topics-hp/.

90 For a comprehensive review of recent research on blogs and other online media, see Hai Tran, 'Online agenda setting: a new frontier for theory development', in *Agenda Setting in a 2.0 World*, ed. T. Johnson (New York: Routledge, 2013). For examples of research showing divergence and convergence among media agendas, see Sharon Meraz, 'The fight for how to think: traditional media, social networks, and issue interpretation', *Journalism: Theory, Practice, and Criticism*, 12 (2011): 107–27; Jae Kook Lee, 'The effect of the internet on homogeneity of the media agenda: a test of the fragmentation thesis', *Journalism and Mass Communication Quarterly*, 84 (2007): 745–60.

91 Matthew Ragas and Spiro Kiousis, 'Intermedia agenda-setting and political activism: MoveOn.org and the 2008 presidential election', *Mass Communication and Society*, 13 (2010): 560–83.

92 Leonard Pitts, 'Objectivity might be impossible, so we strive for fairness', *Austin American-Statesman*, 17 December 2001, p. A13.

93 Stuart N. Soroka, 'Schindler's List's intermedia influence: exploring the role of "entertainment" in media agenda-setting', *Canadian Journal of Communication*, 25 (2000): 211–30.

8 Consequences of Agenda Setting

1 Eugene F. Shaw, 'Agenda-setting and mass communication theory', *International Communication Gazette*, 25, 2 (1979): 101. A creative example of a very early foray in this area is Lee Becker, 'The impact of issue saliences', in *The Emergence of American Political Issues*, eds. Donald Shaw and Maxwell McCombs (St Paul, MN: West, 1977), pp. 121–32.

2 Carl Hovland, Irving Janis, and Harold Kelley, *Communication and Persuasion* (New Haven, CT: Yale University Press, 1953). See also: Nathan Maccoby, 'The new "scientific" rhetoric', in *The Science of Human Communication*, ed. Wilbur Schramm (New York: Basic Books, 1963), pp. 41–53.

3 Shanto Iyengar and Donald R. Kinder, *News That Matters: Television and American Opinion* (Chicago: University of Chicago Press, 1987), p. 63. Although the evidence reported in this book concerns only television news, the bracketed words 'and the other news media' were inserted because there is substantial evidence that all the news media can prime judgements of public performance.

4 Gerd Gigerenzer, Ralph Hertwig, and Thorsten Pachur, eds., *Heuristics: The Foundations of Adaptive Behavior* (New York: Oxford University Press, 2011).

5 A classic presentation of heuristic information processing is Amos Tversky and Daniel Kahneman, 'Availability: a heuristic for judging frequency and probability', *Cognitive Psychology*, 5 (1973): 207–32.

6 Iyengar and Kinder, *News That Matters*, chapters 7–11.

7 An alternative explanation to media priming is the 'projection' hypothesis, which predicts that citizens exposed to issue news align their rating of the president on that issue with their prior overall approval of presidential performance. A population-based survey experiment was conducted to test these competing hypotheses, the results of which demonstrated that 'the causal arrow runs from issue approval to overall approval (media priming), not the reverse (projection).' See Austin Hart and Joel A. Middleton, 'Priming under fire: reverse causality and the classic media priming hypothesis', *Journal of Politics*, 76 (2014): 581–92. Quote is from p. 581.

8 Jon A. Krosnick and Donald R. Kinder, 'Altering the foundations of support for the president through priming', *American Political Science Review*, 84 (1990): 497–512.

9 Ibid., p. 505.

10 Nicholas A. Valentino, Vincent L. Hutchings, and Ismail K. White, 'Cues

that matter: how political ads prime racial attitudes during campaigns',
American Political Science Review, 96 (2002): 75–90.

11 Diana C. Mutz, *Impersonal Influence: How Perceptions of Mass Collectives Affect Political Attitudes* (Cambridge, UK: Cambridge University Press, 1998).

12 Sebastián Valenzuela, 'Variations in media priming: the moderating role of knowledge, interest, news attention, and discussion', *Journalism and Mass Communication Quarterly*, 86 (2009): 756–74.

13 Jon A. Krosnick and Laura Brannon, 'The impact of war on the ingredients of presidential evaluations: George Bush and the Gulf conflict', *American Political Science Review*, 87 (1993): 963–75; Shanto Iyengar and Adam Simon, 'News coverage of the Gulf crisis and public opinion', in *Do the Media Govern?*, eds. Shanto Iyengar and Richard Reeves (Thousand Oaks, CA: Sage, 1997), pp. 248–57.

14 Studies conducted outside the United States include: Robert Anderson, 'Do newspapers enlighten preferences? Personal ideology, party choice, and the electoral cycle: the United Kingdom, 1992–1997', *Canadian Journal of Political Science*, 36 (2003): 601–19; David Nicolas Hopmann, Rens Vliegenthart, Claes de Vreese, and Erik Albaek, 'Effects of television news coverage: how visibility and tone influence party choice', *Political Communication*, 27 (2010): 389–405; Tamir Sheafer and Gabriel Weimann, 'Agenda building, agenda setting, priming, individual voting intentions, and the aggregate results: an analysis of four Israeli elections', *Journal of Communication*, 55 (2005): 347–65; Gunnar Thesen, Christoffer Green-Pedersen, and Peter B. Mortensen, 'Priming, issue ownership, and party support: the electoral gains of an issue-friendly media agenda', *Political Communication*, 34 (2017): 282–301; Lars Willnat and Jian-Hua Zhu, 'Newspaper coverage and public opinion in Hong Kong: a time-series analysis of media priming', *Political Communication*, 13 (1996): 231–46.

15 Scott L. Althaus and Young Mie Kim, 'Priming effects in complex information environments: reassessing the impact of news discourse on presidential approval', *Journal of Politics*, 68 (2006): 960–76.

16 See Sungtae Ha, 'Attribute priming effects and presidential candidate evaluation: the conditionality of political sophistication', *Mass Communication and Society*, 14 (2011): 315–42; Sebastián Valenzuela, 'Variations in media priming.'

17 Iyengar and Simon, 'News coverage of the Gulf crisis and public opinion', p. 250.

18 For additional discussion, see Lars Willnat, 'Agenda setting and priming: conceptual links and differences', in *Communication and Democracy*, eds. M. McCombs, D. Shaw, and D. Weaver (Mahwah, NJ: Lawrence Erlbaum, 1997), pp. 51–66.

19 Iyengar and Simon, 'News coverage of the Gulf crisis and public opinion.'

20 Frank R. Baumgartner and Bryan D. Jones, *Agendas and Instability in American Politics*, 2nd edn (Chicago: University of Chicago Press, 2009).

21 Hans Mathias Kepplinger, Wolfgang Donsbach, Hans Bernd Brosius, and Joachim Friedrich Staab, 'Media tone and public opinion: a longitudinal study of media coverage and public opinion on Chancellor Kohl',

International Journal of Public Opinion Research, 1 (1989): 326–42; Daron R. Shaw, 'The impact of news media favorability and candidate events in presidential campaigns', *Political Communication*, 16 (1999): 183–202.

22 Sungtae Ha, 'Attribute priming effects and presidential candidate evaluation: the conditionality of political sophistication', *Mass Communication and Society*, 14 (2011): 315–42.

23 The relationship between news coverage and favourability ratings is probabilistic rather than deterministic. As we saw in Chapter 5 with the Clinton/Lewinsky scandal and Trump's impeachment inquiry, attribute media priming failures have been documented as well. See Spiro Kiousis, 'Job approval and favorability: the impact of media attention to the Monica Lewinsky scandal on public opinion of President Bill Clinton', *Mass Communication and Society*, 6 (2003): 435–51.

24 Esteban López-Escobar, Maxwell McCombs, and Antonio Tolsá, 'Measuring the public images of political leaders: a methodological contribution of agenda-setting theory', paper presented to the Congress for Political Communication Investigation, Madrid, 2007.

25 Kihan Kim and Maxwell McCombs, 'News story descriptions and the public's opinions of political candidates', *Journalism and Mass Communication Quarterly*, 84 (2007): 299–314.

26 Meital Balmas and Tamir Sheafer, 'Candidate image in election campaigns: attribute agenda setting, affective priming, and voting intentions', *International Journal of Public Opinion Research*, 22 (2010): 204–29. See also: Tamir Sheafer, 'How to evaluate it: the role of story-evaluation tone in agenda setting and priming', *Journal of Communication*, 57 (2007): 21–39.

27 Stuart Soroka, 'Good news and bad news: asymmetric responses to economic information', *Journal of Politics*, 68 (2006): 372–85. For other studies using the issue of the economy, see Deborah J. Blood and Peter C. B. Phillips, 'Economic headline news on the agenda: new approaches to understanding causes and effects', in *Communication and Democracy*, eds. McCombs, Shaw, and Weaver, pp. 97–114; Joe Bob Hester and Rhonda Gibson, 'The economy and second-level agenda setting: a time-series analysis of economic news and public opinion about the economy', *Journalism and Mass Communication Quarterly*, 80 (2003): 73–90.

28 Gunho Lee, 'Who let priming out? Analysis of first and second-level agenda-setting effects on priming', *International Communication Gazette*, 72 (2010): 759–76.

29 Victoria Y. Chen and Paromita Pain, 'What changed public opinion on the same-sex marriage issue? New implications of attribute measures and attribute priming in media agenda setting', *Newspaper Research Journal*, 39 (2018): 453–69.

30 Spiro Kiousis, 'Agenda-setting and attitudes: exploring the impact of media salience on perceived salience and public attitude strength of US presidential candidates from 1984 to 2004', *Journalism Studies*, 12 (2011): 359–74.

31 Spiro Kiousis and Maxwell McCombs, 'Agenda-setting effects and

attitude strength: political figures during the 1996 presidential election', *Communication Research*, 31 (2004): 36–57.

32   Natalie J. Stroud and Kate Kenski, 'From agenda setting to refusal setting: survey nonresponse as a function of media coverage across the 2004 election cycle', *Public Opinion Quarterly*, 71 (2007): 539–59.

33   Patrick Rössler and Michael Schenk, 'Cognitive bonding and the German reunification: agenda-setting and persuasion effects of mass media', *International Journal of Public Opinion Research*, 12 (2000): 29–47.

34   Elihu Katz, 'Media effects', in *International Encyclopedia of the Social and Behavioral Sciences*, eds. Neil J. Smelser an Paul B. Baltes (Oxford, UK: Elsevier, 2001), pp. 9472–9. Quote is on p. 9472.

35   *New York Times*, 17 January 1989, p. 22. Internationally, Population Communications International has assisted in the production of television dramas on family planning, AIDS prevention, gender equality, and a variety of other social topics in developing countries worldwide. See Doris A. Graber, *Processing Politics: Learning from Television in the Internet Age* (Chicago: University of Chicago Press, 2001), p. 127.

36   Kimberly K. Ma, William Schaffner, C. Colmenares, J. Howser, J. Jones, and K. A. Poehling, 'Influenza vaccinations of young children increased with media coverage in 2003', *Pediatrics*, 117 (2006): 157–63.

37   Craig Trumbo, 'The effect of newspaper coverage of influenza on the rate of physician visits for influenza 2002–2008', *Mass Communication and Society*, 15 (2012): 718–38.

38   The investigation was reported in Maxwell McCombs and Donald Shaw, 'A progress report on agenda-setting research', paper presented to the Association for Education in Journalism, San Diego, CA, 1974.

39   Marilyn Roberts, 'Predicting voter behavior via the agenda setting tradition', *Journalism Quarterly*, 69 (1992): 878–92; Marilyn Roberts, Ronald Anderson, and Maxwell McCombs, '1990 Texas gubernatorial campaign influence of issues and images', *Mass Communication Review*, 21 (1994): 20–35. For an application outside the United States, see Sebastián Valenzuela and Maxwell McCombs, 'Agenda-setting effects on vote choice: evidence from the 2006 Mexican election', paper presented to the annual meeting of the International Communication Association, San Francisco, 2007.

40   John R. Petrocik, 'Issue ownership in presidential elections with a 1980 case study', *American Journal of Political Science*, 40 (1996): 825–50. Also see John Petrocik, William Benoit, and G. J. Hansen, 'Issue ownership and presidential campaigning, 1952–2000', *Political Science Quarterly*, 118 (2003): 599–626.

41   Riccardo Puglisi, 'The spin doctor meets the rational voter: electoral competition with agenda-setting effects', available at SSRN: https://ssrn.com/abstract=581881 (2004).

42   Spiro Kiousis, Mike McDevitt, and Xu Wu, 'The genesis of civic awareness: agenda setting in political socialization', *Journal of Communication*, 55 (2005): 756–74; Spiro Kiousis and Michael McDevitt, 'Agenda setting in civic development: effects of curricula and issue importance on youth voter turnout', *Communication Research*, 35 (2008): 481–502.

43 For a study on the indirect effects of agenda setting on political participation beyond voting, see Soo Jung Moon, 'Attention, attitude, and behavior: second-level agenda-setting effects as a mediator of media use and political participation', *Communication Research*, 40 (2013): 698–719.

44 H. Denis Wu and Renita Coleman, 'Advancing agenda-setting theory: the comparative strength and new contingent conditions of the two levels of agenda-setting effects', *Journalism and Mass Communication Quarterly*, 86 (2009): 775–89.

45 Lindita Camaj, 'The consequences of attribute agenda-setting effects for political trust, participation, and protest behaviour', *Journal of Broadcasting and Electronic Media*, 58 (2014): 634–54.

46 Robert L. Stevenson, Rainer Böhme, and Nico Nickel, 'The TV agenda-setting influence on campaign 2000', *Egyptian Journal of Public Opinion Research*, 2, 1 (2001): 29–50.

47 Tsuneo Ogawa, 'Framing and agenda setting function', *Keio Communication Review*, 23 (2001): 71–80.

48 For additional evidence on the parallel between the shifting amounts of news coverage and variations in how much people talked and thought about election news, see Thomas E. Patterson, *The Vanishing Voter: Public Involvement in an Age of Uncertainty* (New York: Alfred A. Knopf, 2002).

49 David H. Weaver, 'Issue salience and public opinion: are there consequences of agenda-setting?', *International Journal of Public Opinion Research*, 3 (1991): 53–68.

50 Nancy Kieffer, 'Agenda-setting and corporate communication issues: can the mass media influence corporate stock prices?', unpublished master's thesis, Syracuse University, 1983.

51 Craig Carroll, ed., *Corporate Reputation and the News Media: Agenda-setting within News Coverage in Developed, Emerging, and Frontier Markets* (New York: Routledge, 2011). Also see M. M. Meijer and Jan Kleinnijenhuis, 'Issue news and corporate reputation: applying the theories of agenda setting and issue ownership in the field of business communication', *Journal of Communication*, 56 (2006): 543–59; Craig Carroll, 'The relationship between media favorability and firms' public esteem', *Public Relations Journal*, 3–4 (2010): 1–32.

52 Spiro Kiousis, Cristina Popescu, and Michael Mitrook, 'Understanding influence on corporate reputation: an examination of public relations efforts, media coverage, public opinion, and financial performance from an agenda building and agenda-setting perspective', *Journal of Public Relations Research*, 19 (2007): 147–65.

53 Roots of the third level of agenda-setting, which is defined by network analysis, are found in Craig Carroll, 'How the mass media influence perceptions of corporate reputation: exploring agenda-setting effects within business news coverage', unpublished doctoral dissertation, University of Texas at Austin, 2004.

54 Coy Callison, 'Media relations and the internet: how *Fortune* 500 company websites assist journalists in news gathering', *Public Relations Review*, 29 (2003): 29–41.

55 Matthew Ragas, 'Issue and stakeholder intercandidate agenda setting among corporate information subsidies', *Journalism and Mass Communication Quarterly*, 89 (2012): 91–111; Coral Ohl, J. David Pincus,Tony Rimmer and Denise Harison, 'Agenda building role of news releases in corporate takeovers', *Public Relations Review*, 21 (1995): 89–101.

9 Communication and Society

1 Harold Lasswell, 'The structure and function of communication in society', in *The Communication of Ideas*, ed. Lyman Bryson (New York: Institute for Religious and Social Studies, 1948), pp. 37–51.

2 Jian-Hua Zhu with William Boroson, 'Susceptibility to agenda setting', in *Communication and Democracy*, eds. M. McCombs, D. Shaw, and D. Weaver (Mahwah, NJ: Lawrence Erlbaum, 1997), p. 82 (emphasis in original).

3 For those familiar with cultivation theory, this process is similar to 'mainstreaming', which occurs when exposure to television and other media diminishes 'differences found in the responses of different groups of people, differences that are associated with the varied cultural, social, and political characteristics of these groups'. Nancy Signorielli, Michael Morgan, and James Shanahan, 'Cultivation analysis: research and practice', in *An Integrated Approach to Communication Theory and Research*, 3rd edn, eds., Don W. Stacks, Michael B. Salwen, and Kristen C. Eichhorn (New York, NY: Routledge, 2019), pp. 113–25. Quote is from p.121. Nevertheless, in agenda setting, this process is perceived as desirable – enabling consensus building. In cultivation, however, 'mainstreaming' is linked to the spread of homogenous, often distorted, public perceptions.

4 Donald Shaw and Shannon Martin, 'The function of mass media agenda setting', *Journalism Quarterly*, 69 (1992): 902–20.

5 Ching-Yi Chiang, 'Bridging and closing the gap of our society: social function of media agenda setting', unpublished master's thesis, University of Texas at Austin, 1995; Esteban López-Escobar, Juan Pablo Llamas, and Maxwell McCombs, 'Una dimensión social de los efectos de los medios de difusión: agenda-setting y consenso' ['A social dimension of media effects: agenda-setting and consensus'] *Comunicación y Sociedad* IX (1996): 91–125; Esteban López-Escobar, Juan Pablo Llamas, and Maxwell McCombs, 'Agenda setting and community consensus: first and second level effects', *International Journal of Public Opinion Research*, 10 (1998): 335–48.

6 Vanessa de Macedo Higgins Joyce, 'Consensus-building function of agenda setting in times of crisis: substantive and affective dimensions', in *Agenda Setting in a 2.0 World*, ed. Thomas J. Johnson (New York: Routledge, 2013).

7 David Weaver, Doris Graber, Maxwell McCombs, and Chaim Eyal, *Media Agenda Setting in a Presidential Election: Issues, Images and Interest* (Westport, CT: Greenwood, 1981).

8 Joseph Cappella and Kathleen Hall Jamieson, *Spiral of Cynicism: The Press*

and the Public Good (New York: Oxford University Press, 1997); Thomas
E. Patterson, *Out of Order* (New York: Random House Vintage Books,
1993).

9 Kyle Huckins, 'Interest-group influence on the media agenda', *Journalism
and Mass Communication Quarterly*, 76 (1999): 76–86.

10 Judith Buddenbaum, 'The media, religion, and public opinion: toward a
unified theory of cultural influence', in *Religion and Popular Culture: Studies
in the Interaction of Worldviews*, eds. Daniel A. Stout and Judith Buddenbaum
(Ames: Iowa State University Press, 2001), p. 27.

11 Jacqueline Harris and Maxwell McCombs, 'The interpersonal/mass
communication interface among church leaders', *Journal of Communication*,
22 (1972): 257–62.

12 Moshe Hellinger and Tsuriel Rashi, 'The Jewish custom of delaying
communal prayer: a view from communication theory', *Review of Rabbinic
Judaism*, 12 (2009): 189–203.

13 See, for example, Michael Robinson, 'Collective memory: from the 20s
through the 90s: the way we think we were', *Public Perspective*, 11, 1 (2000):
14–19, 44–7.

14 Kurt Lang, Gladys Engel Lang, Hans Mathias Kepplinger, and Simone
Ehmig, 'Collective memory and political generations: a survey of German
journalists', *Political Communication*, 10 (1993): 211–29.

15 Yoram Peri, 'The media and collective memory of Yitzhak Rabin's remembrance', *Journal of Communication*, 49, 3 (1999): 106–24.

16 Neta Kliger-Vilenchik, 'Memory setting: applying agenda setting theory to
the study of collective memory' in *On Media Memory: Collective Memory
in a New Media Age*, eds. Motti Neiger, Oren Meyers and Eyal Zandberg
(London: Palgrave Macmillan, 2011), pp. 226–237.

17 Asya Besova and Skye Chance Cooley, 'Foreign news and public opinion:
attribute agenda-setting theory revisited', *Ecquid Novi: African Journalism
Studies*, 30 (2009): 219–242.

18 For an earlier analysis on agenda setting at the country-level, see Wayne
Wanta, Guy Golan, and Cheolhan Lee, 'Agenda setting and international
news: media influence on public perception of foreign nations', *Journalism
and Mass Communication Quarterly*, 81 (2004): 364–77.

19 Raquel Rodriguez Díaz, 'Los profesores universitarios como medios de
comunicación: la agenda setting de los alumnos y profesores' [University
professors as communication media: agenda setting of students and
professors], unpublished doctoral dissertation, Complutense University of
Madrid, 2000.

20 Quoted in John Fortunato, *The Ultimate Assist: The Relationship and
Broadcasting Strategies of the NBA and Television Networks* (Cresskill, NJ:
Hampton Press, 2001), p. 2.

21 Fortunato, *The Ultimate Assist*.

22 Philemon Bantimaroudis, Stelios Zyglidopoulos, and Pavlos Symeou,
'Greek museum media visibility and museum visitation: an exploration
of cultural agenda setting', *Journal of Communication*, 60 (2010): 743–57;
Stelios Zyglidopoulos, Pavlos Symeou, Philemon Bantimaroudis, and

Eleni Kampanellou, 'Cultural agenda setting: media attributes and public attention of Greek museums', *Communication Research*, 39 (2012): 480–98.

23 Pavlos C. Symeou, Philemon Bantimaroudis and Stelios C. Zyglidopoulos, 'Cultural agenda setting and the role of critics: an empirical examination in the market for art-house films', *Communication Research*, 42 (2015): 732–54.

24 Lisa Weidman, 'Consumer knowledge about Oregon wines: applying agenda setting theory to the dissemination of information about consumer products', paper presented to the Midwest Association for Public Opinion Research, Chicago, 2011.

25 Shanto Iyengar, 'A typology of media effects', in the *Oxford Handbook of Political Communication*, eds., Kate Kenski and Kathleen Hall Jamieson (New York: Oxford University Press, 2017), pp. 59–68. Quote is from p. 66.

Bibliography

Ader, Christine, 'A longitudinal study of agenda setting for the issue of environmental pollution', *Journalism and Mass Communication Quarterly*, 72 (1995): 300–11.

Althaus, Scott L. and David Tewksbury, 'Agenda setting and the "new" news: patterns of issue importance among readers of the paper and online versions of the *New York Times*', *Communication Research*, 29 (2002): 180–207.

Althaus, Scott L. and Young Mie Kim, 'Priming effects in complex information environments: reassessing the impact of news discourse on presidential approval', *Journal of Politics*, 68 (2006): 960–76.

Anderson, Alison, 'Sources, media, and modes of climate change communication: the role of celebrities', *Wiley Interdisciplinary Reviews: Climate Change*, 2 (2011): 535–46.

Anderson, John R., *The Architecture of Cognition* (Cambridge, MA: Harvard University Press: 1983).

Anderson, Robert, 'Do newspapers enlighten preferences? Personal ideology, party choice, and the electoral cycle: the United Kingdom, 1992–1997', *Canadian Journal of Political Science*, 36 (2003): 601–619.

Asur, Sitaram, Bernardo A. Huberman, Gabor Szabo, and Chunyan Wang, 'Trends in social media: persistence and decay', Social Computing Lab Hewlett Packard, Palo Alto, CA (2011).

Atwater, Tony, Michael Salwen, and Ronald Anderson, 'Interpersonal discussion as a potential barrier to agenda setting', *Newspaper Research Journal*, 6, 4 (1985): 37–43.

Balmas, Meital and Tamir Sheafer, 'Candidate image in election campaigns: attribute agenda setting, affective priming, and voting intentions', *International Journal of Public Opinion Research*, 22 (2010): 204–29.

Bantimaroudis, Philemon, Stelios Zyglidopoulos, and Pavlos Symeou, 'Greek museum media visibility and museum visitation: an exploration of cultural agenda setting', *Journal of Communication*, 60 (2010): 743–57.

Barberá, Pablo, Andreu Casas, Jonathan Nagler, Patrick J. Egan, Richard Bonneau, John T. Jost,, and Joshua A. Tucker, 'Who leads? Who follows? Measuring issue attention and agenda setting by legislators and the mass public using social media data', *American Political Science Review*, 113 (2019): 883–901.

Barro, Robert J. and Jong-Wha Lee, 'A new data set of educational attainment in the world, 1950–2010', *Journal of Development Economics*, 104 (2013): 184–98.

Bartels, Larry M., *Unequal Democracy: The Political Economy of the New Gilded Age*, 2nd edn (New York: Russell Sage Foundation, 2016).

Baumgartner, Frank R. and Bryan D. Jones, *Agendas and Instability in American Politics*, 2nd edn (Chicago: University of Chicago Press, 2009).

Becker, Lee, 'The impact of issue saliences', in *The Emergence of American Political Issues*, eds. Donald Shaw and Maxwell McCombs (St Paul, MN: West, 1977), pp. 121–32.

Becker, Lee, Maxwell McCombs and Jack McLeod, 'The development of political cognitions', in *Political Communication: Issues and Strategies for Research*, ed. Steven Chaffee (Beverly Hills, CA: Sage, 1975), pp. 21–63.

Becker, Lee and Maxwell McCombs, 'The role of the press in determining voter reactions to presidential primaries', *Human Communication Research*, 4 (1978): 301–7.

Bennett, W. Lance and Shanto Iyengar, 'A new era of minimal effects? The changing foundations of political communication', *Journal of Communication*, 58 (2008): 707–31.

Benton, Marc and P. Jean Frazier, 'The agenda-setting function of the mass media at three levels of information-holding', *Communication Research*, 3 (1976): 261–74.

Besova, Asya and Skye Chance Cooley, 'Foreign news and public opinion: attribute agenda-setting theory revisited', *Ecquid Novi: African Journalism Studies*, 30 (2009): 219–42.

Bettag, Tom, 'What's news? Evolving definitions of news', *Harvard International Journal of Press/Politics*, 5, 3 (2000): 105–107.

Birkland, Thomas, *After Disaster: Agenda Setting, Public Policy, and Focusing Events* (Washington, DC: Georgetown University Press, 1997).

Blood, Warwick, 'Competing models of agenda setting: issue obtrusiveness vs. media exposure', paper presented to the Association for Education in Journalism, Boston, 1980.

Blood, Warwick, 'Unobtrusive issues in the agenda-setting role of the press', unpublished doctoral dissertation, Syracuse University, 1981.

Blumler, Jay G., 'The role of theory in uses and gratifications research', *Communication Research*, 6 (1979): 9–36.

Boczkowski, Pablo J., *News at Work: Imitation in an Age of Information Abundance* (Chicago: University of Chicago Press, 2010).

Boukes, Mark, 'Agenda setting with satire: how political satire increased TTIP'S saliency on the public, media, and political agenda', *Political Communication*, 36 (2019): 426–51.

Bouza, Fermín, 'The impact area of Political Communication: citizenship faced with public discourse', *International Review of Sociology*, 14 (2004): 245–59.

Boyle, Thomas P., 'Intermedia agenda setting in the 1996 presidential primaries', *Journalism and Mass Communication Quarterly*, 78 (2001): 26–44.

Boynton, G. R. and Glenn W. Richardson, Jr, 'Agenda setting in the twenty-first century', *New Media and Society*, 18 (2016): 1916–34.

Brandenburg, Heinz, 'Who follows whom? The impact of parties on media agenda formation in the 1997 British general elections campaign', *Harvard International Journal of Press/Politics*, 7, 3 (2002): 34–54.

Breed, Warren, 'Newspaper opinion leaders and the process of standardization', *Journalism Quarterly*, 32 (1955): 277–84, 328.

Breed, Warren, 'Social control in the newsroom', *Social Forces*, 33 (May 1955): 326–35.

Breen, Michael J., 'A cook, a cardinal, his priests, and the press: deviance as a trigger for intermedia agenda setting', *Journalism and Mass Communication Quarterly*, 74 (1997): 348–56.

Brewer, Marcus and Maxwell McCombs, 'Setting the community agenda', *Journalism and Mass Communication Quarterly*, 73 (1996): 7–16.

Brosius, Hans Bernd and Hans Mathias Kepplinger, 'The agenda setting function of television news: static and dynamic views', *Communication Research*, 17 (1990): 183–211.

Browne, Magdalena and Sebastián Valenzuela, 'Temor a la delincuencia en Chile' ['Fear of crime in Chile'], in *Seguridad, medios y miedos [(In)Security, media and fears]*, eds. Brenda Focás and Omar Rincón (Buenos Aires: Ediciones Imago Mundi, 2018), pp. 63–84.

Bryan, Kenneth, 'Political Communication and agenda setting in local races', unpublished doctoral dissertation, University of Texas at Austin, 1997.

Buddenbaum, Judith, 'The media, religion, and public opinion: toward a unified theory of cultural influence', in *Religion and Popular Culture: Studies in the Interaction of Worldviews*, eds. Daniel A. Stout and Judith Buddenbaum (Ames: Iowa State University Press, 2001).

Bulkow, Kristin, Juliane Urban, and Wolfgang Schweiger, 'The duality of agenda-setting: the role of information processing', *International Journal of Public Opinion Research*, 25 (2012): 43–63.

Burkart, Roland and Uta Russmann, 'Quality of understanding in political campaign communication: an analysis of political parties' press releases and media coverage in Austria (1970–2008)', working paper, University of Vienna, 2013.

Cacciatore, Michael, Dietram Scheufele, and Shanto Iyengar, 'The end of framing as we know it…and the future of media effects', *Mass Communication and Society*, 19 (2016): 7–23.

Callaghan, Karen and Frauke Schnell, 'Assessing the democratic debate: how the news media frame elite policy discourse', *Political Communication*, 18 (2001): 183–212.

Callison, Coy, 'Media relations and the internet: how *Fortune* 500 company websites assist journalists in news gathering', *Public Relations Review*, 29 (2003): 29–41.

Camaj, Lindita, 'Need for orientation, selective exposure, and attribute agenda-setting effects', *Mass Communication and Society*, 17 (2014): 689–712.

Camaj, Lindita, 'The consequences of attribute agenda-setting effects for political trust, participation, and protest behaviour', *Journal of Broadcasting and Electronic Media*, 58 (2014): 634–54.

Camaj, Lindita, 'Motivational theories of agenda-setting effects: an information selection and processing model of attribute agenda-setting', *International Journal of Public Opinion Research*, 31 (2019): 441–62.

Canel, Maria José, Juan Pablo Llamas, and Federico Rey, 'El primer nivel del efecto agenda setting en la información local: los "problemas más importantes" de la ciudad de Pamplona' ['The first level agenda setting effect on local information: the "most important problems" of the city of Pamplona'], *Comunicación y Sociedad*, 9, 1 and 2 (1996): 17–38.

Cao, Xiaoxia, 'Hearing it from Jon Stewart: the impact of The Daily Show on public attentiveness to politics', *International Journal of Public Opinion Research*, 22 (2010): 26–46.

Cappella, Joseph and Kathleen Hall Jamieson, *Spiral of Cynicism: The Press and the Public Good* (New York: Oxford University Press, 1997).

Cardenal, Ana S., Carol Galais, and Silvia Majó-Vázquez, 'Is Facebook eroding the public agenda? Evidence from survey and web-tracking data', *International Journal of Public Opinion Research*, 31 (2019): 589–608.

Carroll, Craig E., 'How the mass media influence perceptions of corporate reputation: exploring agenda-setting effects within business news coverage', unpublished doctoral dissertation, University of Texas at Austin, 2004.

Carroll, Craig E., 'The relationship between media favorability and firms' public esteem', *Public Relations Journal*, 3–4 (2010): 1–32.

Carroll, Craig E., ed., *Corporate Reputation and the News Media: Agenda-setting within News Coverage in Developed, Emerging, and Frontier Markets* (New York: Routledge, 2011).

Carter, Richard F., 'Communication and affective relations', *Journalism Quarterly*, 42 (1965): 203–212.

Casermeiro de Pereson, Alicia, *Los medios en las elecciones: la agenda setting en la ciudad de Buenos Aires* [The media in the elections: agenda setting in the city of Buenos Aires] (Buenos Aires, Argentina, EDUCA, 2003).

Caspi, Dan, 'The agenda-setting function of the Israeli press', *Knowledge: Creation, Diffusion, Utilization*, 3 (1982): 401–14.

Caudill, Edward, 'An agenda-setting perspective on historical public opinion', in *Communication and Democracy*, eds. Maxwell McCombs, Donald Shaw, and David Weaver (Mahwah, NJ: Lawrence Erlbaum, 1997), p. 179.

Chaffee, Steven H. and Donna G. Wilson, 'Media rich, media poor: two studies of diversity in agenda-holding', *Journalism Quarterly*, 54 (1977): 466–76.

Chaffee, Steven H. and M. Metzger, 'The end of mass communication?', *Mass Communication and Society*, 4 (2001): 365–79.

Chen, Victoria Y. and Paromita Pain, 'What changed public opinion on the same-sex marriage issue? New implications of attribute measures and attribute priming in media agenda setting', *Newspaper Research Journal*, 39 (2018): 453–69.

Cheng, Yang, 'The third-level agenda-setting study: an examination of media, implicit, and explicit public agendas in China', *Asian Journal of Communication*, 26 (2016): 319–32.

Chernov, Gennadiy, Sebastián Valenzuela, and Maxwell McCombs, 'An experimental comparison of two perspectives on the concept of need for orientation in agenda-setting theory', *Journalism and Mass Communication Quarterly*, 88 (2011): 142–55.

Chiang, Ching-Yi, 'Bridging and closing the gap of our society: social function of media agenda setting', unpublished master's thesis, University of Texas at Austin, 1995.

Cobb, Roger W., and Charles D. Elder, *Participation in American Politics: The Dynamics of Agenda-Building* (Baltimore: Johns Hopkins University Press, 1972).

Cohen, Bernard C., *The Press and Foreign Policy* (Princeton, NJ: Princeton University Press, 1963).

Cohen, David, 'A report on a non-election agenda setting study', paper presented to the Association for Education in Journalism, Ottawa, Canada, 1975.

Coleman, Renita and Stephen Banning, 'Network TV news' affective framing of the presidential candidates: evidence for a second-level agenda-setting effect through visual framing', *Journalism and Mass Communication Quarterly*, 83 (2006): 313–28.

Coleman, Renita and Maxwell McCombs, 'The young and agenda-less? Age-related differences in agenda setting on the youngest generation, baby boomers, and the civic generation', *Journalism and Mass Communication Quarterly*, 84 (2007): 495–508.

Coleman, Renita and H. Denis Wu, 'Proposing emotion as a dimension of affective agenda setting: separating affect into two components and comparing their second-level effects', *Journalism and Mass Communication Quarterly*, 87 (2010): 315–27.

Collins, Allan M. and Elizabeth F. Loftus, 'A spreading activation theory of semantic processing', *Psychological Review*, 82 (1975): 402–8.

Conway, Michael and Jeffrey R. Patterson, 'Today's top story? An agenda setting and recall experiment involving television and Internet news', *Southwestern Mass Communication Journal*, 24 (2008): 31–48.

Crouse, Timothy, *The Boys on the Bus* (New York: Ballantine, 1973).

Dalton, Russell J., Paul Allen Beck, Robert Huckfeldt, and William Koetzle, 'A test of media-centered agenda setting: newspaper content and public interests in a presidential election', *Political Communication*, 15 (1998): 463–81.

Davies, Nick, *Flat Earth News: An Award-Winning Reporter Exposes Falsehood, Distortion and Propaganda in the Global Media* (London: Chatto and Windus, 2008).

Dearing, James W. and Everett M. Rogers, *Agenda Setting* (Thousand Oaks, CA: Sage, 1996).

Djerf-Pierre, Monika and Adam Shehata, 'Still an agenda setter: Traditional news media and public opinion during the transition from low to high choice media environments', *Journal of Communication*, 67 (2017): 733–57.

Downs, Anthony, 'Up and down with ecology: the "issue-attention cycle"', *The Public Interest*, 28 (1972): 38–50.

Dunn, Scott W., 'Candidate and media agenda setting in the 2005 Virginia gubernatorial election', *Journal of Communication*, 59 (2009): 635–52.

Eaton, Jr, Howard, 'Agenda setting with bi-weekly data on content of three national media', *Journalism Quarterly*, 66 (1989): 942–8.

Edelstein, Alex, Youichi Ito, and Hans Mathias Kepplinger, *Communication and Culture: A Comparative Approach* (New York: Longman, 1989).

Edy, Jill A. and Patrick C. Meirick, 'The fragmenting public agenda: capacity, diversity, and volatility in responses to the "most important problem" question', *Public Opinion Quarterly*, 82 (2018): 661–85.

Einsiedel, Edna F., Kandice L. Salomone, and Frederick Schneider, 'Crime: effects of media exposure and personal experience on issue salience', *Journalism Quarterly*, 61 (1984): 131–6.

Erbring, Lutz, Edie Goldenberg and Arthur Miller, 'Front-page news and real-world cues', *American Journal of Political Science*, 24 (1980): 16–49.

Etter, Michael and Anne Vestergaard, 'Third level of agenda building and agenda setting during a corporate crisis', in *The Power of Information Networks*, eds. Lei Guo and Maxwell McCombs (New York: Routledge, 2016), pp. 175–89.

Evatt, Dixie and Salma Ghanem, 'Building a scale to measure salience', paper presented to the World Association for Public Opinion Research, Rome, Italy, 2001.

Evatt, Dixie and Tamara Bell, 'Upstream influences: the early press releases, agenda setting and politics of a future president', *Southwestern Mass Communication Journal*, 16, 2 (2001): 70–81.

Eyal, Chaim, James Winter, and William DeGeorge, 'The concept of time frame in agenda setting', in *Mass Communication Review Yearbook*, vol. 2, eds. G. Cleveland Wilhoit and Harold de Bock (Beverly Hills, CA: Sage, 1981), pp. 212–18.

Fan, David P., Kathy Keltner, and Robert Wyatt, 'A matter of guilt or innocence: how news reports affect support for the death penalty in the United States', *International Journal of Public Opinion Research*, 14 (2002): 439–52.

Feezell, Jessica T., 'Agenda setting through social media: the importance of incidental news exposure and social filtering in the digital era', *Political Research Quarterly*, 71 (2018): 482–94.

Flyvbjerg, Bent, Todd Landman, and Sanford Schram, eds., *Real Social Science: Applied Phronesis* (Cambridge: Cambridge University Press, 2012).

Folkerts, Jean Lange, 'William Allen White's anti-populist rhetoric as an agenda-setting technique', *Journalism Quarterly*, 60 (1983): 28–34.

Fortunato, John A., *The Ultimate Assist: The Relationship and Broadcasting Strategies of the NBA and Television Networks* (Cresskill, NJ: Hampton Press, 2001).

Frankel, Max, *The Times of My Life and My Life with The Times* (New York: Random House, 1999).

Frensch, Peter A., 'One concept, multiple meanings: on how to define the concept of implicit learning', in *Handbook of Implicit Learning*, eds. Michael A. Stadler and Peter A. Frensch (Thousand Oaks, CA: Sage, 1998), pp. 47–104.

Funkhouser, G. Ray, 'The issues of the sixties', *Public Opinion Quarterly*, 37 (1973): 62–75.

Gamson, William A., *Talking Politics* (New York: Cambridge University Press, 1992).

Gandy, Oscar J., *Beyond Agenda Setting: Information Subsidies and Public Policy* (Norwood, NJ: Ablex, 1982).

Gans, Herbert J., *Deciding What's News: A Study of CBS Evening News, NBC Nightly News, Newsweek and Time* (New York: Pantheon, 1979).

Geiß, Stefan, 'The media's conditional agenda setting power: how baselines and spikes of issue salience affect likelihood and strength of agenda setting', *Communication Research* (2019).

Gentzkow, Matthew, 'Small media, big impact: randomizing news stories reveals broad public impacts', *Science*, 358 (2017): 726–7.

Gerbner, George, Larry Gross, Michael Morgan, Nancy Signorielli, and James Shanahan, 'Growing up with television: cultivation processes', in *Media Effects: Advances in Theory and Research*, 2nd edn, eds. Jennings Bryant and Dolf Zillmann (Mahwah, NJ: Lawrence Erlbaum, 1994), pp. 43–68.

Gigerenzer, Gerd, Ralph Hertwig, and Thorsten Pachur, eds., *Heuristics: The Foundations of Adaptive Behavior* (New York: Oxford University Press, 2011).

Ghanem, Salma, 'Media coverage of crime and public opinion: an exploration of the second level of agenda setting', unpublished doctoral dissertation, University of Texas at Austin, 1996.

Ghanem, Salma, 'Filling in the tapestry: the second level of agenda-setting', in *Communication and Democracy*, eds. Maxwell McCombs, Donald Shaw, and David Weaver (Mahwah, NJ: Lawrence Erlbaum, 1997), pp. 3–14.

Gilberg, Sheldon, Chaim Eyal, Maxwell McCombs, and David Nicholas, 'The State of the Union address and the press agenda', *Journalism Quarterly*, 57 (1980): 584–8.

Glynn, J. Carroll, Michael Huge, James Reineke, Bruce Hardy, and James Shanahan, 'When Oprah intervenes: political correlates of daytime talk show viewing', *Journal of Broadcasting and Electronic Media*, 51 (2007): 228–44.

Gold, David, and Jerry Simmons, 'News selection patterns among Iowa dailies', *Public Opinion Quarterly*, 29 (1965): 425–30.

Gonzenbach, William, *The Media, the President, and Public Opinion: A Longitudinal Analysis of the Drug Issue, 1984–1991* (Mahwah, NJ: Lawrence Erlbaum, 1996).

Gordon, Margaret T. and Linda Heath, 'The news business, crime and fear', in *Reactions to Crime*, ed. Dan Lewis (Beverly Hills, CA: Sage, 1981).

Graber, Doris A., *Processing Politics: Learning from Television in the Internet Age* (Chicago: University of Chicago Press, 2001).

Grassau, Daniela, 'Has TV decreased impact on public opinion due to the transformations of the media environment in the 21st century?', paper presented to the International Association for Media and Communication Research, Madrid, 2019.

Groshek, Jacob and Megan Clough Groshek, 'Agenda-trending: reciprocity and the predictive capacity of social networking sites in intermedia agenda-setting across topics over time', *Media and Communication*, 1, 1, 2013: 15–27.

Gross, Kimberly and Sean Aday, 'The scary world in your living room and neighborhood: using local broadcast news, neighborhood crime rates, and personal experience to test agenda setting and cultivation', *Journal of Communication*, 53 (2003): 411–26.

Gruszczynski, Mike, 'Evidence of partisan agenda fragmentation in the American public, 1959–2015', *Public Opinion Quarterly*, 83 (2020): 749–81.

Gruszczynski, Mike and Michael W. Wagner, 'Information flow in the 21st century: the dynamics of agenda-uptake', *Mass Communication and Society*, 20 (2017): 378–402.

Gumpert, Gary and Robert Cathcart, eds., *Inter/Media: Interpersonal Communication in a Media World* (New York: Oxford University Press, 1986).

Guo, Lei, 'Toward the third level of agenda setting theory: A network agenda setting model', in Thomas J. Johnson, ed., *Agenda Setting in a 2.0 World* (New York: Routledge, 2013), pp. 112–33.

Guo, Lei and Maxwell McCombs, 'Network agenda setting: A third level of media effects', paper presented to the International Communication Association, Boston, 2011.

Guo, Lei and Maxwell McCombs, 'Toward the third-level agenda setting theory: A network agenda setting model', paper presented to the Association for Education in Journalism and Mass Communication, St Louis, 2011.

Guo, Lei, Yi-Ning Katherine Chen, Radoslaw Aksamit, Damian Guzek, Qian Wang, Hong Vu, and Maxwell McCombs, 'How the world pictured the Iraq War: a transnational network analysis', *Journalism Studies*, 16 (2015): 343–62.

Guo, Lei and Maxwell McCombs, eds. *The Power of Information Networks*: New Directions for Agenda Setting (New York: Routledge, 2016)

Gurevitch, Michael and Jay Blumler, 'The construction of election news at the BBC: an observation study', in *Individuals in Mass Media Organizations: Creativity and Constraint*, eds. James Ettema and Charles Whitney (Beverly Hills, CA: Sage, 1982): 179–204.

Gurevitch, Michael and Jay Blumler, 'Political communication systems and democratic values', in *Democracy and the Mass Media*, ed. Judith Lichtenberg (Cambridge: Cambridge University Press, 1990), pp. 269–89.

Ha, Sungtae, 'The intermediary role of news media in the presidential campaign: a mediator, moderator, or political agent?', unpublished paper, University of Texas at Austin, 2001.

Ha, Sungtae, 'Attribute priming effects and presidential candidate evaluation: the conditionality of political sophistication', *Mass Communication and Society*, 14 (2011): 315–42.

Hamilton, James T., *Channeling Violence: The Economic Market for Violent Television Programming* (Princeton, NJ: Princeton University Press, 1998).

Harder, Raymond A., Julie Sevenans, and Peter Van Aelst, 'Intermedia agenda setting in the social media age: How traditional players dominate the news agenda in election times', *Harvard International Journal of Press/Politics*, 22, 3 (2017): 275–293.

Harris, Jacqueline J. and Maxwell E. McCombs, 'The interpersonal/mass communication interface among church leaders', *Journal of Communication*, 22 (1972): 257–62.

Hart, Austin, and Joel A. Middleton, 'Priming under fire: reverse causality and the classic media priming hypothesis', *Journal of Politics*, 76 (2014): 581–92.

Hellinger, Moshe and Tsuriel Rashi, 'The Jewish custom of delaying communal prayer: a view from communication theory', *Review of Rabbinic Judaism*, 12 (2009): 189–203.

Herbst, Susan, 'The cultivation of conversation', in *The Poll with a Human Face: The National Issues Convention Experiment in Political Communication*, eds. Maxwell McCombs and Amy Reynolds (Mahwah, NJ: Lawrence Erlbaum, 1999).

Hester, Joe Bob and Rhonda Gibson, 'The economy and second-level agenda setting: a time-series analysis of economic news and public opinion about the economy', *Journalism and Mass Communication Quarterly*, 80 (2003): 73–90.

Hester, Joe Bob and Rhonda Gibson, 'The agenda setting function of national versus local media: a time-series analysis for the issue of same sex marriage', *Mass Communication and Society*, 10 (2007): 299–172.

Higgins Joyce, Vanessa de Macedo, 'Consensus-building function of agenda setting in times of crisis: substantive and affective dimensions', in *Agenda Setting in a 2.0 World*, ed. Thomas J. Johnson (New York: Routledge, 2013).

Holbrook, R. Andrew and Timothy Hill, 'Agenda setting and priming in prime time television: crime dramas as political cues', *Political Communication*, 22 (2005): 277–95.

Hopmann, David Nicolas, Rens Vliegenthart, Claes de Vreese, and Erik Albaek, 'Effects of television news coverage: how visibility and tone influence party choice', *Political Communication*, 27 (2010): 389–405.

Hovland, Carl, Irving Janis, and Harold Kelley, *Communication and Persuasion* (New Haven, CT: Yale University Press, 1953).

Huckins, Kyle, 'Interest-group influence on the media agenda: a case study', *Journalism and Mass Communication Quarterly*, 76 (1999): 76–86.

Hyun, Ki Deuk, and Soo Jung Moon, 'Agenda setting in the partisan TV news context: attribute agenda setting and polarized evaluation of presidential candidates among viewers of NBC, CNN, and Fox News', *Journalism and Mass Communication Quarterly*, 93 (2016): 509–29.

Inglehart, Ronald, *Culture Shift in Advanced Industrial Society* (Princeton, NJ: Princeton University Press, 1990).

Ingram, Helen, H. Brinton Milward, and Wendy Laird, 'Scientists and agenda setting: advocacy and global warming', in *Risk and Society: The Interaction of Science, Technology and Public Policy*, ed. Marvin Waterstone (Dordrecht, the Netherlands: Springer, 1992).

Iyengar, Shanto, 'A typology of media effects', in the *Oxford Handbook of Political Communication*, eds., Kate Kenski and Kathleen Hall Jamieson (New York: Oxford University Press, 2017), pp. 59–68.

Iyengar, Shanto and Donald R. Kinder, *News That Matters: Television and American Opinion* (Chicago, IL: University of Chicago Press, 1987).

Iyengar, Shanto and Adam Simon, 'News coverage of the Gulf crisis and public opinion', in *Do the Media Govern?*, eds. S. Iyengar and R. Reeves (Thousand Oaks, CA: Sage, 1997), pp. 248–57.

Jackson, Daniel and Kevin Moloney, 'Inside churnalism: PR, journalism and power relationships in flux', *Journalism Studies*, 17 (2015): 1–18.

Jamieson, Kathleen Hall and Karlyn Kohrs Campbell, *The Interplay of Influence:*

News, Advertising, Politics and the Mass Media (Belmont, CA: Wadsworth, 1992).

Jasperson, Amy, Dhavan Shah, Mark Watts, Ronald Faber, and David Fan, 'Framing and the public agenda: media effects on the importance of the federal budget deficit', *Political Communication*, 15 (1998): 205–24.

Jennings, Will and Christopher Wlezien, 'Distinguishing between most important problems and issues', *Public Opinion Quarterly*, 75 (2011): 545–55.

Johnson, Thomas J. and Wayne Wanta, with John T. Byrd and Cindy Lee, 'Exploring FDR's relationship with the press: a historical agenda-setting study', *Political Communication*, 12 (1995): 157–172.

Kahneman, Daniel, and Amos Tversky, 'Choices, values and frames', *American Psychologist*, 39 (1984): 341–50.

Kaplan, Stephen, 'Cognitive maps in perception and thought', in *Image and Environment: Cognitive Mapping and Spacial Behavior*, eds. Roger M. Downs and David Stea (Chicago: Aldine, 1973), pp. 63–78.

Katz, Elihu, 'Media effects', in *International Encyclopedia of the Social and Behavioral Sciences*, eds. Neil J. Smelser and Paul B. Baltes (Oxford, UK: Elsevier, 2001), pp. 9472–9.

Kepplinger, Hans Mathias and Herbert Roth, 'Creating a crisis: German mass media and oil supply in 1973–1974', *Public Opinion Quarterly*, 43 (1979): 285–96.

Kepplinger, Hans Mathias, Wolfgang Donsbach, Hans Bernd Brosius, and Joachim Friedrich Staab, 'Media tone and public opinion: a longitudinal study of media coverage and public opinion on Chancellor Kohl', *International Journal of Public Opinion Research*, 1 (1989): 326–42.

Key, V. O., *The Responsible Electorate: Rationality in Presidential Voting 1936–1960* (Cambridge, MA: Belknap Press of Harvard University Press, 1966).

Kieffer, Nancy, 'Agenda-setting and corporate communication issues: can the mass media influence corporate stock prices?', unpublished master's thesis, Syracuse University, 1983.

Kim, Joohan, Robert O. Wyatt, and Elihu Katz, 'News, talk, opinion, participation: the part played by conversation in deliberative democracy', *Political Communication*, 16 (1999): 361–85.

Kim, Kihan and Maxwell McCombs, 'News story descriptions and the public's opinions of political candidates', *Journalism and Mass Communication Quarterly*, 84 (2007): 299–314.

Kim, Sei-Hill, Dietram Scheufele, and James Shanahan, 'Think about it this way: Attribute agenda-setting function of the press and the public's evaluation of a local issue', *Journalism and Mass Communication Quarterly*, 79 (2002): 7–25.

Kim, Yeojin, Youngju Kim, and Shuhua Zhou, 'Theoretical and methodological trends of agenda-setting theory: A thematic analysis of the last four decades of research', *Agenda Setting Journal*, 1 (2017): 5–22.

King, Gary, Benjamin Schneer, and Ariel White, 'How the news media activate public expression and influence national agendas', *Science*, 358 (2017): 776–80.

King, Pu-Tsung, 'Issue agendas in the 1992 Taiwan legislative election', unpublished doctoral dissertation, University of Texas at Austin, 1994.

King, Pu-Tsung, 'The press, candidate images, and voter perceptions', in *Communication and Democracy*, eds. Maxwell McCombs, Donald Shaw, and David Weaver (Mahwah, NJ: Lawrence Erlbaum, 1997), pp. 29–40.

Kiousis, Spiro, 'Job approval and favorability: the impact of media attention to the Monica Lewinsky scandal on public opinion of President Bill Clinton', *Mass Communication and Society*, 6 (2003): 435–51.

Kiousis, Spiro, 'Compelling arguments and attitude strength – exploring the impact of second-level agenda setting on public opinion of presidential candidate images', *Harvard International Journal of Press/Politics*, 10 (2005): 3–27.

Kiousis, Spiro, 'Agenda-setting and attitudes: exploring the impact of media salience on perceived salience and public attitude strength of US presidential candidates from 1984 to 2004', *Journalism Studies*, 12 (2011): 359–74.

Kiousis, Spiro, Philemon Bantimaroudis, and Hyun Ban, 'Candidate image attributes: experiments on the substantive dimension of second-level agenda setting', *Communication Research*, 26, 4 (1999): 414–28.

Kiousis, Spiro and Maxwell McCombs, 'Agenda-setting effects and attitude strength: political figures during the 1996 presidential election', *Communication Research*, 31 (2004): 36–57.

Kiousis, Spiro, Mike McDevitt, and Xu Wu, 'The genesis of civic awareness: agenda setting in political socialization', *Journal of Communication*, 55 (2005): 756–74.

Kiousis, Spiro, Michael Mitrook, Xu Wu, and Trent Seltzer, 'First and second-level agenda-building and agenda-setting effects: exploring the linkages among candidate news releases, media coverage, and public opinion during the 2002 Florida gubernatorial election', *Journal of Public Relations Research*, 18 (2006): 265–85.

Kiousis, Spiro, Cristina Popescu, and Michael Mitrook, 'Understanding influence on corporate reputation: an examination of public relations efforts, media coverage, public opinion, and financial performance from an agenda building and agenda-setting perspective', *Journal of Public Relations Research*, 19 (2007): 147–65.

Kiousis, Spiro and Michael McDevitt, 'Agenda setting in civic development: effects of curricula and issue importance on youth voter turnout', *Communication Research*, 35 (2008): 481–502.

Kiousis, Spiro and Xu Wu, 'International agenda-building and agenda setting: exploring the influence of public relations counsel on US news media and public perceptions of foreign nations', *International Communication Gazette*, 70 (2008): 58–75.

Kiousis, Spiro, Soo-Yeon Kim, Michael McDevitt, and Ally Ostrowski, 'Competing for attention: information subsidy influence in agenda building during election campaigns', *Journalism and Mass Communication Quarterly*, 86 (2009): 545–62.

Kiousis, Spiro and Jesper Stromback, 'The White House and public relations: examining the linkages between presidential communications and public opinion', *Public Relations Review*, 36 (2010): 7–14.

Kiousis, Spiro, Ji Young Kim, Matt Ragas, Gillian Wheat, Sarab Kochhar, Emma

Svensson, and Maradith Miles, 'Exploring new frontiers of agenda building during the 2012 US presidential election pre-convention period', *Journalism Studies*, 16 (2015): 363–82.

Klapper, Joseph T., *The Effects of Mass Communication* (New York: Free Press, 1960).

Kliger-Vilenchik, Neta, 'Memory setting: applying agenda setting theory to the study of collective memory' in *On Media Memory: Collective Memory in a New Media Age*, eds. Motti Neiger, Oren Meyers, and Eyal Zandberg (London: Palgrave Macmillan, 2011), pp. 226–37.

Kluger, Richard, *The Paper: The Life and Death of the New York Herald Tribune* (New York: Alfred A. Knopf, 1986).

Kosicki, Gerald M., 'Problems and opportunities in agenda setting research', *Journal of Communication*, 43 (1993): 100–27.

Krosnick, Jon A. and Donald R. Kinder, 'Altering the foundations of support for the president through priming', *American Political Science Review*, 84 (1990): 497–512.

Krosnick, Jon A. and Laura Brannon, 'The impact of war on the ingredients of presidential evaluations: George Bush and the Gulf conflict', *American Political Science Review*, 87 (1993): 963–75.

Lane, Robert E., *Political Life: Why and How People Get Involved in Politics* (New York: Free Press, 1959), p. 12.

Lang, Kurt, Gladys Engel Lang, Hans Mathias Kepplinger, and Simone Ehmig, 'Collective memory and political generations: a survey of German journalists', *Political Communication*, 10 (1993): 211–29.

Lasorsa, Dominic L. and Wayne Wanta, 'Effects of personal, interpersonal and media experiences on issue saliences', *Journalism Quarterly*, 67 (1990): 804–13.

Lasswell, Harold D., 'The structure and function of communication in society', in *The Communication of Ideas*, ed. Lyman Bryson (New York: Institute for Religious and Social Studies, 1948), pp. 37–51.

Lazarsfeld, Paul F., Bernard Berelson, and Hazel Gaudet, *The People's Choice* (New York: Duell, Sloan, and Pearce, 1944).

Lazarsfeld, Paul F. and Robert K. Merton, 'Mass communication, popular taste and organized social action', in Guy E. Swanson, Theodore M. Newcomb, and Eugene L. Hartley, eds., *Readings in Social Psychology* (rev. edn) (New York: Henry Holt and Company, 1952), pp. 74–85.

Lee, Gunho, 'Who let priming out? Analysis of first and second-level agenda-setting effects on priming', *International Communication Gazette*, 72 (2010): 759–76.

Lee, Jae Kook, 'The effect of the Internet on homogeneity of the media agenda: a test of the fragmentation thesis', *Journalism and Mass Communication Quarterly*, 84 (2007): 745–60.

Lee, Jae Kook, and Renita Coleman, 'Testing generational, life cycle, and period effects of age on agenda setting', *Mass Communication and Society*, 17, 1 (2014): 3–25.

Lee, Jong-Wha and Hanol Lee, 'Human capital in the long run', *Journal of Development Economics*, 122 (2016): 147–69.

Lee, Na Yeon, 'How agenda setting works: a dual path model and motivated reasoning', *Journalism* (2019).

Lennon, Federico Rey, *Los Diarios Nacionales y la Campaña Electoral: Argentina, 1997 Elecciones* [The national press and the electoral campaign: Argentina, the 1997 elections] (Buenos Aires: Freedom Forum and Universidad Austral, 1998).

Levine, Daniel S., 'Neural population modeling and psychology: a review', *Mathematical Biosciences*, 66 (1983): 1–86.

Lewis, Justin, Andrew Williams, and Bob Franklin, 'A compromised Fourth Estate? UK news journalism, public relations and news sources', *Journalism Studies*, 9 (2008): 1–20.

Lichter, Robert and Ted Smith, 'Why elections are bad news: media and candidate discourse in the 1996 presidential primaries', *Harvard International Journal of Press/Politics*, 1, 4 (1996): 15–35.

Lim, Jeongsub, 'A cross-lagged analysis of agenda setting among online news media', *Journalism and Mass Communication Quarterly*, 83 (2006): 298–312.

Lindsay, Peter H. and Donald A. Norman, *Human Information Processing: An Introduction to Psychology* (New York: Academic Press, 1977).

Lippmann, Walter, *Public Opinion* (New York: Macmillan, 1922).

López-Escobar, Esteban, Juan Pablo Llamas, and Maxwell McCombs, 'Una dimensión social de los efectos de los medios de difusión: agenda-setting y consenso' ['A social dimension of media effects: agenda-setting and consensus'] *Comunicación y Sociedad* IX (1996): 91–125.

López-Escobar, Esteban, Juan Pablo Llamas, and Maxwell McCombs, 'Agenda setting and community consensus: first and second level effects', *International Journal of Public Opinion Research*, 10 (1998): 335–48.

López-Escobar, Esteban, Juan Pablo Llamas, Maxwell McCombs, and Federico Rey Lennon, 'Two levels of agenda setting among advertising and news in the 1995 Spanish elections', *Political Communication*, 15 (1998): 225–38.

López-Escobar, Esteban, Maxwell McCombs, and Antonio Tolsá, 'Measuring the public images of political leaders: a methodological contribution of agenda-setting theory', paper presented to the Congress for Political Communication Investigation, Madrid, 2007.

Lorenz-Spreen, Philipp, Bjarke Mørch Mønsted, Philipp Hövel, and Sune Lehmann, 'Accelerating dynamics of collective attention', *Nature Communications*, 10, 1759 (2019).

Lowry, Dennis T., Tarn Ching Josephine Nio, and Dennis W. Leitner, 'Setting the public fear agenda: a longitudinal analysis of network TV crime reporting, public perceptions of crime, and FBI crime statistics', *Journal of Communication*, 53 (2003): 61–73.

Luo, Yunjuan, Hansel Burley, Alexander Moe, and Mingxiao Sui, 'A meta-analysis of news media's public agenda-setting effects, 1972–2015', *Journalism and Mass Communication Quarterly*, 96 (2019): 150–72.

Ma, Kimberly K., William Schaffner, C. Colmenares, J. Howser, J. Jones, and K. A. Poehling, 'Influenza vaccinations of young children increased with media coverage in 2003', *Pediatrics*, 117 (2006): 157–63.

Maccoby, Nathan, 'The new "scientific" rhetoric', in *The Science of Human*

Communication, ed. Wilbur Schramm (New York: Basic Books, 1963), pp. 41–53.

McCombs, Maxwell, 'Editorial endorsements: a study of influence,' *Journalism Quarterly*, 44 (1967): 545–8.

McCombs, Maxwell, 'Explorers and surveyors: expanding strategies for agenda setting research,' *Journalism Quarterly*, 69 (1992): 815.

McCombs, Maxwell, 'The future agenda for agenda setting research,' *Journal of Mass Communication Studies* [Japan], 45 (1994): 171–81.

McCombs, Maxwell, 'Personal involvement with issues on the public agenda,' *International Journal of Public Opinion Research*, 11 (1999): 152–68.

McCombs, Maxwell, 'Myth and reality in scientific discovery: The case of agenda setting theory,' in *Communication: A Different Kind of Horse Race*, eds. Brenda Dervin and Steven Chaffee (Cresskill, NJ: Hampton Press, 2003), pp. 25–37.

McCombs, Maxwell, 'Civic osmosis: the social impact of media,' *Comunicación y Sociedad*, 25 (2012): 7–14.

McCombs, Maxwell and John Smith, 'Perceptual selection and communication,' *Journalism Quarterly*, 46 (1969): 352–5.

McCombs, Maxwell and Donald Shaw, 'The agenda setting function of mass media,' *Public Opinion Quarterly*, 36 (1972): 176–87.

McCombs, Maxwell and Donald Shaw, 'A progress report on agenda-setting research,' paper presented to the Association for Education in Journalism, San Diego, CA, 1974.

McCombs, Maxwell and Donald Shaw, 'Structuring the unseen environment,' *Journal of Communication*, 26, Spring (1976): 18–22.

McCombs, Maxwell, Sheldon Gilberg, and Chaim Eyal, 'The State of the Union address and the press agenda: a replication,' paper presented to the International Communication Association, Boston, 1982.

McCombs, Maxwell and David Weaver, 'Toward a merger of gratifications and agenda-setting research,' in *Media Gratifications Research: Current Perspectives*, eds. Karl Erik Rosengren, Lawrence Wenner and Philip Palmgreen (Beverly Hills, CA: Sage, 1985), pp. 95–108.

McCombs, Maxwell, Edna Einsiedel, and David Weaver, *Contemporary Public Opinion: Issues and the News* (Hillsdale, NJ: Lawrence Erlbaum, 1991).

McCombs, Maxwell and Dixie Evatt, 'Los temas y los aspectos: explorando una nueva dimensión de la agenda setting' ['Objects and attributes: exploring a new dimension of agenda setting'], *Comunicación y Sociedad*, 8, 1 (1995): 7–32.

McCombs, Maxwell and Jian-Hua Zhu, 'Capacity, diversity and volatility of the public agenda: trends from 1954–1994,' *Public Opinion Quarterly*, 59 (1995): 495–525.

McCombs, Maxwell, Juan Pablo Llamas, Esteban López-Escobar, and Federico Rey, 'Candidate images in Spanish elections: second-level agenda setting effects,' *Journalism & Mass Communication Quarterly*, 74 (1997): 703–17.

McCombs, Maxwell, Esteban López-Escobar, and Juan Pablo Llamas, 'Setting the agenda of attributes in the 1996 Spanish general election,' *Journal of Communication*, 50, 2 (2000): 77–92.

McCombs, Maxwell and Natalie J. Stroud, 'Psychology of agenda-setting effects: Mapping the paths of information processing', *Review of Communication Research*, 2 (2014): 68–93.

McGuire, William J., 'Psychological motives and communication gratification', in *The Uses of Mass Communication: Current Perspectives on Gratifications Research*, eds. J. G. Blumler and Elihu Katz (Beverly Hills, CA: Sage, 1974), pp. 167–96.

McGuire, William J. 'Theoretical foundations of campaigns', in *Public Communication Campaigns*, 2nd edn, eds. Richard E. Rice and Charles K. Atkin (Newbury Park, CA: Sage, 1989), pp. 43–65.

MacKuen, Michael, 'Social communication and the mass policy agenda', in *More Than News: Media Power in Public Affairs*, eds. Michael MacKuen and Steven Coombs (Beverly Hills, CA: Sage, 1981), pp. 19–144.

McLeod, Jack M., Lee B. Becker, and James E. Byrnes, 'Another look at the agenda setting function of the press', *Communication Research*, 1 (1974): 131–66.

Manheim, Jarol B. and Robert B. Albritton, 'Changing national images: international public relations and media agenda setting', *American Political Science Review*, 73 (1984): 641–7.

Martin, Jason, 'Agenda setting, elections and the impact of information technology', in *Agenda Setting in a 2.0 World*, ed. Thomas J. Johnson (New York: Routledge, 2013), pp. 28–52.

Matthes, Jörg, 'The need for orientation towards news media: revising and validating a classic concept', *International Journal of Public Opinion Research*, 18 (2006): 422–44.

Matthes, Jörg, 'Need for orientation as a predictor of agenda-setting effects: causal evidence from a two-wave panel study', *International Journal of Public Opinion Research*, 20 (2008): 440–53.

Mayer, William G., *The Changing American Mind: How and Why American Public Opinion Changed between 1960 and 1988* (Ann Arbor: University of Michigan Press, 1992).

Mazur, Allen, 'Putting radon on the public risk agenda', *Science, Technology, and Human Values*, 12, 3–4 (1987): 86–93.

Meijer, May-May and Jan Kleinnijenhuis, 'Issue news and corporate reputation: applying the theories of agenda setting and issue ownership in the field of business communication', *Journal of Communication*, 56 (2006): 543–59.

Meraz, Sharon, 'The fight for how to think: traditional media, social networks, and issue interpretation', *Journalism: Theory, Practice, and Criticism*, 12 (2011): 107–27.

Meraz, Sharon, 'Using time series analysis to measure intermedia agenda-setting influence in traditional media and political blog networks', *Journalism and Mass Communication Quarterly*, 88 (2011): 176–94.

Merritt, Davis and Maxwell McCombs, *The Two W's of Journalism: The Why and What of Public Affairs Reporting* (Mahwah, NJ: Lawrence Erlbaum, 2003).

Merritt, Richard L., *Symbols of American Community, 1735–1775* (New Haven, CT: Yale University Press, 1966).

Mikami, Shunji, Toshio Takeshita, Makoto Nakada, and Miki Kawabata, 'The media coverage and public awareness of environmental issues in Japan', *International Communication Gazette*, 54 (1995), 209–26.

Miller, George A., 'The magic number seven, plus or minus two: some limits on our capacity for processing information', *Psychological Review*, 63 (1956): 81–97.

Miller, Joanne M., 'Examining the mediators of agenda setting: A new experimental paradigm reveals the role of emotions', *Political Psychology*, 28 (2007): 689–717.

Miller, Mark, Julie Andsager, and Bonnie Riechert, 'Framing the candidates in presidential primaries: issues and images in press releases and news coverage', *Journalism and Mass Communication Quarterly*, 75 (1998): 312–24.

Min, Young, Salma Ghanem, and Dixie Evatt, 'Using a split-ballot survey to explore the robustness of the "MIP" question in agenda setting research: a methodological study', *International Journal of Public Opinion Research*, 19 (2007): 221–36.

Moon, Soo Jung, 'Attention, attitude, and behavior: second-level agenda-setting effects as a mediator of media use and political participation', *Communication Research*, 40 (2013): 698–719.

Mueller, John E., 'Choosing among 133 candidates', *Public Opinion Quarterly*, 34 (1970): 395–402.

Mutz, Diana C., *Impersonal Influence: How Perceptions of Mass Collectives Affect Political Attitudes* (Cambridge, UK: Cambridge University Press, 1998).

Nelson, Barbara, *Making an Issue of Child Abuse: Political Agenda Setting for Social Problems* (Chicago: University of Chicago Press, 1984).

Neuman, W. Russell, 'The threshold of public attention', *Public Opinion Quarterly*, 54 (1990): 159–76.

Neuman, W. Russell, and Lauren Guggenheim, 'The evolution of media effects theory: a six-stage model of cumulative research', *Communication Theory*, 21 (2011): 169–96.

Neuman, W. Russell, Marion R. Just, and Ann N. Crigler, *Common Knowledge: News and the Construction of Political Meaning* (Chicago: University of Chicago Press, 1992).

Nimmo, Dan and Robert L. Savage, *Candidates and their Images* (Pacific Palisades, CA: Goodyear, 1976).

Noelle-Neumann, Elisabeth, 'The spiral of silence: a response', in *Political Communication Yearbook 1984*, eds. Keith Sanders, Lynda Lee Kaid, and Dan Nimmo (Carbondale: Southern Illinois University Press, 1985), pp. 66–94.

Noelle-Neumann, Elisabeth, *The Spiral of Silence: Our Social Skin*, 2nd edn (Chicago: University of Chicago Press, 1993).

Nord, David Paul, 'The politics of agenda setting in late 19th century cities', *Journalism Quarterly*, 58 (1981): 563–74, 612.

O'Shaughnessy, Nicholas, *The Phenomenon of Political Marketing* (London: Macmillan, 1990).

Ogawa, Tsuneo, 'Framing and agenda setting function', *Keio Communication Review*, 23 (2001): 71–80.

Ohl, Coral, J. David Pincus, Tony Rimmer, and Denise Harison, 'Agenda building role of news releases in corporate takeovers', *Public Relations Review*, 21 (1995): 89–101.

Oliver, Mary Beth, Arthur A. Raney, and Jennings Bryant, eds., *Media Effects: Advances in Theory and Research*, 4th edn (New York: Routledge, 2020).

Park, Robert E., 'News as a form of knowledge', *American Journal of Sociology*, 45 (1940): 667–86.

Park, Robert E., 'The city: suggestions for investigation of human behavior in the urban environment', in Robert E. Park and Ernest W. Burgess, eds., *The City* (Chicago, IL: University of Chicago Press, 1925), pp. 1–46.

Patterson, Thomas E., *The Mass Media Election: How Americans Choose Their President* (New York: Praeger, 1980).

Patterson, Thomas E., *Out of Order* (New York: Random House Vintage Books, 1993).

Patterson, Thomas E., *The Vanishing Voter: Public Involvement in an Age of Uncertainty* (New York: Alfred A. Knopf, 2002).

Pavlik, John V., *Public Relations: What Research Tells Us* (Newbury Park, CA: Sage, 1987).

Peri, Yoram, 'The media and collective memory of Yitzhak Rabin's remembrance', *Journal of Communication*, 49 (1999): 106–24.

Peter, Jochen and Claes H. de Vreese, 'Agenda-rich, agenda-poor: a cross-national comparative investigation of nominal and thematic public agenda diversity', *International Journal of Public Opinion Research*, 15 (2003): 44–64.

Peter, Jochen, 'Country characteristics as contingent conditions of agenda setting: the moderating influence of polarized elite opinion', *Communication Research*, 30 (2003): 683–712.

Petrocik, John R., 'Issue ownership in presidential elections with a 1980 case study', *American Journal of Political Science*, 40 (1996): 825–50.

Petrocik, John R., William L. Benoit, and Glenn J. Hansen, 'Issue ownership and presidential campaigning, 1952–2000', *Political Science Quarterly*, 118 (2003): 599–626.

Petty, Richard E. and John T. Cacioppo, *Communication and Persuasion: Central and Peripheral Routes to Attitude Change* (New York: Springer, 1986).

Pingree, Raymond J. and Elizabeth Stoycheff, 'Differentiating cueing from reasoning in agenda setting effects', *Journal of Communication*, 63 (2013): 852–72.

Pingree, Raymond J., Andrea Quenette, John Tchernev, and Ted Dickinson, 'Effects of media criticism on gatekeeping trust and implications for agenda setting', *Journal of Communication*, 63 (2013): 351–72.

Ploughman, Penelope, 'The creation of newsworthy events: an analysis of newspaper coverage of the man-made disaster at Love Canal', unpublished doctoral dissertation, State University of New York at Buffalo, 1984.

Poindexter, Paula, Maxwell McCombs, Laura Smith, and others, 'Need for orientation in the new media landscape', unpublished paper, University of Texas at Austin, 2002.

Popkin, Samuel L., *The Reasoning Voter: Communication and Persuasion in Presidential Campaigns* (Chicago: University of Chicago Press, 1991).

Presser, Stanley, 'Substance and method in *Public Opinion Quarterly*, 1937–2010', *Public Opinion Quarterly*, 75 (2011): 839–45.

Price, Vincent and David Tewksbury, 'News values and public opinion: a theoretical account of media priming and framing' in *Progress in Communication Sciences:Advances in Persuasion*, eds. G. A. Barnett and F. J. Boster (Greenwich, CT: Ablex, 1997), pp. 173–212.

Pritchard, Peter, 'The McPapering of America: an insider's candid account', *Washington Journalism Revue* (1987): 32–7.

Protess, David L. and Maxwell McCombs, eds., *Agenda Setting: Readings on Media, Public Opinion, and Policymaking* (Hillsdale, NJ: Lawrence Erlbaum, 1991).

Protess, David L., Fay L. Cook, Jack C. Doppelt, James S. Ettema, Margaret T. Gordon, Donna R. Leff and Peter Miller, *The Journalism of Outrage: Investigative Reporting and Agenda Building in* America (New York: Guilford, 1991).

Puglisi, Riccardo, 'The spin doctor meets the rational voter: electoral competition with agenda-setting effects', available at SSRN: https://ssrn.com/abstract=581881 (2004).

Ragas, Matthew, 'Issue and stakeholder intercandidate agenda setting among corporate information subsidies', *Journalism and Mass Communication Quarterly*, 89 (2012): 91–111.

Ragas, Matthew and Spiro Kiousis, 'Intermedia agenda-setting and political activism: MoveOn.org and the 2008 presidential election', *Mass Communication and Society*, 13 (2010): 560–83.

Rains, Stephen A., Timothy R. Levine, and Rene Weber, 'Sixty years of quantitative Communication Research summarized: lessons from 149 meta-analyses', *Annals of the International Communication Association*, 42 (2018): 105–24.

Reese, Stephen D. and Lucig Danielian, 'Intermedia influence and the drug issue', in *Communication Campaigns about Drugs*, ed. P. Shoemaker (Hillsdale, NJ: Lawrence Erlbaum, 1989), pp. 29–46.

Reese, Stephen D. and Pamela J. Shoemaker, 'A media sociology for the networked public sphere: the hierarchy of influences model', *Mass Communication and Society*, 19 (2016): 389–410.

Roberts, Marilyn, 'Predicting voter behavior via the agenda setting tradition', *Journalism Quarterly*, 69 (1992): 878–92.

Roberts, Marilyn and Maxwell McCombs, 'Agenda setting and political advertising: origins of the news agenda', *Political Communication*, 11 (1994): 249–62.

Roberts, Marilyn, Ronald Anderson, and Maxwell McCombs, '1990 Texas gubernatorial campaign influence of issues and images', *Mass Communication Review*, 21 (1994): 20–35.

Roberts, Marilyn, Wayne Wanta, and Tzong-Houng (Dustin) Dzwo, 'Agenda setting and issue salience online', *Communication Research*, 29 (2002): 452–65.

Robinson, Michael, 'Collective memory: from the 20s through the 90s: the way we think we were', *Public Perspective*, 11, 1 (2000): 14–19, 44–7.

Rodríguez Díaz, Raquel, 'Los profesores universitarios como medios de comunicación: la agenda setting de los alumnos y profesores' [University professors as communication media: agenda setting of students and professors], unpublished doctoral dissertation, Complutense University of Madrid, 2000.

Rogers, Everett M., James W. Dearing, and Soonbum Chang, 'AIDS in the 1980s: the agenda-setting process for a public issue', *Journalism Monographs*, 126 (1991).

Rogstad, Ingrid, 'Is Twitter just rehashing? Intermedia agenda setting between Twitter and mainstream media', *Journal of Information Technology and Politics*, 13, 2 (2016): 142–58.

Rössler, Patrick and Michael Schenk, 'Cognitive bonding and the German reunification: agenda-setting and persuasion effects of mass media', *International Journal of Public Opinion Research*, 12 (2000): 29–47.

Rumelhart, David E. and Donald A. Norman, 'Accretion, tuning and restructuring: Three modes of learning', in *Semantic Factors in Cognition*, eds. John Wealdon Cotton and Roberta L. Klatzky (Hillsdale, NJ: Lawrence Erlbaum, 1978).

Salwen, Michael, 'Effects of accumulation of coverage on issue salience in agenda setting', *Journalism Quarterly*, 65 (1988): 100–6, 130.

Sánchez-Aranda, José Javier, María José Canel, and Juan Pablo Llamas, 'Framing effects of television political advertising and the selective perception process', papers presented at the World Association for Public Opinion Research regional conference, Pamplona, Spain, 1997.

Sayre, Ben, Leticia Bode, Dhavan Shah, Dave Wilcox, and Chirag Shah, 'Agenda setting in a digital age: tracking attention to California Proposition 8 in social media, online news and conventional news', *Policy and Internet*, 2, 2 (2010): 7–32.

Scharkow, Michael and Jens Vogelgesang, 'Measuring the public agenda using search engine queries', *International Journal of Public Opinion Research*, 23 (2011): 104–113.

Schlozman, Kay Lehman, Sidney Verba, and Henry E. Brady, *The Unheavenly Chorus: Unequal Political Voice and the Broken Promise of American Democracy* (Princeton, NJ: Princeton University Press, 2013).

Schoenbach, Klaus and Holli A. Semetko, 'Agenda setting, agenda reinforcing or agenda deflating? A study of the 1990 German national election', *Journalism Quarterly*, 68 (1992): 837–46.

Schudson, Michael, *The Good Citizen: A History of American Civic Life* (New York: Free Press, 1998), pp. 310–11.

Searles, Kathleen, and Glen Smith, 'Who's the boss? Setting the agenda in a fragmented media environment', *International Journal of Communication*, 10 (2016): 2074–95.

Semetko, Holli A., Jay G. Blumler, Michael Gurevitch, and David H. Weaver, with Steve Barkin and G. Cleveland Wilhoit, *The Formation of Campaign Agendas: A Comparative Analysis of Party and Media Roles in Recent American and British Elections* (Hillsdale, NJ: Lawrence Erlbaum, 1991).

Shaw, Daron R., 'The impact of news media favorability and candidate events in presidential campaigns', *Political Communication*, 16 (1999): 183–202.

Shaw, Donald L. and Maxwell E. McCombs, eds., *The Emergence of American Political Issues* (St Paul, MN: West, 1977).

Shaw, Donald L. and John Slater, 'Press puts unemployment on agenda: Richmond community opinion, 1981–1984', *Journalism Quarterly*, 65 (1988): 407–11.

Shaw, Donald L. and Shannon Martin, 'The function of mass media agenda setting', *Journalism Quarterly*, 69 (1992): 902–20.

Shaw, Donald L., Bradley J. Hamm, and Thomas C. Terry, 'Vertical vs. horizontal media: Using agenda setting and audience agenda-melding to create public information strategies in the emerging Papyrus Society', *Military Review*, 86, 6 (2006): 13–25.

Shaw, Donald L., Milad Minooie, Deb Aikat, and Chris J. Vargo, *Agendamelding: News, Social Media, Audiences and Civic Community* (New York: Peter Lang, 2019).

Shaw, Eugene F., 'Agenda-setting and mass communication theory', *International Communication Gazette*, 25, 2 (1979): 101.

Sheafer, Tamir, 'How to evaluate it: the role of story-evaluation tone in agenda setting and priming', *Journal of Communication*, 57 (2007): 21–39.

Sheafer, Tamir and Gabriel Weimann, 'Agenda building, agenda setting, priming individual voting intentions and the aggregate results: an analysis of four Israeli elections', *Journal of Communication*, 55 (2005): 347–65.

Shehata, Adam, 'Unemployment on the agenda: A panel study of agenda setting effects during the 2006 Swedish national election campaign', *Journal of Communication*, 60 (2010): 182–203.

Shoemaker, Pamela, ed., *Communication Campaigns about Drugs* (Hillsdale, NJ: Lawrence Erlbaum, 1989).

Shoemaker, Pamela, 'Hardwired for news: using biological and cultural evolution to explain the surveillance function', *Journal of Communication*, 46, 3 (1996): 32–47.

Shoemaker, Pamela and Tim Vos, *Gatekeeping Theory* (New York: Routledge, 2009).

Shoemaker, Pamela and Stephen D. Reese, *Mediating the Message in the 21st Century: A Media Sociology Perspective* (New York: Routledge, 2014).

Sigal, Leon V. *Reporters and Officials: The Organization and Politics of Newsmaking* (Lexington, MA: D. C. Heath, 1973).

Signorielli, Nancy, Michael Morgan, and James Shanahan, 'Cultivation analysis: research and practice', in *An Integrated Approach To Communication Theory And Research*, 3rd edn, eds., Don W. Stacks, Michael B. Salwen, and Kristen C. Eichhorn (New York: Routledge, 2019), pp. 113–25.

Smith, Kim, 'Newspaper coverage and public concern about community issues', *Journalism Monographs*, 101 (1987).

Smith, Tom W., 'America's most important problems – a trend analysis, 1946–1976', *Public Opinion Quarterly*, 44 (1980): 164–80.

Snider, Paul, 'Mr Gates revisited: a 1966 version of the 1949 case study', *Journalism Quarterly*, 44 (1967): 419–27.

Son, Young Jun, and David H. Weaver, 'Another look at what moves public opinion: media agenda setting and polls in the 2000 US election', *International Journal of Public Opinion Research*, 18 (2006): 174–97.

Song, Yonghoi, 'Internet news media and issue development: a case study on the roles of independent online news services as agenda-builders for anti-US protests in South Korea', *New Media and Society*, 9 (2007): 71–92.

Soroka, Stuart N., 'Schindler's List's intermedia influence: exploring the role of "entertainment" in media agenda-setting', *Canadian Journal of Communication*, 25 (2000): 211–30.

Soroka, Stuart N., *Agenda-Setting Dynamics in Canada* (Vancouver: UBC Press, 2002).

Soroka, Stuart N., 'Issue attributes and agenda setting by media, the public, and policymakers in Canada', *International Journal of Public Opinion Research*, 14 (2002): 264–85.

Soroka, Stuart N., 'Media, public opinion, and foreign policy', *Harvard International Journal of Press/Politics*, 8 (2003): 27–48.

Soroka, Stuart N., 'Good news and bad news: asymmetric responses to economic information', *Journal of Politics*, 68 (2006): 372–85.

Soroka, Stuart N. and Stephen McAdams, 'News, politics, and negativity', *Political Communication*, 32, 1 (2015): 1–22.

Stacks, Don W., Michael B. Salwen, and Kristen C. Eichhorn, eds., *An Integrated Approach to Communication Theory and Research*, 3rd edn (New York: Routledge, 2019).

Stevenson, Robert L., Rainer Böhme, and Nico Nickel, 'The TV agenda-setting influence on campaign 2000', *Egyptian Journal of Public Opinion Research*, 2, 1 (2001): 29–50.

Stoycheff, Elizabeth, Raymond J. Pingree, Jason T. Peifer, and Mingxiao Sui, 'Agenda cueing effects of news and social media', *Media Psychology*, 21, 2 (2018): 182–201.

Stromback, Jesper and Spiro Kiousis, 'A new look at agenda setting effects – Comparing the predictive power of overall political news consumption and specific news media consumption across different media channels and media types', *Journal of Communication*, 60 (2010): 271–92.

Stromback, Jesper and Spiro Kiousis, eds., *Political Public Relations: Principles and Applications* (New York: Routledge, 2011).

Stroud, Natalie J., *Niche News: The Politics of News Choice* (New York: Oxford University Press, 2011).

Stroud, Natalie J. and Kate Kenski, 'From agenda setting to refusal setting: survey nonresponse as a function of media coverage across the 2004 election cycle', *Public Opinion Quarterly*, 71 (2007): 539–59.

Swanson, David and Paolo Mancini, eds., *Politics, Media, and Modern Democracy: An International Study of Innovations in Electoral Campaiging and their Consequences* (Westport, CT: Praeger, 1996).

Symeou, Pavlos C., Philemon Bantimaroudis, and Stelios C. Zyglidopoulos, 'Cultural agenda setting and the role of critics: an empirical examination in the market for art-house films', *Communication Research*, 42 (2015): 732–54.

Takeshita, Toshio, 'Agenda setting effects of the press in a Japanese local election', *Studies of Broadcasting*, 29 (1993):193–216.

Takeshita, Toshio, 'Expanding attribute agenda setting into framing: an application of the problematic situation scheme', paper presented to the International Communication Association, Seoul, Korea, 2002.

Takeshita, Toshio, 'Current critical problems in agenda-setting research', *International Journal of Public Opinion Research*, 18 (2006): 275–96.

Takeshita, Toshio, 'Agenda setting and framing: two dimensions of attribute agenda-setting', *Mita Journal of Sociology* [Japan], 12 (2007): 4–18.

Takeshita, Toshio and Shunji Mikami, 'How did mass media influence the voters' choice in the 1993 general election in Japan?: a study of agenda setting', *Keio Communication Review*, 17 (1995): 27–41.

Tan, Yue and David H. Weaver, 'Agenda diversity and agenda setting from 1956 to 2004: what are the trends over time?', *Journalism Studies*, 14 (2013): 773–89.

Tedesco, John C., 'Issue and strategy agenda setting in the 2000 presidential primaries', unpublished paper, Virginia Technological University, 2001.

Tedesco, John C., 'Intercandidate agenda setting in the 2004 Democratic presidential primary', *American Behavioral Scientist*, 49 (2005): 92–113.

Thesen, Gunnar, Christoffer Green-Pedersen, and Peter B. Mortensen, 'Priming, issue ownership, and party support: the electoral gains of an issue-friendly media agenda', *Political Communication*, 34 (2017): 282–301.

Tolman, Edward C., *Purposive Behavior in Animals and Men* (New York: Appleton-Century-Crofts, 1932).

Tolman, Edward C., 'Cognitive maps in rats and men', *Psychological Review*, 55 (1948): 189–208.

Tran, Hai, 'Online agenda setting: a new frontier for theory development', in *Agenda Setting in a 2.0 World*, ed. Thomas J. Johnson (New York: Routledge, 2013), pp. 205–29.

Trumbo, Craig, 'Longitudinal modelling of public issues: an application of the agenda-setting process to the issue of global warming', *Journalism Monographs*, 152 (1995).

Trumbo, Craig, 'The effect of newspaper coverage of influenza on the rate of physician visits for influenza 2002–2008', *Mass Communication and Society*, 15 (2012): 718–38.

Tuchman, Gaye, 'Telling stories', *Journal of Communication*, 26, 4 (1976): 93–7.

Tversky, Amos and Daniel Kahneman, 'Availability: a heuristic for judging frequency and probability', *Cognitive Psychology*, 5 (1973): 207–32.

Valentino, Nicholas A., Vincent L. Hutchings, and Ismail K. White, 'Cues that matter: How political ads prime racial attitudes during campaigns', *American Political Science Review*, 96 (2002): 75–90.

Valenzuela, Sebastián, 'Variations in media priming: the moderating role of knowledge, interest, news attention, and discussion', *Journalism and Mass Communication Quarterly*, 86 (2009): 756–74.

Valenzuela, Sebastián, 'Materialism, post-materialism and agenda-setting effects: the values-issues consistency hypothesis', *International Journal of Public Opinion Research*, 23 (2011): 437–63.

Valenzuela, Sebastián, 'Value resonance and the origins of issue salience', in *Agenda Setting in a 2.0 World*, ed. Thomas J. Johnson (New York: Routledge, 2013), pp. 53–64.

Valenzuela, Sebastián, 'Agenda setting and journalism', in *Oxford Research Encyclopedia of Communication*, ed. Jon F. Nussbaum (New York: Oxford University Press, 2019).

Valenzuela, Sebastián and Maxwell McCombs, 'Agenda-setting effects on vote choice: evidence from the 2006 Mexican election', paper presented to the annual meeting of the International Communication Association, San Francisco, 2007.

Valenzuela, Sebastián and Arturo Arriagada, 'Competencia por la uniformidad en noticieros y diarios chilenos 2000–2005' ['The competition for similarity in Chilean news broadcast and newspapaers 2000–2005'], *Cuadernos.info*, 24 (2009): 41–52.

Valenzuela, Sebastián and Arturo Arriagada, 'Politics without citizens? Public opinion, television news, the president, and real-world factors in Chile, 2000–2005', *Harvard International Journal of Press/Politics*, 16 (2011): 357–81.

Valenzuela, Sebastián and Gennadiy Chernov, 'Explicating the values-issue consistency hypothesis through need for orientation', *Canadian Journal of Communication*, 41, 1 (2016).

Valenzuela, Sebastián, Soledad Puente, and Pablo M. Flores, 'Comparing disaster news on Twitter and television: an intermedia agenda setting perspective', *Journal of Broadcasting and Electronic Media*, 61 (2017): 615–37.

van Aelst, Peter and Stefaan Walgrave, 'Political agenda setting by the mass media: ten years of research, 2005–2015', in *Handbook of Public Policy Agenda Setting*, ed. Nikolaos Zahariadis (Cheltenham, UK: Edward Elgar, 2016), pp. 157–78.

Váně, Jan and František Kalvas, 'Focusing events and their effect on agenda setting', paper presented to the World Association for Public Opinion Research, Hong Kong, 2012.

VanSlyke Turk, Judy, 'Information subsidies and influence', *Public Relations Review*, 11 (1985): 10–25.

VanSlyke Turk, Judy, 'Information subsidies and media content: a study of public relations influence on the news', *Journalism Monographs*, 100 (1986).

VanSlyke Turk, Judy, 'Public relations influence on the news', *Newspaper Research Journal*, 7 (1986): 15–27.

Vargo, Chris J., Lei Guo, Maxwell McCombs, and Donald L. Shaw, 'Network issue agendas on Twitter during the 2012 US presidential election', *Journal of Communication*, 64 (2014): 296–316.

Vargo, Chris J. and Lei Guo, 'Exploring the network agenda setting model with big social data', in Lei Guo and Maxwell McCombs, eds. *The Power of Information Networks*: New Directions for Agenda Setting (New York, Routledge: 2016), pp. 55–65.

Vargo, Chris J. and Lei Guo, 'Networks, big data, and intermedia agenda setting: an analysis of traditional, partisan, and emerging online US news', *Journalism and Mass Communication Quarterly*, 94 (2017): 1031–55.

Vargo, Chris J., Lei Guo, and Michelle A. Amazeen, 'The agenda-setting power of fake news: A big data analysis of the online media landscape from 2014 to 2016', *New Media and Society*, 20 (2018): 2028–49.

Vonbun, Ramona, Katharina Kleinen-von Königslöw, and Klaus Schoenbach,

'Intermedia agenda-setting in a multimedia news environment', *Journalism*, 17 (2016): 1054–73.

Vu, Hong, Nga Nguyen, and Volker Gehrau, 'Agenda diffusion: an integrated model of agenda setting and interpersonal communication', *Journalism and Mass Communication Quarterly*, 87 (2010): 100–16.

Vu, Hong Tien, Lei Guo, and Maxwell E. McCombs, 'Exploring "the world outside and the pictures in our heads": A network agenda setting study', *Journalism and Mass Communication Quarterly*, 91 (2014): 669–86.

Wallsten, Kevin, 'Agenda setting and the blogosphere: an analysis of the relationship between mainstream media and political blogs', *Review of Policy Research*, 24 (2007): 567–87.

Wang, Tai-Li, 'Agenda setting online: an experiment testing the effects of hyperlinks in online newspapers', *Southwestern Mass Communication Journal*, 15, 2 (2000): 59–70.

Wanta, Wayne, *The Public and the National Agenda: How People Learn about Important Issues* (Mahwah, NJ: Lawrence Erlbaum, 1997).

Wanta, Wayne and Joe Foote, 'The president–news media relationship: a time-series analysis of agenda setting', *Journal of Broadcasting and Electronic Media*, 38 (1994): 437–48.

Wanta, Wayne and Salma Ghanem, 'Effects of agenda setting', in *Mass Media Effects Research: Advances through Meta-Analysis*, eds. Raymond W. Preiss, Barbara Mae Gayle, Nancy Burrell, Mike Allen, and Jennings Bryant (Mahwah, NJ: Lawrence Erlbaum, 2006), pp. 37–51.

Wanta, Wayne, Guy Golan and Cheolhan Lee, 'Agenda setting and international news: media influence on public perception of foreign nations', *Journalism and Mass Communication Quarterly*, 81 (2004): 364–77.

Wanta, Wayne and Yu-Wei Hu, 'Time-lag differences in the agenda setting process: an examination of five news media', *International Journal of Public Opinion Research*, 6 (1994): 225–40.

Wanta, Wayne, Mary Ann Stephenson, Judy VanSlyke Turk, and Maxwell McCombs, 'How president's State of Union talk influenced news media agendas', *Journalism Quarterly*, 66 (1989): 537–41.

Watt, James H., Mary Mazza, and Leslie Synder, 'Agenda-setting effects of television news coverage and the memory decay curve', *Communication Research*, 20 (1993): 408–35.

Watts, Liz, 'Coverage of polio and AIDS: agenda setting in reporting cure research on polio and AIDS in newspapers, news magazines and network television', *Ohio Journalism Monograph Series* [School of Journalism, Ohio University], 4 (1993).

Weart, Spencer R., *The Discovery of Global Warming* (Cambridge, MA: Harvard University Press, 2008).

Weaver, David H., 'Political issues and voter need for orientation', in *The Emergence of American Political Issues*, eds. Donald Shaw and Maxwell McCombs (St Paul, MN: West, 1977), pp. 107–19.

Weaver, David H., 'Audience need for orientation and media effects', *Communication Research*, 7 (1980): 361–76.

Weaver, David H., 'Issue salience and public opinion: are there consequences of agenda-setting?', *International Journal of Public Opinion Research*, 3 (1991): 53–68.

Weaver, David H. and Maxwell McCombs, 'Voters' need for orientation and choice of candidate: mass media and electoral decision making', paper presented to the American Association for Public Opinion Research, Roanoke, VA, 1978.

Weaver, David H., Doris A. Graber, Maxwell E. McCombs, and Chaim H. Eyal, *Media Agenda Setting in a Presidential Election: Issues, Images and Interest* (Westport, CT: Greenwood, 1981).

Weaver, David H. and Swanzy Nimley Elliot, 'Who sets the agenda for the media? A study of local agenda-building', *Journalism Quarterly*, 62 (1985): 87–94.

Webster, James G. and Thomas B. Ksiazek, 'The dynamics of audience fragmentation: public attention in an age of digital media', *Journal of Communication*, 62 (2012): 39–56.

Weeks, Brian and Brian Southwell, 'The symbiosis of news coverage and aggregate online search behavior: Obama, rumors, and presidential politics', *Mass Communication and Society*, 13 (2010): 341–60.

Weidman, Lisa, 'Consumer knowledge about Oregon wines: applying agenda setting theory to the dissemination of information about consumer products', paper presented to the Midwest Association for Public Opinion Research, Chicago, 2011.

Weiss-Blatt, Nirit, 'Role of tech bloggers in the flow of information', in *The Power of Information Networks*, eds. Lei Guo and Maxwell McCombs (New York: Routledge, 2016), pp.88–103.

Westley, Bruce and Lee Barrow, 'An investigation of news seeking behavior', *Journalism Quarterly*, 36 (1959): 431–8.

White, David Manning, 'The "gate keeper": a case study in the selection of news', *Journalism Quarterly*, 27 (1950): 383–90.

White, Theodore, *The Making of the President, 1972* (New York: Bantam, 1973).

Whitney, D. Charles and Lee Becker, '"Keeping the gates" for gatekeepers: the effects of wire news', *Journalism Quarterly*, 59 (1982): 60–5.

Williams, Bruce A. and Michael X. Delli Carpini, 'Monica and Bill all the time and everywhere: the collapse of gatekeeping and agenda setting in the new media environment', *American Behavioral Scientist*, 47 (2004): 1208–30.

Willnat, Lars, 'Agenda setting and priming: conceptual links and differences', in *Communication and Democracy*, eds. M. McCombs, D. Shaw, and D. Weaver (Mahwah, NJ: Lawrence Erlbaum, 1997), pp. 51–66.

Willnat, Lars and Jian-Hua Zhu, 'Newspaper coverage and public opinion in Hong Kong: a time-series analysis of media priming', *Political Communication*, 13 (1996): 231–46.

Winter, James P., 'Contingent conditions in the agenda-setting process', in *Mass Communication Review Yearbook*, eds. G. Cleveland Wilhoit and Harold de Bock (Beverly Hills, CA: Sage, 1981), pp. 235–43.

Winter, James P., and Chaim H. Eyal, 'Agenda setting for the civil rights issue', *Public Opinion Quarterly*, 45 (1981): 376–83.

Winter, James P., Chaim H. Eyal, and Ann Rogers, 'Issue-specific agenda setting: the whole as less than the sum of the parts', *Canadian Journal of Communication*, 8, 2 (1982): 1–10.

Wirth, Werner, Jörg Matthes, Christian Schemer, Martin Wettstein, Thomas Friemel, Regula Hänggli, and Gabriele Siegert, 'Agenda building and setting in a referendum campaign: investigating the flow of arguments among campaigners, the media, and the public', *Journalism and Mass Communication Quarterly*, 87 (2010): 328–45.

Wu, H. Denis and Renita Coleman, 'Advancing agenda-setting theory: the comparative strength and new contingent conditions of the two levels of agenda-setting effects', *Journalism and Mass Communication Quarterly*, 86 (2009): 775–89.

Wu, H. Denis and Lei Guo, 'Beyond salience transmission: linking agenda networks between media and voters', *Communication Research* (2017).

Yang, Jin, and Gerald Stone, 'The powerful role of interpersonal communication on agenda setting', *Mass Communication and Society*, 6 (2003): 57–74.

Yioutas, Julie, and Ivana Segvic, 'Revisiting the Clinton/Lewinsky scandal: the convergence of agenda setting and framing', *Journalism and Mass Communication Quarterly*, 80 (2003): 567–82.

Young, Lori and Stuart Soroka, 'Affective news: the automated coding of sentiment in political texts', *Political Communication*, 29 (2012): 205–31.

Zhang, Guoliang, Guosong Shao, and Nicholas David Bowman, 'What is most important for my country is not most important for me: agenda-setting effects in China', *Communication Research*, 39 (2012): 662–78.

Zhu, Jian-Hua with William Boroson, 'Susceptibility to agenda setting', in *Communication and Democracy*, eds. M. McCombs, D. Shaw, and D. Weaver (Mahwah, NJ: Lawrence Erlbaum, 1997).

Zhu, Jian-Hua, 'Issue competition and attention distraction: a zero-sum theory of agenda setting', *Journalism Quarterly*, 68 (1992): 825–36.

Zucker, Harold, 'The variable nature of news media influence', in *Communication Yearbook 2*, ed. Brent Ruben (New Brunswick, NJ: Transaction Books, 1978), pp. 225–40.

Zyglidopoulos, Stelios, Pavlos Symeou, Philemon Bantimaroudis, and Eleni Kampanellou, 'Cultural agenda setting: media attributes and public attention of Greek museums', *Communication Research*, 39 (2012): 480–98.

Index